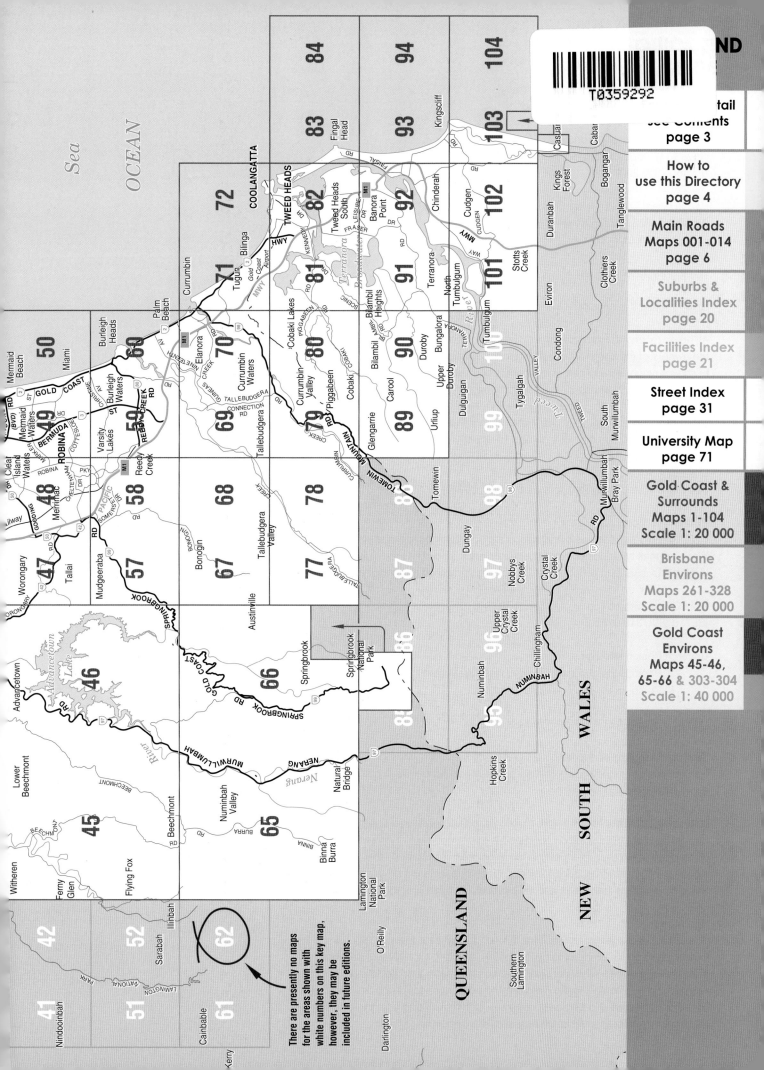

Sea

OCEAN

84
83
94
104

T0359292

tail
~~See Contents~~
page 3

How to
use this Directory
page 4

Main Roads
Maps 001-014
page 6

Suburbs &
Localities Index
page 20

Facilities Index
page 21

Street Index
page 31

University Map
page 71

Gold Coast &
Surrounds
Maps 1-104
Scale 1: 20 000

Brisbane
Environs
Maps 261-328
Scale 1: 20 000

Gold Coast
Environs
Maps 45-46,
65-66 & 303-304
Scale 1: 40 000

There are presently no maps
for the areas shown with
white numbers on this key map,
however, they may be
included in future editions.

First published in 1997

Published in 2024 by Hardie Grant Travel,
a division of Hardie Grant Publishing

Hardie Grant Travel (Sydney)
Level 7, 45 Jones Street
Ultimo, NSW 2007

Hardie Grant Travel (Melbourne)
Building 1, 658 Church Street
Richmond, Victoria 3121

hardiegranttravel.com.au

UBD Gregory's is an imprint of Hardie Grant Travel

Publishers note

UBD Gregory's welcomes contributions and feedback on the contents of this directory.
Please e-mail us at upsales@hardiegrant.com.au. Hardie Grant Travel is Australia's
largest publisher and distributor of Street Directories, Maps, Travel and Guide Books.

Gold Coast 25th edition
ISBN 9780 7319 3286 3

Cover: Design pfisterer + freeman
         Photo Burleigh Heads, Gold Coast, Queensland
         Photography by AzmanL/istockphoto

Printed in China by Leo Paper Products Ltd

Custom Mapping services

For any custom mapping requirements please contact our head office
on +61 2 9857 3700

Acknowledgments

The revision of the information contained in this street directory could not be carried out
without the assistance given by the following organisations and their representatives
Nearmap; Australia Post, local government authorities, land developers, Federal and
State government authorities, tourist information offices and the general public

Disclaimer

The publisher disclaims any responsibility or duty of care towards any person for
loss or damage suffered from any use of this directory for whatever purpose and
in whatever manner. While considerable care has been taken by the publisher in
researching and compiling the directory, the publisher accepts no responsibility for
errors or omissions. No person should rely upon this directory for the purpose of
making any business investment or real estate decision.

CONTENTS

Gregory's

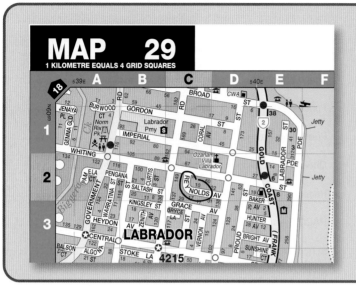

HOW TO FIND A STREET

1. Look up the street name and suburb in the Street Index (e.g. Reynolds Avenue, Labrador).

2. Note its map number and reference (29,C2).

3. Turn to the appropriate map (29) and locate the street by following the grid lines down from the reference letter (C) and across from the number (2) to where they meet, as shown on the diagram above.

REYNELLA
rd. Tallebudgera........69 D17
REYNOLDS
av. Labrador 29 C2
rd. Currumbin Vy 78 P15

CAN'T FIND A STREET?

If the Street Index does not list the street you are seeking under a particular suburb, check to see if the street is actually in an adjoining suburb.To do this, refer to the Suburbs and Localities Index and find on which map the suburb appears. Turn to that map and note the names of surrounding suburbs. Now return to the Street Index and look for the street in one of these suburbs.

MAP FEATURES

Direction

For all practical purposes Grid North and True North are always to the top of the maps. Each map features a directional arrow pointing to the city.

Grid Lines

The blue grid lines serve two purposes:
- they form the reference squares for locating streets and facilities etc.
- they allow easy calculation of distances (see Map Scales).

Map Symbols

Most of the map symbols are self-explanatory. However, to ensure that you gain maximum information from the street maps, we recommend that you familiarise yourself with all the map symbols used (see opposite page).

Overlap Areas & Map Borders

The street maps have an overlap area on each edge to assist in maintaining position when moving to an adjoining map. Adjoining map numbers are shown in the borders and corners.

Future Maps

Maps covering areas that may be included in future editions are indicated with white numbers on the Key Map at the beginning of this directory. They allow for future expansion of the directory without renumbering existing maps & still allow sequential map numbering.

Continuing Maps

When map numbers are not in sequential order, then a note will appear under the map number indicating the previous or following map number.

MAP SCALES

The maps are drawn to various scales, allowing more detail to be shown in very congested areas.

Orange Borders

Scale 1:20 000 - Grid squares measure 250m
Maps 1–104 Gold Coast & Surrounds

Blue Borders

Scale 1:20 000 - Grid Squares measure 250m
Maps 261–328 Brisbane Environs

Orange & Aqua Borders

Scale 1:40 000 (Outer Areas) - Grid Squares measure 500m
Maps 45–46, 65–66, 303–304 Gold Coast Environs

AUSTRALIAN MAP GRID

The small numbers in the map borders refer to the co-ordinates of the Australian Map Grid (AMG) which are spaced at 1000 metre (1km) intervals.The co-ordinates for Gold Coast are derived from Zone 56 of the International Universal Transverse Mercator System and is based on the Australian Geodetic Datum of 1966 (AGD66). All of the street maps are aligned with the AMG.

✱	Ambulance Station
⚜	Barbecue
M16 •	Beach Access Number
⛴	Boat Ramp
♋	Bowling Club
🚌	Bus Station
▲	Camping Area
⛺	Caravan Park
Ⓟ	Car Park
■ Cncl Off	Council Office
▽	Drive-In Theatre
☎	Emergency Phone
F	Fire Station
♣	Girl Guides
⛳	Golf Course
✚	Hospital
Ⓗ	Hotel
ⓘ	Information Centre
𝒊	Information Centre (accredited)
📖	Library
⚓	Lighthouse
☀	Lookout – 360° view
☀	– 180° view
⚒	Masonic Centre
▲	Memorial / Monument
⛫	Motel
⛩	Picnic Area
■ Museum	Place of Interest
♦	Place of Worship
⛲	Playground
■ PCYC	Pol & Citizens Youth Club
★	Police Station
✉	Post Office
🗘	Quarry
■ QT	Queensland Transport
■ RFB	Rural Fire Brigade
Ⓢ	School – Private
Ⓢ	– State
⚘	Scouts
🛢	Service Station
🛒	Shopping Centre
🚌	South East Busway Station
■ SES	State Emergency Service
⚑	Swimming Pool
🚕	Taxi Stand
☎	Telephone
Ⓒ	Tertiary Institution – Private
Ⓒ	– State
🚻	Toilets
Ⓦ	Weighbridge
🍇	Winery

Freeway/Motorway	
Motorway Route and Exit Ramp Numbers	
Highway or Main Traffic Route & Footbridge	
Alternative Traffic Route	
Trafficable Road	
Untrafficable/Proposed Road	
Traffic Light, Roundabout and Red Light Camera	
Road, Railway Bridge & Level Crossing	
Bridge Clearance Heights	
One-Way Traffic Route	
National, State & Tourist Route Numbers	
Proposed Arterial	
Direction to Brisbane City Centre	
Distance by road from GPO	
House or Building Number / Apartment Number	
Railway Line with Station (distance from Central Rly Stn)	
Transmission Lines – Energex	
– Powerlink Queensland	
Suburb Name	
Postcode Number	
Suburb Boundary	
Locality Name	
Local Government – Name	
– Boundary	
Ferry Route	
Cycleway, Walking Track and Equestrian Trail	
Park, Reserve, Golf Course, etc	
School or Hospital	
Caravan Park, Cemetery, Shopping Centre, etc	
Building	
Mall, Plaza	
Swamp / Mangroves	
Land Subject to Inundation	
Pine Plantation	

PACIFIC M1 EXIT 45 MWY
Fbr
GOLD COAST | HWY
SUMNERS | RD
WESTLAKE | DR
ELLERBY | RD

5.2m | 4.7m

1 15 26 A4

Proposed | Arterial

CITY

26

20 | 108

Ormeau 53.3

E — 750 — E
808

NERANG

4211

West Burleigh

Gold Coast

SCALE
0   5   10 km

LIMIT OF MAPS

Kin Kin

State Forest

Mt Mooloo +

Big Baldy +
+ Little Baldy

Long Flat

Mary

Kybong

A1
BRUCE

Tandur

Woodum Forest Reserve

Sandy

NOOSA

Pinbarren

Gilldora

BURGESS RD

BROOLOO RD

GYMPIE

51

Green Ridge

TANDUR

TANDUR - TRAVESTON

SIX MILE

Traveston

Mt Pinbarren +

Cootharaba

State Forest

CREEK

BLACK GATE

KANDANGA - AMAMOOR

Amamoor

TRAVESTON CROSSING RD

COORAN

Mile

Cooran

ARTHIS RD

POMONA - KIN KIN

Pinbarren

SIX

MILE

BAZZO

Amamoor

HAPPY VALLEY RD

Kandanga

Kandanga

51

COOLOY

GYMPIE

BRUCE

A1

Coles

COLES CREEK

Ck

SCHREIBERS

JAMROT

CREEK

Mt Cooroora + 439m

POMONA

4

YUROL

State Forest

Melawondi

Nobby Glen

Mary River

KENILWORTH

SKYRING

+ Mt Tuchekoi

Federal

MIDDLE CREEK

SANKEYS

POMONA CONNECTION

PIONEER RD

ELM

HWY

A1

BRUCE

Mary

KADANGA CREEK

Bergins Pocket

Tuchekoi

Black Mountain

ANDERSONS RD

BLACK MTN

Creek

COOROY - BELLI CREEK

State Forest

BROOLOO

51

TUCHEKOI RD

Carters Ridge

Happy

Jack

Creek

Ridgewood

COOROY

BELLI

CREEK

LAWNVILLE RD

Eerwah Vale

Imbil

IMBIL RD

Bollier

POULSEN RD

13

Blackfellow

BELLI CREEK

TOP FORESTRY (North Branch)

(South Branch)

OLD CEYLON RD

14

Bella

BROOLOO RD

Belli

NEWSPAPER HILL RD

SKYRING CREEK

Blackfellow State Forest

Derrier Flat

YABBA CREEK

Borumba Dam

GYMPIE - KENILWORTH

51

Brooloo

MOY POCKET

Belli Park

BOYLE RD

Creek

EUMUNDI - KENILWORTH

BROWNS CREEK RD

Borumba Mountain

Imbil

+ Kenilworth Bluff

Oaky

OAKY CREEK

33

Belli

CEDAR CREEK

Mapleton

Cooloolabin Dam

Range

Cooloolabi

BUCKBY RD

State

KENILWORTH

WILCOX

51

Gheerulla

SAM KELLY RD

Gheerulla

National

COOLOOLABIN RD

Rocky Ck

Forest

EUMUNDI

BEACON HILL RD

Kiamba

31

Kenilworth

Coolabine

COOLABINE

Ck

Park

Mapleton

KUREELPA RD

Yabba

KENILWORTH RD

Obi

Obi

Obi Obi

53

Blackall

MAPLETON FOREST

Kureelpa

SUNDAY CREEK

MALENY - KENILWORTH

WALLI MOUNTAIN

Mary

Forest Reserve

Kidaman Creek

Obi Obi

HUNSLEY RD

PENCIL CREEK

Mapleton Falls National Park

Ck

MAPLETON RD

FLAXTON

Mapleton

54

DULONG

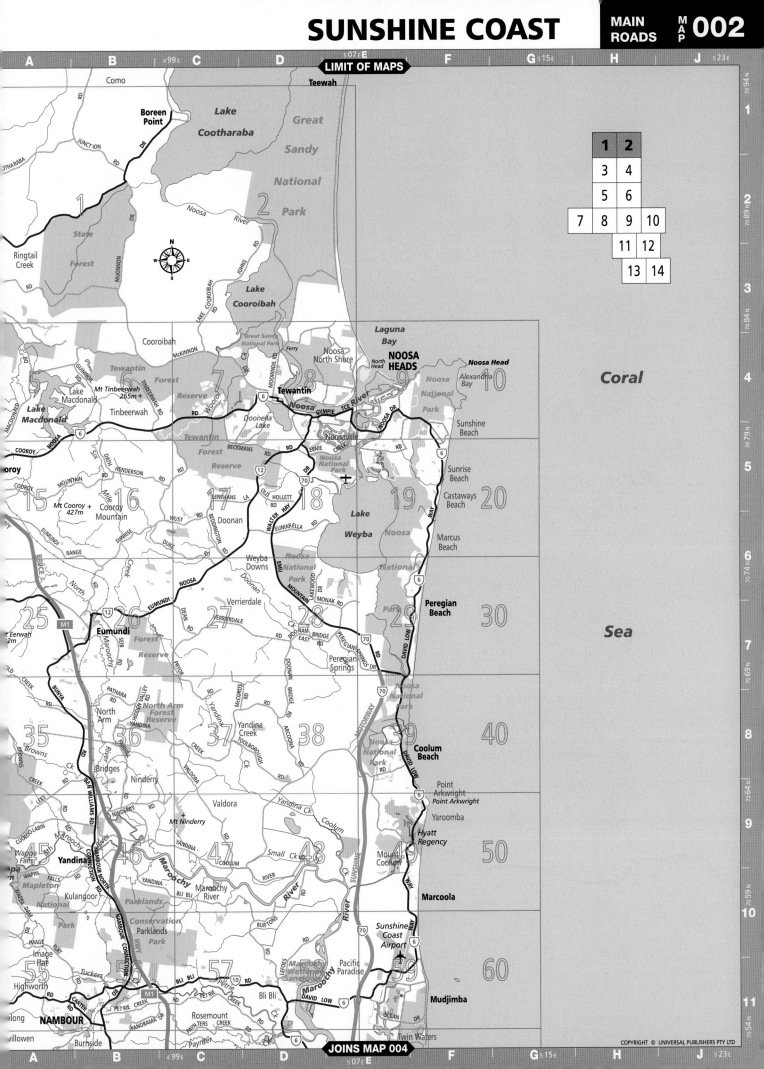

LIMIT OF MAPS

Como

Teewah

Boreen Point

Lake Cootharaba

Great Sandy National Park

Noosa River

Ringtail Creek

State Forest

Lake Cooroibah

Cooroiban

Great Sandy National Park

Noosa North Shore

North Head

NOOSA HEADS

Laguna Bay

Noosa Head

Alexandria Bay

Coral

Tewantin Forest Reserve

Mt Tinbeerwah 265m

Tewantin

Noosa

Tinbeerwah

Lake Macdonald

Noosa National Park

Sunshine Beach

Lake Macdonald

Doonella Lake

Noosaville

Cooroy

Tewantin Forest Reserve

Beckmans

Noosa National Park

Sunrise Beach

Castaways Beach

Cooroy

Mt Cooroy 427m

Cooroy Mountain

Lenehans La

Old Hollett

Walter Hay

Doonan

Lake Weyba

Noosa

Marcus Beach

Eumundi

Weyba Downs

Noosa National Park

Doonan

Verrierdale

Noosa National Park

Peregian Beach

Sea

Eumundi

Forest Reserve

Verrierdale

Peregian Springs Dr

Peregian Springs

North Arm

North Arm Forest Reserve

Yandina

Yandina Creek

Toolborough

Noosa National Park

Coolum Beach

Browns

Bridges

Ninderry

Valdora

Point Arkwright

Point Arkwright

Yaroomba

Mt Ninderry

Yandina

Valdora

Coolum

Small Ck

Coolum

Mount Coolum

Hyatt Regency

Yandina

Maroochy

Maroochy River

Bli Bli

Marcoola

Wappa Falls

Mapleton

Kulangoor

Parklands

Maroochy River

Conservation Parklands Park

Burtons

Maroochy Wetland Sanctuary

Sunshine Coast Airport

Pacific Paradise

Image Flat

Tuckers

Bli Bli

Rosemount

Bli Bli

Mudjimba

Highworth

NAMBOUR

Petrie Creek

Panorama Dr

Rosemount

David Low

Twin Waters

Burnside

Paynter

JOINS MAP 004

SCALE
0   5   10 km

JOINS MAP 001

Conondale National Park

Kenilworth National Reserve

Conondale

Range

LIMIT OF MAPS

Cambroon

Forest Reserve

Curramore

Witta

Lake Baroon

Elaman Creek

Conondale

Mary

Harper

Reesville

Maleny

North Maleny

Chenre Institute Wisdo Cultu

Balmoral Ridge

Wootha

Forest Reserve

Candle Mountain 293m

Crohamhurst

Mt Blanc 245m

Booroobin

Stanley

Peachester

River

Cedarton

Bellthorpe State Forest

Forest Reserve

Commissioners Flat

Bellthorpe

Mt Mary Smokes 657m

+ Mt McLean

Bellthorpe Forest Reserve

Stanmore

Stanley

Beerburrum State Forest

Beerwah 556m

Glass House Mtns Nat Pk

Stony Creek

Blackrock

D'Aguilar

Stanley

River

Lake Somerset

Forest Reserve

Neurum

Neurum Mtn + 509m

Woodford

Beerburrum State Forest

D'Aguilar

Beerburrum State Forest

Tunbubu (The Twi

JOINS MAP 005

32 73 74 53 54 92 93 94 32 33 34 43 35 36

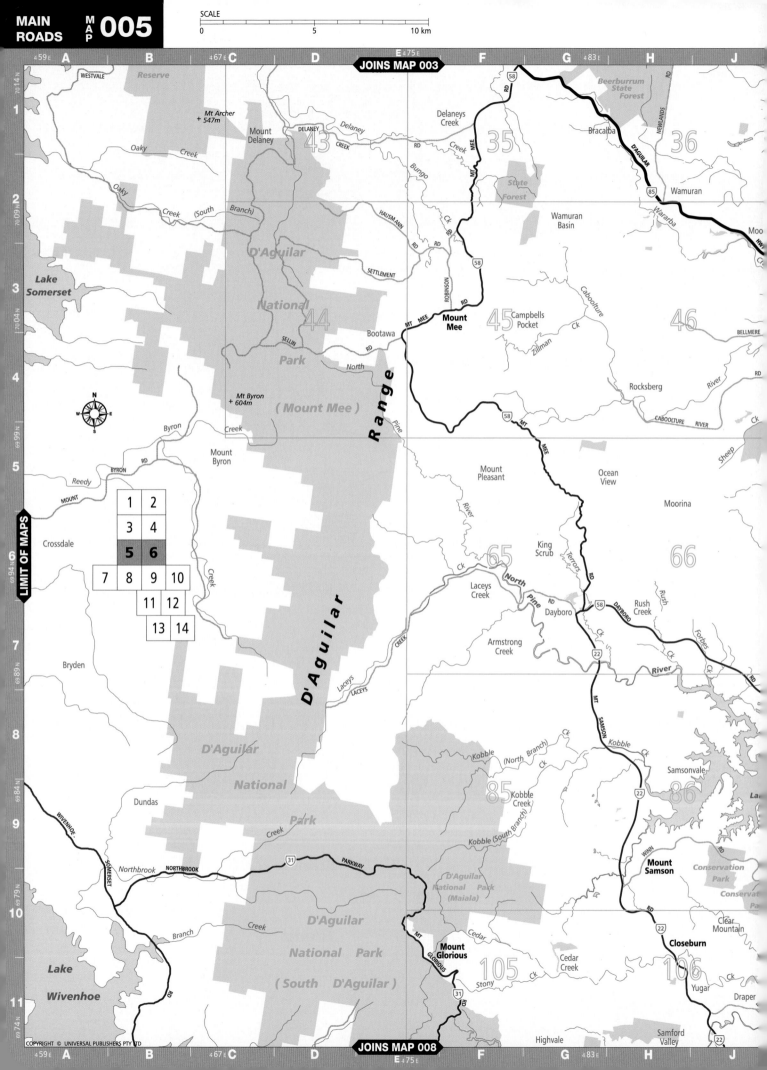

SCALE

0   5   10 km

WESTVALE

Reserve

Mt Archer
+ 547m

Mount
Delaney

DELANEY

Delaney

Delaneys
Creek

Beerburrum
State
Forest

58
RD

Bracalba

NEWLANDS RD

36

DAGUILAR

85

Wamuran

43

DELANEY
CREEK

Oaky

Creek

Oaky

Creek   (South

Branch)

D'Aguilar

HAUSMANN

Bungo

Ck

State

Forest

35

Wararba

Moo

Ck

Lake
Somerset

National

44

SETTLEMENT

RD

RD

ROBINSON

58
RD

Wamuran
Basin

45

Campbells
Pocket

Caboolture

Zillman

Ck

46

BELLMERE

Bootawa

Mount
Mee

MT MEE

Park

SELLIN

RD

North

Rocksberg

River

RD

Sheep

CABOOLTURE   RIVER

Ck

Mt Byron
+ 604m

(Mount Mee)

Byron

Creek

Range

Pine

MT

MEE

58

Mount
Pleasant

Ocean
View

Moorina

Mount
Byron

LIMIT OF MAPS

Crossdale

BYRON   RD

Reedy

MOUNT

1	2
3	4
5	**6**

River

65

King
Scrub

Terors

RD

66

Byron

| 7 | 8 | 9 | 10 |

Ck

North

Laceys
Creek

Pine

RD

Dayboro

58

DAYBORO

Rush
Creek

Rush

Ck

| 11 | 12 |
| 13 | 14 |

Creek

D'Aguilar

22

Armstrong
Creek

River

Forbes

Ck

RD

Bryden

Range

CREEK

Laceys

LACEYS

D'Aguilar

National

Park

Dundas

Creek

D'Aguilar

Kobble

(North Branch)

Ck

MT

SAMSON

Kobble

Samsonvale

86

La

85

Kobble
Creek

Kobble

Ck

Kobble (South Branch)

Creek

31

PARKWAY

D'Aguilar
National Park
(Maiala)

22

WINN

Mount
Samson

Conservation
Park

Conserva

Pa

Northbrook

NORTHBROOK

WIVENHOE

SOMERSET

Branch

Creek

D'Aguilar

National   Park

(South   D'Aguilar)

MT

GLORIOUS

Mount
Glorious

105

Cedar

Cedar
Creek

RD

22

Closeburn

Clear
Mountain

106

Lake

Wivenhoe

RD

31
RD

Stony

Ck

Highvale

Yugar

Samford
Valley

Draper

Ck

22

JOINS MAP 004

JOINS MAP 009

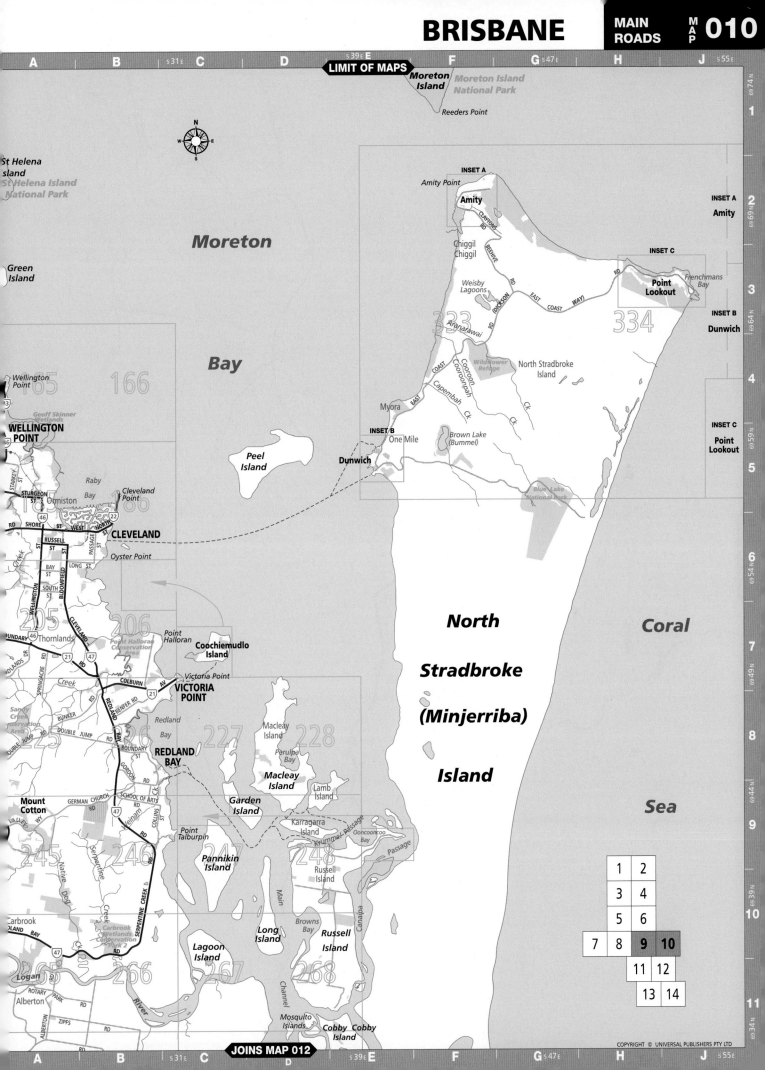

Moreton Island

Moreton Island National Park

Reeders Point

St Helena Island

St Helena Island National Park

Moreton

Bay

INSET A

Amity Point

Amity

Chiggil Chiggil

Weisby Lagoons

333

Aranarawai

Myora

Capembah Ck

North Stradbroke Island

Wildflower Refuge

INSET C

Point Lookout

Frenchmans Bay

334

INSET A

Amity

INSET B

Dunwich

INSET C

Point Lookout

Green Island

Wellington Point

165

166

Geoff Skinner Wetlands

WELLINGTON POINT

Raby Bay

Ormiston

185

186

Cleveland Point

CLEVELAND

Oyster Point

Peel Island

Dunwich

INSET B

One Mile

Brown Lake (Bummel)

Blue Lake National Park

Coral

205

206

Thornlands

Point Halloran Conservation Area

Point Halloran

Coochiemudlo Island

Victoria Point

VICTORIA POINT

North

Stradbroke

(Minjerriba)

Island

Sea

Sandy Creek Conservation Area

225

226

Redland Bay

227

228

Macleay Island

Perulpa Bay

Macleay Island

Lamb Island

Karragarra Island

Garden Island

Point Talburpin

REDLAND BAY

Mount Cotton

245

246

247

248

Pannikin Island

Krummel Passage

Ooncooncoo Bay

Passage

Russell Island

Carbrook

Carbrook Wetlands Conservation

Lagoon Island

Long Island

Browns Bay

Russell Island

Logan

265

266

267

268

Alberton

Mosquito Islands

Cobby Cobby Island

1	2
3	4
5	6
7	8	9	10
	11	12
	13	14

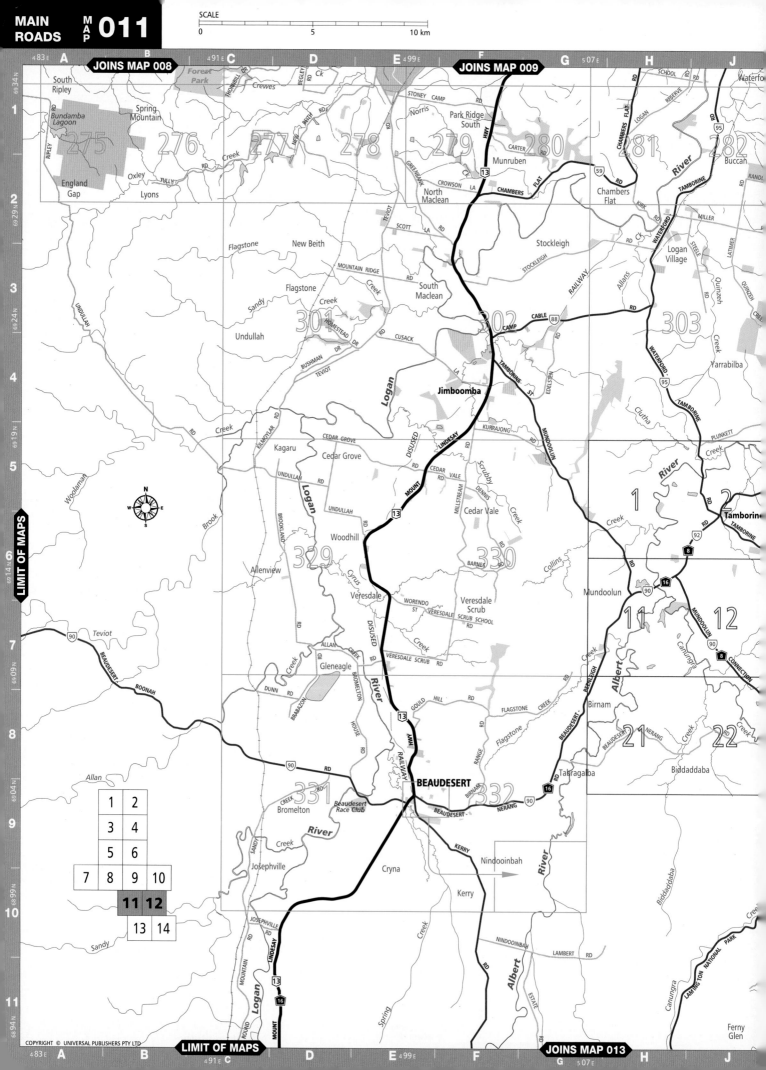

JOINS MAP 009

JOINS MAP 010

JOINS MAP 013

JOINS MAP 014

MAP 013

SCALE

0   5   10 km

A   B   C   D   E   F   G   H   J

499 E   507 E   515 E   523 E

68 94 N

68 89 N

68 84 N

68 79 N

68 74 N

68 69 N

68 64 N

68 59 N

68 54 N

LIMIT OF MAPS

N
W · E
S

Kerry

Kerry

Cainbable

Sarabah

Mt Cainbable
656m

Ferny
Glen

Flying
Fox

Flying Fox

Land
Warfare
Centre

45

Advancetown
Lake

46

Beechmont

Illinbah

Numinbah

Correctional

Centre

65

Numinbah
Valley

Numinbah

Forest

Reserve

Springbrook

Little Nerang
Dam   Austinville

Springbrook

66   National

Park

Springbrook

Christmas
Creek

Albert

Hillview

Darlington

O'Reilly

Binna
Burra

Binna Burra
Lodge

Lamington

Natural Bridge

Springbrook

Lamington

O'Reilly's
Guesthouse

National

Mt Wanungara
1180m

River

Natural
Bridge

Natural Bridge
Section

Numinbar

Nature Reserve

Upper
Crystal Creek

Lost World

Little Widgee Mtn
760m

Park

Range

Hopkins
Creek

Numinbah

Chinghee
Creek

Neglected Mtn

Southern
Lamington

Mt Throakban
1150m

Limpinwood
Nature Reserve

Limpinwood

Zara

Chillingham

Crys
Cree

Lamington

Running

Mount
Gipps

Plateau

McPherson

Mt Hutley
790m

Border

Gradys

New

Queensland

South

Wales

Tyalgum
Creek

Oxley

River

Zara

Brindle

Ranges   Creek

Tweed

Pumpenbil

Pumpenbil

Back
Creek

Tyalgum

Wollumbin

State

Forest

Mount

Warning

National

Mount
Warning

Sheepstation

National

The Pinnacle
919m

Back

Mebbin

Range

Brays

Brays
Creek

Mt Warning
1156m

Park

Cedar
Creek

Lynchs

Warrazambil

Park

National

Mebbin

Byrrill

Byrrill Creek

Terragon

Tweed

Do

A   B   C   D   E   F   G   H   J

499 E   507 E   515 E   523 E

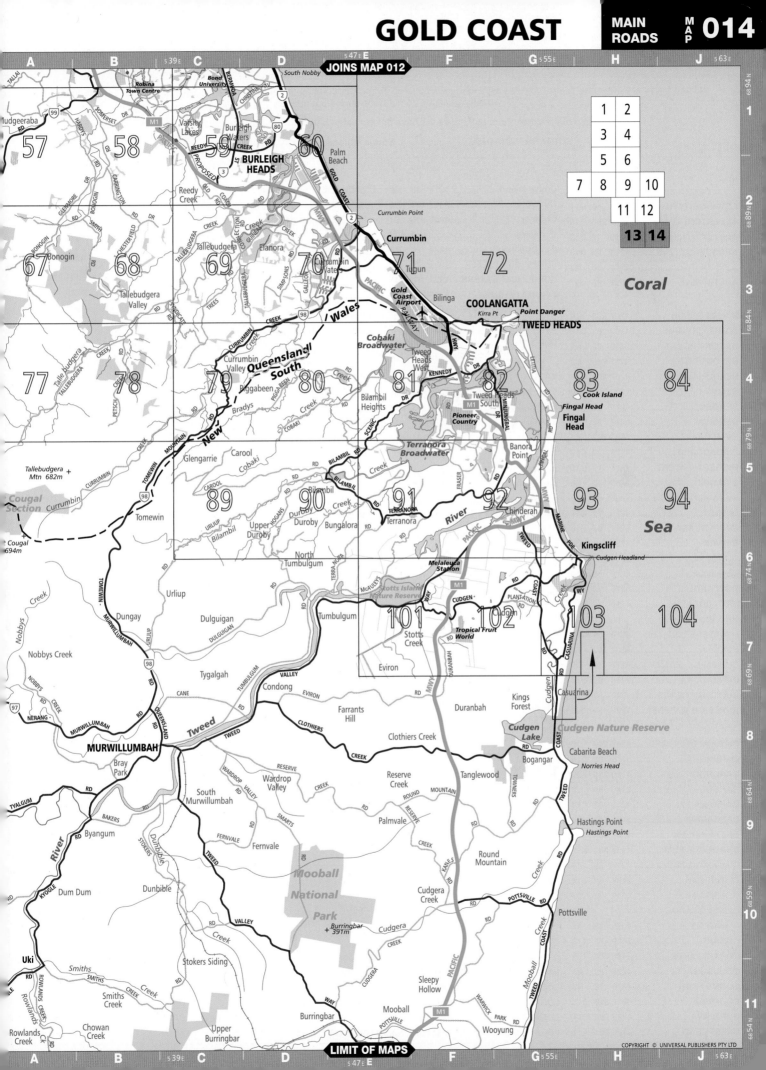

SUBURBS & LOCALITIES INDEX

Listed below are the suburbs and localities within the area covered by the Street Maps, together with their postcodes and map references. Many localities do not have official boundaries.

With the help of the appropriate authorities we have differentiated between suburbs and localities as follows –

SURFERS PARADISE ..... Suburb   Studio Village.... Locality or unofficial suburb

	Map	Ref
A		
ADVANCETOWN 4211	46	M11
ALBERTON....................4207	265	G16
Anglers Paradise 4216	19	B13
ARUNDEL....................4214	18	D16
ASHMORE 4214	38	M2
AUSTINVILLE 4213	66	Q7
B		
BAHRS SCRUB 4207	283	G9
BANNOCKBURN.............4207	283	Q19
BANORA POINT 2486	92	N4
BEECHMONT 4211	65	C2
BEENLEIGH..................4207	264	B16
BELIVAH 4207	283	G19
BENOBBLE 4275	33	H2
BENOWA 4217	38	L9
BETHANIA 4205	263	E9
BIDDADDABA 4275	22	C17
BIGGERA WATERS..........4216	19	D15
BILAMBIL 2486	90	K9
BILAMBIL HEIGHTS 2486	81	B15
BILINGA......................4225	71	Q17
BINNA BURRA 4211	65	E16
BIRNAM 4285	21	C4
BONOGIN 4213	67	P9
Boykambil 4212	8	D10
BOYLAND 4275	23	G2
BROADBEACH...............4218	39	R17
BROADBEACH		
WATERS...................4218	39	G17
BUCCAN....................4207	282	L9
BUNDALL 4217	39	B9
BUNGALORA 2486	90	Q15
BURLEIGH HEADS 4220	60	C12
BURLEIGH WATERS.......4220	59	N8
C		
Cabbage Tree Point.........4207	287	Q8
CANUNGRA...................4275	33	E16
CARBROOK 4130	265	D5
CAROOL 2486	89	L3
CARRARA 4211	38	C14
CASUARINA 2487	103	C14
CEDAR CREEK 4207	304	J13
CHAMBERS FLAT...........4133	281	K15
Chevron Island..............4217	39	K4
CHINDERAH 2487	92	J17
CLAGIRABA 4211	35	D7
CLEAR ISLAND		
WATERS...................4226	49	A5
COBAKI 2486	80	K16
COBAKI LAKES 2486	80	L6
COOLANGATTA 4225	29	E3
COOMBABAH 4216	18	H3
COOMERA 4209	328	B13
CORNUBIA 4130	264	K1
CRESTMEAD.................4132	261	L11

	Map	Ref
Cronin Island...................4217	39	J2
CUDGEN 2487	102	K10
Cupania 4208	305	C1
Currigee......................	9	K16
CURRUMBIN 4223	71	B8
CURRUMBIN VALLEY 4223	79	M8
CURRUMBIN WATERS 4223	70	M11
Cypress Gardens............4218	38	R18
D		
DURANBAH..................2487	102	C20
DUROBY 2486	90	J14
E		
EAGLEBY 4207	264	M9
Eagle Heights 4271	14	B8
EDENS LANDING............4207	263	F16
ELANORA 4221	70	B8
EVIRON 2484	101	F19
F		
FERNY GLEN 4275	45	B8
FINGAL HEAD 2487	92	R6
Florida Gardens............4218	39	L15
FLYING FOX 4275	45	E13
G		
GAVEN 4211	27	H9
GILBERTON 4208	285	Q14
GILSTON.....................4211	36	L17
GLENGARRIE 2486	89	D5
GUANABA 4210	15	F15
H		
HELENSVALE.................4212	17	G4
Heydon Heights 4215	29	B5
HIGHLAND PARK 4211	37	D11
HOLLYWELL..................4216	8	Q19
HOLMVIEW...................4207	263	H19
HOPE ISLAND 4212	8	E14
I		
ILLINBAH....................4275	65	B5
Isle of Capri 4217	39	J10
J		
JACOBS WELL 4208	308	E10
JIMBOOMBA.................4280	303	B15
K		
KAIRABAH 4207	303	M18
KINGSCLIFF 2487	103	H6
KINGS FOREST..............2487	102	H16
KINGSHOLME 4208	304	N14
KINGSTON...................4114	262	B2
Kirra 4225	82	B1
Koala Park 4220	60	C11
L		
LABRADOR 4215	29	B3
LOGANHOLME................4129	263	P10
LOGANLEA 4131	262	F4
LOGAN RESERVE 4133	261	L17
LOGAN VILLAGE............4207	303	N3

	Map	Ref
LOWER BEECHMONT.....4211	46	A4
LUSCOMBE..................4207	304	L5
M		
MAIN BEACH.................4217	29	P17
MARSDEN 4132	261	H2
MAUDSLAND 4210	16	F15
MERMAID BEACH...........4218	50	B7
MERMAID WATERS 4218	49	K6
MERRIMAC 4226	48	C11
MIAMI 4220	50	D16
Miami Keys 4218	39	J20
MOLENDINAR 4214	28	D13
MOUNT NATHAN 4211	35	P5
Mount Tamborine 4272	23	Q13
MOUNT WARREN PARK..4207	284	A6
MUDGEERABA 4213	57	G6
MUNDOOLUN 4285	11	C6
Musgrave Hill 4215	29	A8
N		
NATURAL BRIDGE 4211	65	P17
NERANG 4211	37	H5
NERANWOOD 4213	66	Q1
Nobby Beach.................4218	50	C12
North Tamborine 4272	13	K11
NORTH TUMBULGUM 2490	101	G2
NORWELL 4208	307	F15
NUMINBAH VALLEY........4211	65	R9
O		
O'REILLY 4211	65	A16
ORMEAU.....................4208	305	K5
ORMEAU HILLS 4208	305	A15
OXENFORD 4210	16	N8
P		
PACIFIC PINES...............4211	17	C16
PALM BEACH.................4221	60	M13
PARADISE POINT 4216	8	N13
Paradise Waters.............4217	39	J1
PARKWOOD 4214	28	F6
PIGGABEEN 2486	80	D9
PIMPAMA...................4209	326	M2
R		
REDLAND BAY...............4165	266	N7
REEDY CREEK 4227	59	B19
Rialto.......................4218	39	E16
Rio Vista 4218	39	H14
ROBINA 4226	49	D11
RUNAWAY BAY 4216	18	Q4
RUSSELL ISLAND 4184	268	G8
S		
Sanctuary Cove 4212	8	A1
Santa Barbara 4212	7	Q7
Sorrento....................4217	39	C13
SOUTHERN MORETON		
BAY ISLANDS	8	P4
SOUTHPORT..................4215	29	D13

	Map	Ref
SOUTH STRADBROKE....4216	9	K3
SPRINGBROOK 4213	66	K14
STAPYLTON 4207	285	H7
STEIGLITZ 4207	287	P11
STOCKLEIGH 4280	293	E9
STOTTS CREEK 2487	101	N12
Studio Village................4210	17	A11
SURFERS PARADISE......4217	39	Q6
T		
TABRAGALBA...............4285	21	E14
TALLAI 4213	47	F16
TALLEBUDGERA 4228	69	J9
TALLEBUDGERA		
VALLEY 4228	68	Q12
TAMBORINE 4270	2	G10
TAMBORINE MOUNTAIN..4272	23	Q7
TANAH MERAH 4128	263	J1
TERRANORA.................2486	91	G15
The Spit 4217	29	M1
TUGUN.....................4224	71	F13
TUMBULGUM 2490	101	C11
TWEED HEADS 2485	82	C4
TWEED HEADS SOUTH ..2486	82	D15
TWEED HEADS WEST....2485	81	P6
U		
UPPER COOMERA 4209	6	E10
UPPER DUROBY..............2486	89	N17
Upper Hairpin Bend........4275	33	H9
URLIUP 2484	89	G14
V		
VARSITY LAKES 4227	59	D10
W		
WATERFORD..................4133	263	B20
WATERFORD WEST 4133	262	K12
Wedge Bluff Lookout 4213	66	N16
West Burleigh 4219	59	Q14
WILLOW VALE 4209	325	M13
Wilsons Lookout............4272	24	H12
WINDAROO 4207	284	A13
WITHEREN 4275	33	P10
WOLFFDENE 4207	304	D5
WONGAWALLAN 4210	4	L11
WONGLEPONG 4275	23	J11
WOONGOOLBA 4207	287	D7
WORONGARY 4213	47	F2
Y		
Yalbaroo 4211	65	B10
Yangahla Lookout..........4211	65	K18
YARRABILBA 4207	300	C8
YATALA....................4207	284	Q15

Map Ref

Aged Care, Nursing Homes & Retirement Communities

Acare Aged Care
2 Halcyon Dr,
Pimpama 326 Q5
Arcare Helensvale
103 Lindfield Rd............... 17 F12
Arcare Hope Island
10 Halcyon Wy 8 E12
Arcare Logan Reserve
17 Halcyon Wy 262 C15
Arcare Regency
38 Caseys Rd,
Hope Island 7 R5
Arcare St James
40 Helensvale Rd,
Helensvale...................... 17 B2
Ashmore Retreat
19 Allunga Av................. 28 J18
Auscare House
208 Cotlew St,
Ashmore 28 H20
Aveo Amity Gardens
5 Lochinvar Ct,
Ashmore 38 B1
Aveo Banora Point
57 Leisure Dr................... 92 G1
Aveo Pine Lake
11 Araucaria Wy,
Elanora............................ 70 L6
Aveo Robina
1 Glenside Dr.................. 48 Q16
Aveo Southport
4 Beryl St 29 D17
Aveo The Domain
Country Club
74 Wardoo St,
Ashmore 28 N19
Aveo Tranquility Gardens
5 Mildura Dr,
Helensvale....................... 17 J9
Bangalor Retreat
3 Stott St,
Tweed Heads West.......... 81 F13
Bayview Place,
Tricare
86 Bayview St,
Runaway Bay 19 C10
Beenleigh Nursing Home
45 York St 264 C19
Bethania Gardens
87 Station Rd................. 263 C7
Bethania Retirement Court
8 Page St....................... 263 B8
Blue Care,
Arundel Woodlands Lodge
29 Melbourne Rd 28 M1
Beenleigh Bethania
Haven Aged Care Facility
67 Station Rd............... 263 B8
Carbrook Wirunya
Aged Care Facility
559 Beenleigh-
Redland Bay Rd............ 265 B4
Elanora Pineshaven
Aged Care
17 Applecross Wy............ 70 K2
Kingscliff Aged Care Facility
24a Kingscliff St 93 C18
Kirrahaven Aged Care
24 Coolangatta Rd,
Coolangatta..................... 82 C2
Labrador Gardens
83 Muir St 29 D4
Talleyhaven Hostel
54 Dudgeon Dr,
Tallebudgera................... 69 P17

Tweed Heads Amaroo
Aged Care Facility
68 Keith Compton Dr 82 L8
Bupa Banora Point
18 Ballymore Ct 91 R2
Bupa Merrimac
3 Glenhaven Ct............... 48 F10
Bupa Runaway Bay
376 Pine Ridge Rd,
Coombabah..................... 18 M9
Bupa Tugun
6 Croft Ct........................ 71 C14
Cypress Gardens
Retirement Community &
Nursing Centre,
Tricare
Gooding Dr,
Clear Island Waters......... 48 Q1
De Paul Manor Estate
1 Edmund Rice Dr,
Southport........................ 28 L15
De Paul Villa
27 Edmund Rice Dr,
Southport........................ 28 L15
Earle Haven
Retirement Village
62 Lawrence Dr,
Nerang 37 M4
Emerald Gardens
70 Hansford Rd,
Coombabah..................... 18 K2
Estia Health Mudgeeraba
27 Old Coach Rd,
Tallai 47 P19
Estia Health Southport
40 William St 29 C8
Galleon Harbour
Retirement & Leisure Resort
174 Galleon Wy,
Currumbin Waters........... 70 J16
Golden Age
Retirement Village,
Church of Christ Care
60 Ridgeway Av,
Southport........................ 29 D19
Golden Crest Manors
1 McKenzie Dr,
Highland Park 37 J11
Golden Grove Hostel
164 High St,
Southport........................ 29 E9
Grande Pacific,
Lifestyle Retirement Resorts
70 Marine Pde,
Southport........................ 29 G10
Halcyon Greens
7 Halcyon Dr,
Pimpama 326 R4
Halcyon Waters
Halcyon Wy,
Hope Island 8 D15
Hibiscus House
Nursing Home,
Earle Haven
Retirement Village
70 Lawrence Dr,
Nerang 37 M5
Hill View House Aged Care
Residence
135 Cotlew St,
Ashmore 28 M20
239 Gooding Dr,
Merrimac 48 H3
Homesteads Aged Care,
Churches of Christ Care
64 Billabirra Cr,
Nerang 36 R1
Ingenia Lifestyle
Bethania 263 A5
Jeta Garden
27 Clarendon Av,
Bethania 262 Q10

Jimbelunga Nursing Centre
259 River Hills Rd,
Eagleby 264 N16
Kingscliff Beach
Retirement Village
1 Blue Jay Cct,
Kingscliff 93 C19
Lady Small Haven
Retirement Village,
Churches of Christ Care
60 Allchurch Av,
Benowa........................... 38 Q8
Lions Haven for the Aged
Pendraat Pde,
Hope Island 8 B10
McKenzie Aged Care,
Raffles
Peregrine Dr,
Tweed Heads South 82 G15
Sandbrook
10 Executive Dr,
Burleigh Waters............... 59 L10
The Terraces
74 University Dr,
Varsity Lakes 49 G19
Magnolia Homestead
Aged Care
142 Reserve Rd,
Upper Coomera 6 K8
Marana Gardens
Aged Care Services,
Churches of Christ Care
10 Ridgeway Av,
Southport........................ 29 D18
Marsden Gardens
8 Cove St...................... 261 H4
Masonic Care Queensland,
South Coast Hostel
101 Allied Dr,
Arundel 18 K20
Melody Park
Retirement Resort,
Wisteria Lodge
261 Gilston Rd,
Nerang 37 A10
Mermaid Beach
Nursing Centre,
Tricare
2424 Gold Coast Hwy 49 Q7
Merrimac Park Private Care
50 Macadie Wy,
Merrimac 48 F7
Miami Retirement Village
170 Bardon Av,
Burleigh Waters............... 49 K16
Mudgeeraba Nursing Centre
21 Old Coach Rd,
Tallai 47 P18
Nerang Nursing Centre
6 Mylor St 37 F2
Noble Lakeside Australia
34 Monarch Dr,
Kingscliff 93 A19
Noyea Riverside
Retirement Village
5 Martens St,
Mount Warren Park 284 J5
Ocean View Banora Point
cnr Pacific Hwy &
Terranora Rd 92 L4
Opal Ashmore
100 Wardoo St............... 28 P19
Opal Florence Tower
7 Florence Pl,
Tweed Heads................... 82 K4
Opal Kirra Beach
6 Ocean St,
Coolangatta.................... 82 C2
Opal Leamington
55 Worendo St,
Southport........................ 29 D9
Opal Retirement Village
42 Quinzeh Creek Rd,
Logan Village 293 R2

Opal Tweed Heads
1 Carramar Dr,
Tweed Heads West.......... 81 J12
Opal Varsity Rise
14 Lake St,
Varsity Lakes 49 G20
Oxford Crest,
Eagleby
145 Fryar Rd................. 264 H14
Ozcare,
Keith Turnbull Place
52 Imperial Pde,
Labrador......................... 29 D2
Ozanam Villa Burleigh
20 Matilda St,
Burleigh Heads............... 60 C10
Parkwood Gardens
100 Usher Av,
Labrador......................... 28 N1
Palm Lake Resort
40 Riverbrooke Dr,
Upper Coomera 6 K14
Banora Point
67 Winders Pl 82 H18
Bethania
43 Goodooga Dr............. 262 R12
Eagleby
84 Eagleby Rd 264 F9
Mount Warren Park
1 Mt Warren Bvd........... 284 A4
Tweed River
2 Barneys Point Rd,
Banora Point 92 P4
Waterford
29 High Rd..................... 263 A14
Palm Lake
Retirement Village,
Bethania
3 Goodooga Dr 262 R11
Paradise Lake Care Centre
360 Oxley Dr,
Coombabah..................... 18 L6
Paradise Palms
Leisure Villas
35 St Kevins Av,
Benowa........................... 38 Q8
Pimpama Nursing Centre,
Tricare
Anembo Av,
Kingsholme.................... 305 Q16
PresCare Roslyn Lodge
24 Main Western Rd,
Tamborine Mountain....... 13 N15
Regal Waters
16 Holzheimer Rd,
Bethania 263 D8
River Glen Over 50's Village
30 Beutel St,
Waterford West............. 262 E10
River Lodge Aged Care
71 Walton St,
Southport........................ 29 C8
RSL Care,
Darlington Retirement
Community
126 Leisure Dr,
Banora Point 92 E1
Galleon Gardens
Retirement Community
126 Galleon Wy,
Currumbin Waters........... 70 J14
Talbarra Retirement
Community
150 Old Logan Village Rd,
Waterford...................... 262 R14
Winders Retirement
Community
Winders Pl,
Banora Point 92 J1
Ruby Gardens
225 Logan St,
Eagleby 264 K17

Runaway Bay Village,
Tricare
98 Bayview St 19 B9
St Andrews
Lutheran Aged Care
2 Sullivan Rd,
Tallebudgera 59 R20
St Cuthberts
Retirement Living Complexes
20 Banks Av,
Tweed Heads................... 82 L6
Seachange
Riverside Coomera
29 Ghostgum Gr,
Upper Coomera 6 J15
Seachange Village Arundel
299 Napper Rd................. 27 N2
Sequana Retirement
Community
409 Tamborine-
Oxenford Rd,
Upper Coomera 16 E3
Southern Cross Care,
Edens Landing
20 Loane Dr 263 H13
Southern Cross
St Josephs Villas
55 Blundell Bvd,
Tweed Heads South 82 J15
Southern Cross
St Marthas Hostel
3 Leisure Dr,
Banora Point 92 H1
Southern Cross
St Marthas Villas
81 Leisure Dr,
Banora Point 92 F1
Southport Lodge
37 Jimmieson Av,
Labrador......................... 28 R6
Spiritus Abri
cnr Bauer & Heath Sts,
Southport...................... 29 H16
SunnyCove Bethania
3 Snedden St................. 263 B7
Sunny Ridge Gardens
470 Pine Ridge Rd,
Coombabah..................... 18 L11
Terranora Valley
Assisted Living Apartments
Carramar Dr,
Tweed Heads West.......... 81 J12
The Palms Village
112 Dry Dock Rd,
Tweed Heads South 82 C13
Tricare Labrador Aged Care
71 Brighton St,
Biggera Waters............... 19 D16
Trinity Gardens
Retirement Hostel
135 Nerang St,
Southport........................ 29 D14
Victoria Towers
34 Scarborough St,
Southport........................ 29 G13
Villa La Salle
Retirement Village
32 Bauer St,
Southport........................ 29 G16
Villa Serena,
Advanced Aged Care Services
cnr Laver & Easthill Drs,
Robina........................... 58 K2
Vision by Halcyon
27 Grant Av,
Hope Island 8 D11
Westminster House Robina
5 Bourton Rd,
Merrimac 48 B8

Airports / Airfields

Caravan, Tourist & Mobile Home Parks

Map Ref

Advancetown
Advancetown Caravan Park,
376 Nerang-
Murwillumbah Rd 36 B17
Biggera Waters
Treasure Island
Holiday Park,
117 Brisbane Rd 18 Q17
Burleigh Heads
Burleigh Beach
Tourist Park,
Goodwin Tce 60 G7
Burleigh Town Village,
3 Township Dr 59 R15
Burleigh Waters
Bungalows Village Park,
325 Reedy Creek Rd 59 K10
Carbrook
Aquatic Gardens
Caravan Park,
833 Beenleigh-
Redland Bay Rd............. 265 M8
Carrara
Casino Village
Caravan Park,
524 Nerang-
Broadbeach Rd................ 38 F11
River Gardens
Caravan Park,
672 Nerang-
Broadbeach Rd................ 38 K12
Riverside Home Park,
456 Nerang-
Broadbeach Rd............... 38 E10
Chambers Flat
Chambers Pines
Lifestyle Resort,
cnr Chambers Flat &
Koplick Rds 281 G3
Chinderah
Chinderah Village
Caravan Park,
20 Chinderah Bay Dr....... 92 P11
Homestead Caravan Park,
Chinderah Bay Dr............ 92 P8
Ingenia Holidays Kingscliff,
46 Wommin Bay Rd 92 R12
Royal Pacific Tourist
Retreat & Caravan Park,
109 Chinderah Rd............ 92M14
Tweed River Hacienda
Holiday Park,
37 Chinderah Bay Dr....... 92 P9
Tweed Shores & Chinderah
Lakes Caravan Park,
92 Chinderah Bay Dr.... 92 K14
Coolangatta
Kirra Beach Tourist Park,
Charlotte St 82 A2
Coombabah
Emerald Gardens,
70 Hansford Rd 18 K2
Lakeview Caravan Park,
11 Esplanade 8 F20
Pine Ridge Caravan Village,
570 Pine Ridge Rd 18 H13
Fingal Head
Tweed Holiday Parks,
9 Prince St 83 B13
Helensvale
BIG4 Gold Coast
Holiday Park & Motel,
66 Siganto Dr 17 A1
Jacobs Well
Jacobs Well Tourist Park,
Jacobs Well Rd 308 D9
Kingscliff
Tweed Holiday Park,
Kingscliff North,
Marine Pde 93 C13

Map Ref

Tweed Holiday Parks,
Kingscliff Beach,
Marine Pde 93 F19
Labrador
Southport Tourist Park,
6 Frank St....................... 29 D6
Main Beach
Main Beach Tourist Park,
Main Beach Pde 29M16
Mermaid Waters
Nobby Beach
Holiday Village,
2200 Gold Coast Hwy...... 49 Q13
Miami
Ocean Beach
Tourist Park Miami,
2 Hythe St 50 B17
Nerang
Nerang Caravan Park,
73 Nerang St 37 J3
Palm Beach
Tallebudgera Creek
Tourist Park,
1544 Gold Coast Hwy...... 60 H11
Southport
Broadwater Tourist Park,
Gold Coast Hwy 29 F7
Tamborine Mountain
Tamborine Mountain
Caravan & Camping,
Thunderbird Park
Tourist Complex,
Tamborine Mountain Rd 13 M4
Tweed Heads South
BIG4 Tweed Billabong
Holiday Park,
Holden St 82 D13
Boyds Bay Holiday Park,
cnr Pacific Hwy &
Dry Dock Rd 82 G10
Colonial Tweed
Caravan Park,
cnr Philp Pde &
Fraser Dr 82 A13
River Retreat
Caravan Park,
8 Philp Pde 81 R12
Tweed Broadwater Village,
250 Kirkwood Rd W......... 81 Q13
Tweed Heads West
Pyramid Holiday Park,
Kennedy Dr 82 A9
Upper Coomera
Coomera Village
Caravan Park,
2 Reserve Rd 6 Q8

Cemeteries & Crematoria

Alberton Cemetery 265 N18
Allambe Memorial Park
Cemetery &
Crematorium................... 37 Q6
Beenleigh Cemetery 264 D14
Canungra Cemetery.......... 33 K17
Catholic Cemetery 300 G20
Chambers Flat
Cemetery 281 F9
Chinderah Cemetery 92 N16
Coomera Cemetery 6 P3
Eagleby Cemetery 264 G11
Eco Memorial Park 285 D5
Henry Jordan
Private Cemetery 262 N13
Logan Reserve Bethel
Lutheran Cemetery 262 A19
Logan Village Cemetery .. 293M11
Marian Valley Shrine 45 J11
Melaleuca Station
Memorial Gardens........ 102 B1
Mudgeeraba Cemetery 48 B19
Nerang Cemetery 37 F1
Norwell Cemetery 307 J6
Parkhouse Cemetery 304 D11
Pimpama Cemetery 305 P20

Map Ref

St Johns Cemetery............ 11 G3
Southport General
Cemetery 28 R13
Southport Lawn
Cemetery 28 L7
Tallebudgera Cemetery 69 M2
Tamborine Catholic
Cemetery 2 G1
Tamborine Mountain
Cemetery 13 L17
Tamborine Village
Cemetery 304 B18
Tweed Crematorium &
Memorial Gardens........... 82 E14
Tweed Heads Cemetery..... 82 G4
Tygum Pioneer
Cemetery 262 J13
Upper Coomera
Cemetery 6 A19
Wonglepong Cemetery...... 23 E16

Churches & Other Places of Worship

Other Congregations

Arundel
Serbian Orthodox,
114 Allied Dr 18 L19
Beenleigh
Rivergate,
10 Plantation Rd 284 J4
Seventh-day Baptist,
Church St 284 E3
Broadbeach Waters
Church of Christ,
Iglesia Ni Cristo,
4 Sunshine Bvd............... 39 L19
Carbrook
Interdenominational,
"Youth with a
Mission Island Breeze",
cnr Beenleigh-
Redland Bay &
Ferry Rds 265 L7
Carrara
Dream Centre
Christian Church,
cnr Nerang-Broadbeach &
Chisholm Rds 38 A7
Reach out for Christ,
International Ministries,
288 Gooding Dr 48 J2
Marsden
Apostolic Christian
Church Nazarene,
Second Av 261 J4
Maudsland
Apostolic Church Australia,
City on Hill,
60 Gaven Arterial Rd 16 H13
Robina
St Andrews Heritage
Queensland Church,
Great Southern Dr 49 C18
Southport
Gospel Chapel,
cnr Scarborough St &
High St............................ 29 E9
Tallebudgera
Gold Coast
Revival Fellowship,
cnr Tallebudgera
Creek Rd & Heather St ... 59 R20

Anglican

Beenleigh
St Georges,
cnr Kent &
Tansey Sts 284 D2
Burleigh Heads
St Johns,
14 Park Av 60 E6

Map Ref

Canungra
St Lukes,
Kidston St....................... 33 D14
Coolangatta
St Peters,
32 Lanham St 82 G2
Kingscliff
St James,
120 Marine Pde 93 E19
Labrador
St James,
41 Brighton St 19 D17
Southport,
All Saints,
Chirn Cr........................... 29 B6
Mudgeeraba
Church of the
Good Shepherd,
4 Tarrant Dr 57 M5
Mundoolun
Mundoolun Rd 11 G3
Nerang
St Margarets,
Beaudesert-Nerang Rd.... 37 C3
Oxenford
Tamborine-Oxenford Rd ... 6 H19
Palm Beach
St Pauls,
65 Palm Beach Av 70 M1
Robina
Trinity Mission,
Robina Town Centre Dr .. 58 K1
Southport
St Peters,
69 Nerang St 29 F13
Surfers Paradise
Holy Spirit,
73 Salerno St.................. 39 H12
St John the Evangelist,
Hamilton Av 40M15
Tamborine Mountain
St Georges,
Dapsang Dr 14 A13
Tugun
All Saints,
24 Toolona St................... 71 F11
Tweed Heads
St Cuthberts,
cnr Florence &
Powell Sts....................... 82 K5

Anglican Catholic

Mermaid Beach
St Johns,
Dolphin Av....................... 49 R12
Upper Coomera
Chapel of St Stephen
Protomartyr,
Saint Stephens College,
Reserve Rd 6 N9

Australian Christian Churches

Arundel
New Life Centre,
16 Dunkirk Cl................... 18 K19
Coombabah
Runaway Bay,
456 Pine Ridge Rd 18M11
Coomera
Jowett St........................... 6 R10
Miami
23 Christine Av 50 B20
Ormeau
Highway Christian,
Creek St 305 L16
Reedy Creek
Kings Christian Centre,
68 Gemvale Rd 58 R10
Southport
116 Ridgeway Av 39 B1
Surfers Paradise
Surf City,
Surfers Paradise Bvd...... 40M13
Tweed Heads
3 Beryl St 82 J3

Map Ref

Tweed Heads South
Machinery Dr 82 H17
Waterford West
Logan Christian Fellowship,
Kingston Rd 262 G9

Baptist

Beenleigh
Beenleigh District,
79 Pheasant Av 264 B15
Crestmead
Logan City,
229 Chambers Flat Rd .. 261 M9
Helensvale
Helensvale & District,
cnr Discovery Dr &
Careel Cl 17 J10
Labrador
Coast Life Community,
cnr Gold Coast Hwy &
Billington St 19 C18
Mudgeeraba
Gold Coast
Christian Family,
120 Mudgeeraba Rd........ 47 R14
Reedy Creek
10 Gemvale Rd 59 A11
Southport
170 Nerang St 29 C15
Tugun
Tugun-Tweed Community,
cnr Toolona & Atkin Sts.. 71 F11

Baptist Independent

Mount Warren Park
Beenleigh,
Harvest,
135 Mt Warren Bvd........ 284 F5
Nerang
Gold Coast,
22 White St 37 G2
Worongary
Hinterland,
405 Hinkler Dr................. 47 P4

Buddhist

Marsden
Cambodian Khmer,
44 Third Av 261 G3

Catholic

Beechmont
St Johns,
Windabout Rd 45 G18
Beenleigh
St Patricks,
70 Tobruk St 264 C18
Broadbeach
Stella Maris,
268 Hedges Av 49 Q3
Burleigh Heads
Infant Saviour,
Park Av............................ 60 E6
Canungra
St Margaret Mary,
Kidston St....................... 33 E15
Clear Island Waters
Sacred Heart,
50 Fairway Dr 49 B3
Coolangatta
St Augustines,
cnr McLean &
Tweed Sts 82 F2
Kingscliff
St Anthonys,
Pearl St 103 F1
Labrador
St Joseph the Worker,
Imperial Pde.................... 29 D2
Marsden
St Maximilian Kolbe,
26 Macarthy Rd.............. 261 H2
Miami
Calvary,
Santa Monica Rd............. 50 A15

Churches & Other Places of Worship

Parks, Reserves & Sporting Venues

Places of Interest

	Map Ref
Mudgeeraba Showground	
Mudgeeraba Rd,	
Worongary	47 Q13
Norwell Motorplex	
75 Norwell Rd,	
Woongoolba	286 H14
Numinbah Environmental	
Education Centre	
1721 Nerang-Murwillumbah Rd,	
Numinbah Valley	46 C17
Opal Shed Mining Company	
164 Siganto Dr,	
Helensvale	6 R18
Paradise Country	
Entertainment Rd,	
Oxenford	16 Q7
Purling Brook Falls	
Lloyds Rd,	
Springbrook	66 H15
Putt Putt Golf	
2492 Gold Coast Hwy,	
Mermaid Beach	49 Q6
Ripleys Believe It	
Or Not Museum	
Soul Surfers Paradise Beach,	
Cavill Av,	
Surfers Paradise	40 N10
Sanctuary Cove	
Masthead Wy,	
Hope Island	8 A1
Sea World	
Seaworld Dr,	
Main Beach	29 L8
SkyPoint Observation Deck	
Q1,	
Surfers Paradise Bvd,	
Surfers Paradise	40 N14
Springbrook Glow Worms	
2509 Springbrook Rd	66 H18
Springbrook Research	
Observatory	
2337 Springbrook Rd	66 F15
Superbee Honey World	
35 Tomewin St,	
Currumbin	71 D6
Surf World	
35 Tomewin St,	
Currumbin	71 D6
Tamborine Mountain	
Heritage Centre	
Wongawallan Rd	14 E11
Tamborine Rainforest Skywalk	
Tamborine Mountain Rd,	
Tamborine Mountain	13 N6
The Star Casino	
Broadbeach Island,	
Casino Dr,	
Broadbeach	49 N1
The Strawberry Farm	
Pimpama-Jacobs Well Rd,	
Pimpama	326 D5
Thunderbird Park	
cnr Tamborine Mountain &	
Cedar Creek Falls Rd,	
Tamborine Mountain	13 N4
Tweed Maritime & Heritage	
Museum,	
Tweed River	
Regional Museum	
230 Kennedy Dr,	
Tweed Heads West	81 M11
Visitor Information Centre,	
Beenleigh Information &	
Booking Centre	
209 Main St	284 H4
Canungra	
cnr Kidston &	
ppel Sts	33 E14
Coolangatta	
The Strand,	
Griffith St	82 G1
Surfers Paradise	
cnr Cavill Av &	
Surfers Paradise Bvd	40 M10
Tamborine Mountain	
Tamborine Mountain Rd,	
Tamborine Mountain	13 N14
Warner Bros Movie World	
Entertainment Rd,	
Oxenford	16 Q5

	Map Ref
Wax Museum	
cnr Ferny & Elkhorn Avs,	
Surfers Paradise	40 L7
Wet 'n' Wild Water World	
Entertainment Rd,	
Oxenford	17 A8
WhiteWater World	
Dreamworld Pky,	
Coomera	6 R6
Witches Chase	
Cheese Company	
165 Long Rd,	
Tamborine Mountain	14 C13
Witches Falls	
Tamborine National Park,	
Main Western Rd,	
Tamborine Mountain	13 H17

Police Stations

	Map Ref
Arundel Police Beat	27 Q2
Beenleigh	284 D1
Broadbeach	
Police Shopfront	49 M2
Broadwater Police Beat	7 R2
Burleigh Heads	60 C10
Canungra	33 E15
Coolangatta	82 F1
Coomera	6 R10
Crestmead	261 D4
Eagleby Police Beat	264 H15
Edens Landing	
Police Beat	263 G13
Harbour Town	
Police Beat	18 N17
Jacobs Well Police Beat	308 B11
Kingscliff	93 E18
Logan Village Yarrabilba	293 P4
Mudgeeraba	48 C19
Nerang	37 H2
Norfolk Village	
Police Beat	305 B5
North Tamborine	13 N12
Pacific Pines Police Beat	27 D1
Palm Beach	70 Q2
Robina Police Shopfront	48 L20
Robina Police Station	58 Q7
Runaway Bay	19 A7
Southport	29 G12
Surfers Paradise	40 N8
Tweed Heads	82 H7
Water Police	29 M13

Police & Citizens Youth Clubs

	Map Ref
Ashmore	
Dominions Rd	28 L18
Beenleigh	
Alamein St	264 E18
Bornhoffen	
Nerang-Murwillumbah Rd,	
Natural Bridge	65 Q20
Crestmead	
26 Lilly Pilly St	261 K9
Gold Coast	
180 Monaco St,	
Broadbeach Waters	39 F14
Nerang	
Cayuga St	37 J8
Tweed Heads	
Florence St	82 G4

Qld Transport Customer Service Centres

	Map Ref
Beenleigh	
Customer Service Centre	
24 Kent St	284 D1
Bundall	
Customer Service Centre	
30 Upton St	39 E11

	Map Ref
Burleigh Waters	
Customer Service Centre	
1 Santa Maria Ct	49 K20
Currumbin Waters	
Customer Service Centre	
109 Currumbin	
Creek Rd	70 N13
Helensvale	
Customer Service Centre	
Helensvale Plaza,	
12 Sir John Overall Dr	17 H12
Southport	
Customer Service Centre	
265 Nerang Rd	28 Q16

Racecourses & Trotting Tracks

	Map Ref
Border Park Raceway	
Binya Av,	
Tweed Heads	82 A3
Gold Coast Turf Club	
Racecourse Dr,	
Bundall	39 C8

RACQ Branch Offices

	Map Ref
Oxenford Service Centre	
50 Siganto Dr,	
Helensvale	17 A3
RACQ Beenleigh	
Beenleigh Mall,	
40 Main St	284 D2
RACQ Elanora	
The Pines Shopping Centre,	
Guineas Creek Rd	70 M6
RACQ Nerang	
My Centre Nerang,	
57 Station St	37 J5
RACQ Robina	
Robina Town Centre,	
Arbour La	48 L20
RACQ Southport West	
239 Southport-Nerang Rd,	
Southport	28 Q16
Tamborine Mountain	
Auto Clinic	
41 Main St	13 N12

Schools & Colleges - Private

	Map Ref
A B Paterson College	
Arundel	18 A14
Aquinas College	
Southport	28 L15
Assisi Catholic College	
Upper Coomera	6 L3
Bethania Lutheran	
Primary	263 B11
Calvary Christian College,	
Carbrook Campus	265 B5
Canterbury College	
Waterford	262 Q17
Coomera	
Anglican College	6 M3
Emmanuel College	
Carrara	38 F13
Gainsborough Primary	
Pimpama	326 N8
Gold Coast Christian College	
Reedy Creek	59 A13
Guardian Angels Catholic	
Primary	
Southport	28 L14
Hillcrest Christian College	
Reedy Creek	58 R12
Josiah College	
Carrara	38 F12
Jubilee Primary	
Pacific Pines	17 A14
Kimberley College	
Carbrook	265 A4

	Map Ref
Kings Christian College	
Reedy Creek	58 R9
Logan Village Campus	
Logan Village	293 L4
Pimpama Campus	326 J2
Lindisfarne Grammar,	
Junior Campus	
Tweed Heads	82 F13
Middle & Senior Campus	
Terranora	91 L10
Livingstone	
Christian College	
Ormeau	305 N14
Lutheran Ormeau Rivers	
District School	
Pimpama	306 D17
Marymount Catholic College	
Burleigh Waters	59 N10
Mother Teresa Primary	
Ormeau	305 R10
Pacific Coast	
Christian College,	
High School	
Tweed Heads South	82 A14
Queensland	
Independent College	
Merrimac	48 D8
Rivermount College	
Yatala	284 C16
St Andrews Lutheran College	
Tallebudgera	59 Q20
St Anthonys	
Catholic Primary	
Kingscliff	103 F1
St Augustines Primary	
Currumbin Waters	70 J13
St Brigids Catholic Primary	
Nerang	37 A5
St Clares Primary	
Yarrabilba	293 Q20
St Francis College	
Crestmead	261 D10
St Francis Xavier Primary	
Runaway Bay	19 B6
St Hildas	
Southport	29 E12
St James Primary	
Banora Point	82 G20
St Josephs College	
Banora Point	82 G19
Coomera	327 G12
St Josephs Primary	
Beenleigh	264 C19
Tweed Heads	82 J3
St Kevins Primary	
Benowa	38 P8
St Michaels Catholic	
Secondary College	
Merrimac	48 D5
St Philomena	
Park Ridge	281 E1
St Stephens College	
Upper Coomera	6 P8
St Vincents Primary	
Clear Island Waters	49 C2
San Damiano College	
Yarrabilba	300 B1
Silkwood Steiner	
Nerang	36 F8
Somerset College	
Mudgeeraba	58 G7
Tamborine	
Mountain College	13 J14
The Southport Preparatory	
Southport	29 E19
The Southport School	29 G20
Trinity Lutheran College,	
Middle & Senior Schools	
Molendinar	28 C17
Primary School	
Ashmore	28 G19
Trinity Secondary College	
Beenleigh	264 B18

	Map Ref
Arundel Primary	28 C2
Ashmore Primary	38 K2
Banora Point High	92 B2
Banora Point Primary	92 K5
Beechmont Primary	65 G1
Beenleigh High	264 E20
Beenleigh Primary	284 C2
Beenleigh Special School	
Mount Warren Park	284 C4
Bellevue Park	
Ashmore	38 R4
Benowa High	38 N9
Benowa Primary	38 P9
Biggera Waters Primary	18 R14
Bilambil Primary	90 M5
Broadbeach Primary	49 Q2
Burleigh Heads Primary	60 D5
Burrowes Primary	
Marsden	261 H3
Caldera School	
Tweed Heads South	82 H19
Caningeraba Primary	
Burleigh Waters	59 N4
Canungra Primary	33 D14
Carbrook Primary	265 A3
Carool Primary	89 M8
Cedar Creek Primary	304 E15
Centaur Primary	
Banora Point	92 C2
Clover Hill Primary	
Mudgeeraba	58 H7
Coolangatta Primary	82 D2
Coombabah High	18 J12
Coombabah Primary	8 N19
Coomera Primary	7 A8
Coomera Rivers	
State School	
Coomera	327 E18
Coomera Springs Primary	
Upper Coomera	326 K18
Coomera State	
Special School	327 L19
Crestmead Primary	261 G8
Cudgen Primary	102 P3
Currumbin Community	
Special School	
Currumbin Waters	70 P14
Currumbin Primary	70 Q8
Currumbin Valley	
Primary	78 Q18
Duranbah Primary	101 Q14
Eagleby Learning	
Centre	264 H11
Eagleby Primary	264 H10
Eagleby South Primary	
Eagleby	264 J15
Edens Landing Primary	263 G15
Elanora High	70 D4
Elanora Primary	70 L4
Fingal Head Primary	83 B14
Foxwell Secondary College	
Coomera	7 F2
Gaven Primary	
Oxenford	16 N11
Gilston Primary	46 R2
Helensvale High	17 E1
Helensvale Primary	17 F9
Highland Reserve	
State School	
Upper Coomera	6 C18
Ingleside Primary	
Tallebudgera Valley	68 K20
Keebra Park High	
Southport	29 B19
Kingscliff High	103 D5
Kingscliff Primary	103 G1
Labrador Primary	29 B1
Loganholme Primary	263 M7
Loganlea High	262 N2
Logan Reserve Primary	262 A20
Logan Village Primary	293 P2

Map Ref

Marsden High
  Waterford West 261 R7
Marsden Primary 261 P7
Merrimac High
  Mermaid Waters 49 H4
Merrimac Primary 48 H4
Miami High 50 A14
Miami Primary
  Mermaid Waters 49 L13
Mt Warren Park Primary .. 284 E5
Mudgeeraba Creek Primary
  Mudgeeraba 57 N5
Mudgeeraba Primary 47 Q19
Mudgeeraba
  Special School 58 C1
Musgrave Hill Primary
  Southport 28 Q8
Nerang High 37 E7
Nerang Primary 37 J1
Norfolk Village Primary
  Ormeau 305 E5
Numinbah Valley Primary . 65 Q6
Ormeau Primary
  Pimpama 306 A18
Ormeau Woods High 305 M5
Oxenford Primary 16 M2
Pacific Pines High 27 A1
Pacific Pines Primary 17 B19
Palm Beach-Currumbin High
  Palm Beach 70 Q4
Palm Beach Primary 60 K15
Park Lake Primary
  Pacific Pines 16 L18
Picnic Creek Primary
  Coomera 327 K15
Pimpama Primary 326 A5
Pimpama
  State Primary College .. 327 C12
Pimpama State
  Secondary College 327 A13
Robina High 48 H19
Robina Primary 49 A18
St Bernard Primary
  Tamborine Mountain 24 B13
Southport High 29 C10
Southport Primary 29 A13
Southport
  Special School 28 Q9
South Rock Primary
  Yarrabilba 300 J10
Springbrook Primary 66 F15
Surfers Paradise Primary . 39 K12
Tallebudgera Primary 69 N9
Tamborine Mountain
  High 13 Q16
Tamborine Mountain
  Primary 14 C15
Terranora Primary 91 H13
Tweed Heads Primary 82 J2
Tweed Heads
  South Primary 82 H13
Tweed River High
  Tweed Heads South 82 H13
Upper Coomera College ... 6 J9
Varsity College,
  Middle & Senior Campus
  Varsity Lakes 59 F1
  Primary & Junior Campus
  Varsity Lakes 59 E5
Waterford Primary 262 N11
Waterford West Primary .. 262 J9
William Duncan Primary
  Highland Park 37 G12
Windaroo Primary
  Mount Warren Park 284 A8
Windaroo Valley High
  Bahrs Scrub 283 Q11
Woongoolba Primary 287 B13
Worongary Primary 37 L16
Yarrabilba Primary 294 A20
Yarrabilba
  Secondary College 294 D20

Scouts

Map Ref

Ashmore 28 L17
Beenleigh 283 P5
Burleigh Heads 60 C6
Canungra 45 G4
Chinderah 92 N14
Coomera 6 R8
Helensvale 17 B6
Labrador 19 C19
Marsden 262 A3
Mudgeeraba 48 B13
Nerang 27 H20
Palm Beach 70 P6
Parkwood Heights 28 K6
Point Danger 82 H2
Southport 29 D10
Twin Rivers 264 G15

Shopping Complexes - Major

Ashmore City
  Shopping Centre 28 K17
Ashmore Plaza 28 L20
Australia Fair
  Shopping Centre
  Southport 29 H12
Beenleigh Marketplace
  Shopping Centre 284 F1
Bell Central Shopping Centre
  Mudgeeraba 58 D1
Benowa Gardens
  Shopping Centre
  Benowa 38 P11
Burleigh Homespace
  Burleigh Waters 49 K20
Chevron Renaissance
  Surfers Paradise 40 L8
Circle on Cavill
  Surfers Paradise 40 L10
Coomera City Centre
  Upper Coomera 326 L20
Harbour Town
  Biggera Waters 18 N16
Helensvale Plaza 17 H12
Holmview Central
  Shopping Centre
  Holmview 263 D18
Homeworld Helensvale 7 A16
Hope Island Marketplace
  Hope Island 8 C12
Marina Mirage
  Main Beach 29 M12
Marsden Park
  Shopping Centre 262 B4
Metro Market
  Biggera Waters 19 B16
Monte Carlo
  Surfers Paradise 40 M8
Mudgeeraba Market
  Shopping Centre 58 D1
Nerang Mall
  Shopping Centre 37 J6
Niecon Plaza
  Broadbeach 39 P19
Pacific Fair Shopping Centre
  Broadbeach Waters 49 M2
Paradise Centre
  Surfers Paradise 40 M10
Piazza on the Boulevard
  Surfers Paradise 40 M7
Pimpama City
  Shopping Centre
  Pimpama 326 H4
Pimpama Junction 327 A9
Q Super Centre
  Mermaid Waters 49 D6
Robina Town Centre 48 M20
Runaway Bay
  Shopping Village 19 B8

Map Ref

Sanctuary Cove
  Marine Village
  Hope Island 8 C1
Soul Surfers
  Paradise Beach
  Surfers Paradise 40 N10
Southport Central 29 G13
Southport Park
  Shopping Centre 29 E20
Stockland Burleigh Heads
  Burleigh Waters 60 B9
The Mark Centre
  Surfers Paradise 40 N10
The Oasis Shopping Centre
  Broadbeach 39 P19
The O.C. @ Exit 35
  Eagleby 284 L4
The Pines
  Shopping Centre
  Elanora 70 M6
The Strand
  Coolangatta 82 H1
Treetops Plaza
  Shopping Centre
  Burleigh Waters 59 L10
Tweed City
  Shopping Centre
  Tweed Heads South 82 K16
Tweed Mall
  Tweed Heads 82 K3
Vicinity Centres Oxenford ... 6 Q18
Westfield,
  Helensvale 17 H14
Westfield Coomera 6 R2
Westfield Coomera 326 R20

Swimming Pools

Bethania
  Aquatic Centre 263 B7
Bond University
  Swimming Pool 49 J19
Club Banora
  Swimming Pool 92 G1
Eagleby Aquatic Centre ... 264 G15
Gold Coast
  quatic Centre 29 H11
Gullivers Coomera Indoor
  Swim Gym &
  Sports Centre 6 M10
Helensvale
  Swimming Pool 17 F2
Kingscliff
  Swimming Centre 103 D3
Miami Olympic
  Swimming Pool 49 N14
Moriarty Community
  Sporting Complex 33 B14
Mudgeeraba
  Swimming Pool 58 C1
Nerang Swimming Pool 37 G2
Palm Beach Olympic
  Swimming Pool 70 Q5
Rob Nay Memorial Pool ... 264 D18
Southport
  Swimming Enclosure 29 J12
South Tweed Indoor
  Swimming Complex 82 J13
Tamborine Mountain
  Swimming Pool 13 M14
Woongoolba
  Swimming Pool 286 M10

Tertiary Institutions

Australian Industry
  Trade College,
  Robina
  Scottsdale Dr 58 P7
Bond University
  University Dr,
  Robina 49 G19

Map Ref

Central Queensland University,
  Gold Coast International
  Campus
  60 Marine Pde,
  Southport 29 G11
Griffith University,
  Centre for Medicine &
  Oral Health
  16 High St,
  Southport 29 E14
Gold Coast Campus
  Parklands Dr,
  Southport 28 J9
Queensland Academies
  Health Sciences Campus
  Edmund Rice Dr,
  Southport 28 K11
Harvest Bible College
  2 Mieke Ct,
  Burleigh Heads 59 L19
New York Film Academy
  Australia,
  Gold Coast Campus
  Southport Central Towers,
  5 Lawson St,
  Southport 29 G13
Shafston College,
  Gold Coast Campus
  13 Nerang St,
  Southport 29 G12
Southern Cross University,
  Gold Coast
  Southern Cross Dr,
  Bilinga 81 R1
Lakeside
  Caloola Dr,
  Tweed Heads 82 B5
Riverside
  Brett St,
  Tweed Heads 82 J5
TAFE NSW Kingscliff
  Cudgen Rd 103 C4
TAFE Queensland,
  Ashmore Campus
  cnr Heeb St &
  Benowa Rd 38 P4
  Coolangatta Campus
  5 Scott St 82 H2
  Coomera Creative Campus
  198 Foxwell Rd 7 B1
  Southport Campus
  91 Scarborough St 29 G12

Theatres & Cinemas

Arts Theatre,
  The Arts Centre
  Gold Coast
  135 Bundall Rd,
  Surfers Paradise 39 H7
Beenleigh Twin Drive-In
  100 Jacobs Well Rd,
  Stapylton 285 B7
Event Cinemas,
  Australia Fair Cinemas
  Australia Fair
  Shopping Centre,
  Scarborough St,
  Southport 29 H12
  Coolangatta
  The Strand,
  cnr Griffith &
  Warner Sts 82 H1
  Pacific Fair
  Pacific Fair Shopping Centre,
  Hooker Bvd,
  Broadbeach Waters 49 N3
  Robina
  Robina Town Centre,
  Robina Town Centre Dr .. 48 L20
Gold Coast Little Theatre
  21 Scarborough St,
  Southport 29 H14

Map Ref

Hoyts Cinemas,
  Tweed City
  54 Minjungbal Dr,
  Tweed Heads South 82 L15
Javeenbah Theatre
  cnr Ferry & Stevens Sts,
  Nerang 37 G1
Nerang Cinemas
  Earle Plaza,
  52 Price St 37 H3
Reading Cinemas,
  Harbour Town
  Harbour Town Shopping
  Centre,
  cnr Brisbane Rd &
  Oxley Dr,
  Biggera Waters 18 N16
Village Theatre
  Sanctuary Cove
  Masthead Wy,
  Hope Island 8 C1

Weighbridges

Gold Coast City Council,
  Reedy Creek Landfill
  89 Hutchinson St,
  Burleigh Heads 59 G16
Gold Coast
  City Council Landfill
  Herbertson Dr,
  Molendinar 27 R19
Sims Metal Management
  12 Hope St,
  Nerang 27 G20
Stonemaster Quarries Pty Ltd
  3 Stonemaster Dr,
  Stapylton 285 E3

Wharf & Marina

Horizon Shores Marina 287 N16

Wineries

Albert River Wines 11 Q6
Cedar Creek Estate
  Vineyard & Winery 13 Q18
Hampton Estate 23 P9
Mason Wines 13 M18
Mount Nathan Winery 35 L6
O'Reillys Vineyards
  Canungra Valley 33 A20
Witches Falls Winery 13 L16

Publishing Dates

1st Edition 1997
2nd Edition 1999
3rd Edition 2000
4th Edition 2001
5th Edition 2002
6th Edition 2003
7th Edition 2004
8th Edition 2005
9th Edition 2006
10th Edition 2007
11th Edition 2008
12th Edition 2009
13th Edition 2010
14th Edition 2011
15th Edition 2012
16th Edition 2013
17th Edition 2014
18th Edition 2015
19th Edition 2016
20th Edition 2017
21st Edition 2018
22nd Edition 2019
23rd Edition 2020
24th Edition 2021
25th Edition 2024

Street Listings

All the streets in this index are listed alphabetically and then by suburb. It is most important to have the correct name when looking for a particular street. If any difficulty is experienced with the suburb name, refer to the Suburbs and Localities Index.

Mc and **Mac:** Names beginning with 'Mc' are treated as though they are spelt 'Mac' and indexed accordingly.

Mt: Names beginning with 'Mt' are treated as though they are spelt 'Mount' and indexed accordingly.

St: Names beginning with 'St' are treated as though they are spelt 'Saint' and indexed accordingly.

The: Names beginning with 'The' are treated with 'The' first and are indexed accordingly.

Streets not Named on Maps

For reasons of clarity it is not always possible to show and name every street on the map itself. Any street or lane that is not shown on the map face is listed in italic (sloping) type and referenced to its approximate position.

Alphabet Indicators

These are the street names in capitals located on the top left and right hand corners of each page of the street index. The indicator on the left page represents the first named street in the first column on this page, while the indicator on the right page represents the last named street in the last column on this page.

ABBREVIATIONS FOR DESIGNATIONS

Alley .... al	Circus .... crc	Edge .... edg	Hike .... hk	Place .... pl	Square .... sq
Approach ...... app	Close cl	Elbow .... elb	Hill .... hill	Plaza .... plz	Strand .... sd
Arcade .... arc	Common ...... cmn	End .... end	Junction .... jnc	Pocket .... pkt	Street .... st
Avenue .... av	Concourse ..... cnc	Entrance ...... ent	Key .... key	Port/Point ...... pt	Tarn .... tn
Bend .... bnd	Copse .... cps	Esplanade .... esp	Lane .... la	Promenade .... prm	Terrace .... tce
Boardwalk ..... bwk	Corner .... cnr	Expressway ... exp	Link .... lk	Quadrant .... qd	Tollway .... twy
Boulevard ...... bvd	Corso .... cso	Fairway .... fy	Lookout .... lkt	Quay/s .... qy	Top .... top
Bowl .... bl	Court .... ct	Freeway .... fwy	Loop .... lp	Ramble .... ra	Tor .... tor
Brace .... br	Courtyard ...... cyd	Frontage .... fr	Mall .... ml	Reach .... rch	Track .... tr
Brae .... br	Cove .... cov	Garden/s ...... gdn	Mead .... md	Reserve .... res	Trail .... trl
Break .... brk	Crescent .... cr	Gate/s .... gte	Meander .... mdr	Rest .... rst	Turn .... trn
Brook .... brk	Crest .... cst	Gateway .... gwy	Mews .... mw	Retreat .... rt	Underpass ..... ups
Broadway ...... bwy	Cross .... cs	Glade .... gld	Motorway ..... mwy	Return .... rtn	Vale .... va
Brow .... brw	Crossing .... csg	Glen .... gln	Nook .... nk	Ridge .... rdg	Valley .... vy
Bypass .... bps	Curve .... cve	Grange .... gra	North .... n	Rise .... ri	View .... vw
Central c	Dale .... dle	Green .... grn	Outlook .... out	Road .... rd	Vista .... vst
Centre .... ctr	Down/s .... dn	Grove .... gr	Parade .... pde	Roadway .... rdy	Walk .... wk
Chase .... ch	Drive .... dr	Grovet .... gr	Park .... pk	Route .... rte	Walkway .... wky
Circle .... cir	Driveway .... dwy	Haven .... hvn	Parkway .... pky	Row .... row	Way .... wy
Circuit .... cct	East .... e	Heights .... hts	Pass .... ps	Serviceway .... swy	West .... w
		Highway .... hwy	Pathway .... pwy	South .... s	Wynd .... wyn

ABBREVIATIONS FOR SUBURB NAMES

Airport .... Aprt	Crossing .... Csg	Head/s .... Hd	Lower .... Lr	Pocket .... Pkt	South .... S
Basin .... Bsn	Down/s .... Dn	Headland ...... Hd	Meadow/s .... Mdw	Point/Port ..... Pt	Terminal ...... Term
Bay .... B	East .... E	Heights .... Ht	Mount .... Mt	Range .... Rge	University ...... Uni
Beach .... Bch	Field/s .... Fd	Hill/s .... Hl	Mountain/s .... Mtn	Reach .... Rch	Upper .... Up
Bridge .... Br	Flat .... Fl	Island I	North .... N	Reserve .... Res	Valley .... Vy
Central .... Ctrl	Forest .... Frst	Junction .... Jctn	Paradise ...... Pdse	Ridge .... Rdg	Vale .... Va
Chase .... Ch	Garden/s .... Gdn	Lagoon .... Lgn	Park .... Pk	River .... R	Village Vill
Corner .... Cnr	Grove .... Gr	Lakes L	Peninsula ...... Pen	Rocks .... Rks	Waters .... Wtr
Court .... Ct	Gully .... Gly	Lodge .... Ldg	Plain/s .... Pl	Saint .... St	West .... W
Creek .... Ck	Harbor/our .... Hbr	Lookout .... Lkt	Plateau .... Plat		

Map Ref

A

AARON
st. Coomera 328 C18
ABALONE
av. Paradise Pt 8 P14
av. Russell I 268 J7
ABBEYFEALE
st. Crestmead 261 G6
ABBEY RIDGE
rd. Reedy Creek 68 M2
ABBEY ROSE
wy. Nerang 37 C9
ABBEYTREE
ct. Robina 58 R6
ABBOTT
ct. Guanaba 15 K15
ABBY
cct. Maudsland 16 E11
cr. Ashmore 38 N2
ABELE
ct. Elanora 70 G3
ABELIA
dr. Waterford W 262 M14
st. Palm Beach 60 G14
ABEL TASMAN
pl. Hollywell 9 A18
ABERCROMBIE
cr. Up Coomera 6 A15
ABERDEEN
ct. Banora Pt 92 C7
ct. Benowa 39 A12
ct. Highland Pk 37 H11
ABETE
ct. Nerang 37 B7
ABILENE
pl. Reedy Creek 58 P20
A B PATERSON
dr. Arundel 18 B14
ABRAHAM
rd. Up Coomera 6 M8
ABRAHAM ROAD EXIT
Up Coomera 6 N5
ABRAHEIM
ct. Mudgeeraba 57 R4
ACACIA
av. Surfers Pdse 39 M3
av. Surfers Pdse 40 L2
ct. Beechmont 45 H20
ct. Robina 58 Q7
st. Bahrs Scrub 283 J6
st. Tweed Hd S 81 R13
ACADEMIC
dr. Up Coomera 6 L9
ACADEMY
st. Oxenford 16 R11
ACANTHUS
av. Burleigh Hd 60 A7
av. Burleigh Hd 60 C5
av. Burleigh Wtr 59 R6
ACCESS
av. Yatala 284 M9
ACERO
ct. Nerang 37 B8
ACHIEVEMENT
dr. Ormeau 305 M11
ACKLIN
ct. Varsity Lakes 59 E6
ACMENA
ct. Elanora 70 C10
ACOLUS
ct. Casuarina 103 H16
ACOMA
tce. Mudgeeraba 57 R1
ACORN
la. Robina 58 P6
ACRON
st. Elanora 70 D2
ACTIVA
wy. Hope Island 7 P10
ACTIVITY
cr. Molendinar 28 B13
ct. Yatala 304 N1
ACTON
dr. Varsity Lakes 59 C2
pl. Up Coomera 16 C1
st. Buccan 282 F3
ADA
cr. Logan Res 281 R5
ADA BELL
wy. Southport 29 J14
ADALONG
pl. Nerang 37 B6
ADAM
st. Oxenford 16 Q11
ADAMINABY
dr. Helensvale 17 C2
ADAMS
av. Miami 49 R18
ADDISYN
st. Pimpama 326 R13
ADDLEY
la. Up Coomera 326 H19
ADELAIDE
cct. Beenleigh 263 Q20
cct. Beenleigh 283 Q1
cr. Ormeau Hills 305 G18
ct. Tamborine Mtn 33 M4
st. Tweed Heads 82 G7
ADELE
cr. Bahrs Scrub 283 J12
ADELIZA
ct. Arundel 18 C19
ADELONG
cl. Up Coomera 6 C14
ADEN
pl. Ormeau 305 P10
ADINA
av. Bilinga 71 K15
pl. Banora Pt 92 N3
ADIOS
ct. Mudgeeraba 57 N12
ADLER
cct. Yarrabilba 293 L19
ct. Benowa 38 R12
ADMIRAL
cr. Tugun 71 E14
ADMIRALTY
dr. Hope Island 8 D13
dr. Surfers Pdse 39 K2
pl. Banora Pt 92 K10
ADORI
st. Surfers Pdse 39 K5
ADRIAN
ct. Jacobs Well 308 D8
ADROSE
ct. Beenleigh 283 N2
ADVANCETOWN
rd. Advancetown 46 J2
ADVANCETOWN-MUDGEERABA
rd. Gilston 46 Q2
rd. Tallai 46 Q2
rd. Tallai 47 B8
rd. Worongary 47 B8
ADVENTURE
av. Oxenford 16 R10
ADVOCATE
pl. Banora Pt 92 F2
AEGEAN
st. Waterford W 262 G8
wy. Currumbin Wtr 70 K8
AEOLUS
la. Casuarina 103 J16
AETHALIA
st. Currumbin Wtr 70 H8
AGATHA
ct. Oxenford 16 Q12
AGAVE
st. Elanora 70 E3
AGESTON
rd. Alberton 285 R2
AGNES
st. Tweed Hd S 82 H11
AGNEW
st. Labrador 29 C7
AHERN
st. Labrador 29 D5
AILSA
st. Redland Bay 266 R1
st. Redland Bay 267 A1
AINGEAL
pl. Oxenford 16 J11
AINSLEE
ct. Mt Warren Pk 284 G8
AINSLEY
av. Ashmore 38 D3
cct. Marsden 261 F2
AINSLIE
st. Marsden 261 E3
st. Pacific Pines 16 N15
AINSWORTH
st. Pacific Pines 16 Q20
AIRD
ct. Highland Pk 37 H10
AIRLIE
pl. Helensvale 17 G10
AJAX
ct. Currumbin Wtr 70 P17
AKAMA
ct. Mudgeeraba 57 M9
AKES
av. Southport 29 G17
AKOONAH
dr. Beechmont 65 H10
st. Hope Island 7 Q2
ALABASTER
dr. Carrara 38 B11
dr. Logan Res 262 A18
ALAMAU
st. Benowa 38 P7
ALAMEIN
st. Beenleigh 264 D20
st. Beenleigh 284 D1
st. Beenleigh 284 D2
ALAN WILKE BRIDGE
Yatala 304 H3
ALASKA
av. Broadbeach Wtr 39 C20
ALAWARA
dr. Tallai 47 P16
ALBA
ct. Maudsland 16 E12
ALBANY
av. Currumbin 71 A8
la. Currumbin 71 A8
ALBATROSS
av. Mermaid Bch 50 A10
cct. Tweed Hd W 81 L13
ct. Carbrook 264 L2
ALBERT
av. Broadbeach 39 P19
st. Bethania 262 M10
st. Bethania 263 A11
st. Burleigh Hd 60 G7
st. Coomera 7 M2
st. Eagleby 264 H18
st. Logan Vill 293 P4
st. Redland Bay 267 A7
st. Redland Bay 267 A8
st. Waterford 262 M10
ALBERTA
pl. Surfers Pdse 39 J8
ALBERT EVANS
dr. Worongary 47 C7
ALBERTON
rd. Alberton 265 K14
rd. Alberton 265 K20
rd. Alberton 285 J1
ALBERT RIVER
pl. Tamborine 2 D3
ALBERT VALLEY
dr. Bahrs Scrub 283 P10
ALBICORE
st. Mermaid Wtr 49 R12
ALBION
av. Miami 49 R17
ALBIZIA
ct. Ormeau 305 B5
st. Cornubia 264 D1
ALBRECHT
ct. Edens Landing 263 D15
ALCES
cl. Up Coomera 6 N10
ALCOTT
ct. Parkwood 28 A9
ALDER
ct. Currumbin Wtr 70 G12
st. Logan Res 261 N14
ALDERLEY
la. Southport 29 E11
ALDERNEY
ct. Varsity Lakes 59 C6
ALDGATE
cr. Pacific Pines 26 K6
ALDRIN
av. Benowa 38 Q6
ALEC
av. Mermaid Wtr 49 P11
av. Miami 49 P11
ALECTURA
cr. Bahrs Scrub 283 E8
ALESSANDRA
cct. Coomera 327 G14
ALEX
la. Pimpama 326 N9
ALEXA
ri. Up Coomera 5 Q19
ALEXANDER
ct. Chambers Ft 281 L14
ct. Tweed Hd S 82 L18
dr. Highland Pk 37 H12
dr. Nerang 37 C7
dr. Ormeau 305 K6
ALEXANDRA
av. Broadbeach 49 P2
av. Mermaid Bch 49 P2
st. Beenleigh 263 N19
ALEXANDRINA
dr. Varsity Lakes 59 D2
st. Coomera 7 N2
ALEX FISHER
dr. Burleigh Hd 59 E12
ALEXIS
pl. Park Ridge 261 K14
ALEX KEITH
ct. Burleigh Hd 59 L20
ALFA
dr. Up Coomera 6 H1
dr. Up Coomera 326 H20
ALFORD
la. Pacific Pines 16 Q18
st. Waterford W 262 D9
ALFRED
rd. Stockleigh 293 A9
st. Mermaid Bch 49 R8
ALFRED RAYMOND HULSE
dr. Up Coomera 326 J19
ALF RUSH MEMORIAL
dr. Tweed Hd S 82 N18
ALGONA
st. Labrador 29 A4
ALICE
st. Beenleigh 283 Q2
ALICE BOWDEN
ct. Worongary 47 E8
ALICIA
st. Southport 29 B18
ALICIAJAY
cct. Luscombe 304 M1
ALINJARRA
dr. Tugun 71 B13
ALISMA
ct. Ormeau 305 L9
ALISON
ct. Buccan 282 N6
rd. Carrara 37 P15
rd. Carrara 38 C16
st. Surfers Pdse 39 M8
st. Surfers Pdse 40 M12
ALKIRA
av. Palm Beach 60 J12
st. Tugun 71 C10
wy. Worongary 47 N4
ALLAMANDA
av. Banora Pt 92 P2
gr. Bundall 39 B6
st. Russell I 268 K1
ALLAMBI
av. Broadbeach Wtr 39 K15
ALLAN
st. Loganholme 263 Q4
st. Southport 29 E15
ALLANDALE
ent. Mermaid Wtr 49 E7
ALLARA
av. Palm Beach 60 L16
ALLARDYCE
cr. Gaven 17 E14
cr. Pacific Pines 17 E14
ALLART
ct. Marsden 261 M1
ALLAWAH
av. Palm Beach 60 H13
ct. Logan Vill 294 A6
st. Bundall 39 C12
ALLCHIN
ct. Currumbin Wtr 70 M13
ALLCHURCH
av. Benowa 38 P9
ALLDEN
av. Labrador 29 A6
ALLEENA
ct. Mudgeeraba 57 J4
ALLEGRO
pl. Varsity Lakes 59 G6
ALLENBY
cr. Windaroo 283 R16
ALLERTON PARK
dr. Park Ridge 261 E19
ALLEY
wy. Kingscliff 103 G7
ALLIANCE
st. Coomera 7 F1
st. Coomera 327 F20
ALLIED
dr. Arundel 28 H2
ALLINGA
av. Russell I 268 L13
st. Coombabah 8 H20
ALLINGTON
cct. Maudsland 16 F11
ALLOAH
rd. Witheren 45 G3
rd. Witheren 45 J4
ALLORA
cr. Ormeau Hills 305 K16
st. Waterford W 262 J9
ALLOY
st. Yatala 284 Q20
st. Yatala 304 R1
ALLSPICE
dr. Ashmore 38 P3
st. Crestmead 261 E8
ALLUM
wy. Logan Res 261 Q15
ALLUNGA
av. Ashmore 28 J19
ALLY
ct. Marsden 261 H4
ALLYN
st. Ormeau Hills 305 H18
ALMA
st. Broadbeach Wtr 49 J1
st. Southport 28 R11
ALMANDIN
st. Logan Res 261 K16
ALMOND
ct. Elanora 60 E19
ALOE
ct. Elanora 70 F3
ALOHA
la. Main Beach 29 N18
ALOISI
pl. Clagiraba 25 D8
ALPHA
av. Crestmead 261 J11
av. Currumbin 70 R9
wy. Banora Pt 82 J19
ALPINA
pl. Banora Pt 92 D2
ALPINE
la. Pimpama 326 M4
tce. Tamborine Mtn 23 Q11
tce. Tamborine Mtn 24 B12
ALTAIR
st. Coomera 327 D15
st. Tweed Hd S 82 K13
ALTER
ct. Merrimac 48 A12
ALTISSIMO
cl. Varsity Lakes 59 F5
ALTITUDE
bvd.Terranora 92 B8
dr. Pimpama 326 J11
ALTJIRA
la. Coomera 327 F15
ALTMAN
ct. Logan Res 261 N15
ALTO
tce. Yatala 284 F14
tce. Yatala 284 F15
ALTONA
cl. Robina 49 C12
rd. Chinderah 102 M1
st. Pimpama 326 F9
ALTOS
ct. Mudgeeraba 57 K4
ALUMNI
pl. Southport 28 K9
ALVA
st. Tweed Heads 82 E8
ALVARADO
ct. Broadbeach Wtr 39 G15
ALVEY
ct. Mudgeeraba 58 L6
ALVINE
dr. Eagleby 264 K10
ALZINO
pl. Carrara 37 Q14
AMA
av. Runaway Bay 19 B4
AMADEUS
st. Elanora 70 E4
AMALFI
av. Russell I 268 H10
dr. Surfers Pdse 39 K13
AMANDA
st. Up Coomera 16 F3
AMANU
cr. Pacific Pines 17 A20
AMARANTH
cr. Up Coomera 326 J17
AMARAY
dr. Up Coomera 6 H13
AMARI
st. Holmview 263 D20
AMAROO
dr. Banora Pt 92 C6
st. Biggera Wtr 18 R17
AMAZON
cct. Helensvale 17 L15
AMBASSADOR
dr. Burleigh Hd 59 E12
AMBAT
ct. Tanah Merah 263 H4
AMBER
av. Russell I 268 P10
cr. Jimboomba 293 A20
ct. Bethania 262 R7
rd. Tweed Hd S 82 J16
AMBERMERLE
wy. Coomera 328 H13
AMBERWOOD
dr. Up Coomera 6 J10
AMBITION
st. Ormeau 305 N11
AMBOINA
av. Palm Beach 70 N4
AMBON
ct. Tamborine Mtn 24 L11
AMBROSE
st. Chambers Ft 281 F6
AMELIA
st. Beenleigh 264 C17
st. Marsden 261 N1
st. Up Coomera 6 D18
AMETHYST
ct. Carrara 38 A11
AMITY
rd. Coomera 327 J13
AMORA
rd. Yarrabilba 300 K9
AMORETTE
av. Varsity Lakes 59 G5
AMSONIA
ct. Arundel 17 Q13
AMULLA
ct. Mudgeeraba 57 N11
AMUNDSEN
dr. Logan Res 261 R13
dr. Logan Res 262 A13
AMY
dr. Beenleigh 283 N2
dr. Coomera 327 G10
ANAHEIM
dr. Helensvale 7 B15
ANCHOR
ct. Mermaid Wtr 49 Q12
ANCHORAGE
tce. Hope Island 8 E2
wy. Biggera Wtr 18 P13
wy. Runaway Bay 18 P13
ANCHUSA
st. Ashmore 38 P4
ANCONA
st. Carrara 37 N12
ANCONIA
av. Tweed Hd W 81 L10
ANCORA
cr. Hope Island 8 F11
ANDALUSIAN
dr. Up Coomera 6 M7
ANDAMOOKA
av. Worongary 37 N16
ANDANTE
av. Nerang 37 C13
ANDERSON
ct. Bonogin 67 K16
st. Banora Pt 92 M2
ANDERSONS
rd. Duranbah 102 A20
ANDORRA
pl. Varsity Lakes 59 C9
ANDREA
av. Broadbeach Wtr 39 K18
ANDREW
av. Broadbeach Wtr 39 E18
ANDREWS
ct. Chambers Ft 281 E7
rd. Mt Nathan 36 B2
rd. Tallebudgera 69 H7
st. Southport 29 G15
ANDROMEDA
av. Tanah Merah 263 F2
av. Tanah Merah 263 G3
dr. Coomera 327 F18
pde.Robina 49 D19
ANDROS
ct. Clear I Wtr 48 Q4
ANEMBO
av. Pimpama 305 Q15
ct. Logan Vill 294 A7
st. Surfers Pdse 39 H5
ANEMONE
av. Hollywell 19 A2

Map Ref

BAILEY
cr. Southport 28 N16
ct. Ormeau 305 N12
rd. Tweed Hd W 81 H11
st. Yarrabilba 293 P20
BAILEYS
rd. Tallai 47 K20
BAILEYS MOUNTAIN
rd. Up Coomera 6 A3
rd. Willow Vale 6 A3
BAINES
ct. Pimpama 327 D10
BAINS
rd. Currumbin Vy 78 R17
BAIRNSDALE
ct. Helensvale 17 H10
BAJADA
pl. Carrara 37 P12
BAKARA
la. Up Coomera, off Coomerong Cr 6 A17
BAKER
av. Labrador 29 E2
BAKERANA
ct. Ormeau 305 C4
BAKERS
rd. Natural Br 65 Q20
BAKERS RIDGE
dr. Oxenford 16 F8
BALBOA
ct. Hollywell 8 R19
st. Yarrabilba 300 L10
BALCATTA
ct. Elanora 70 J2
BALDWIN
cr. Pimpama 327 D13
BALFOUR
cr. Highland Pk 37 G10
st. Tweed Hd S 82 G12
BALFOURS
rd. Bungalora 90 M16
BAL HARBOUR
Broadbeach Wtr 39 K18
BALI
av. Palm Beach 70 M2
av. Russell I 268 K3
ct. Tamborine Mtn 24 K8
BALINTORE
st. Up Coomera 6 K3
BALLA BALLA
cr. Ormeau Hills 305 F18
BALLAH
cr. Highland Pk 37 D15
BALLANDRA
ct. Mermaid Wtr 49 H7
BALLANTRAE
rd. Tamborine 2 C14
BALLARAT
ct. Tallai 57 N1
BALLARD
pl. Coombabah 18 K1
BALLERINA
st. Burleigh Wtr 59 L5
BALLIDU
cl. Elanora 70 J4
BALLOW
st. Coolangatta 82 F4
BALLYBUNION
dr. Parkwood 28 H7
BALLYBUNYON
cr. Hope Island 8 D8
BALLYHOO
la. Coomera 328 C17
BALLYLIFFEN
ct. Robina 49 A20
BALLYMORE
ct. Banora Pt 91 R3
BALMAIN
st. Varsity Lakes 59 F9
BALMARA
pl. Coomera 328 F16
BALMORAL
av. Bundall 39 B12
st. Eagleby 264 K8
wk. Banora Pt 92 G1
BALONNE
ct. Up Coomera 6 B10
st. Holmview 283 G3
BALOO
cr. Nerang 37 A4
BALRANALD
ct. Helensvale 17 J3
BALSA
st. Crestmead 261 K6
st. Elanora 70 G4
BALSON
ct. Labrador 28 R3
BALTIMORE
ct. Carrara 48 B1
BALWYN
ct. Arundel 28 L1
pl. Robina 48 R12
BALYANDO
dr. Nerang 27 D20
BAMADI
ct. Nerang 27 E19
BAMBAROO
cr. Tweed Heads 82 C5
BAMBARRA
st. Southport 28 R14
BAMBERRY
st. Fingal Head 83 C16
st. Russell I 268 K5
BAMBI
cl. Up Coomera 6 M10
BAMBIL
st. Crestmead 261 J5
st. Marsden 261 J5
BAMBLING
rd. Boyland 23 B8
rd. Wonglepong 23 B8
BAMBOO
av. Benowa 38 Q5
av. Benowa 39 A6
av. Bundall 39 A6
BANBROOK
ct. Molendinar 28 F12
BANDANA
dr. Piggabeen 80 C10
BANDAR
ct. Tanah Merah 263 H5
BANDICOOT
ct. Coombabah 18 M4
dr. Bahrs Scrub 283 D8
la. Springbrook 66 G20
BANFF
ct. Robina 49 B19
BANGALOW
av. Banora Pt 82 M20
cct. Bahrs Scrub 283 H7
dr. Steiglitz 287 R10
st. Russell I 268 E11
BANJO
cr. Gilston 36 Q19
cr. Terranora 91 J12
st. Burleigh Hd 60 B10
BANK
la. Tamborine Mtn 13 N13
BANKA
av. Jacobs Well 308 A8
BANKS
av. Tweed Heads 82 L6
dr. Ormeau 305 L14
wy. Logan Res 261 R13
BANKSIA
bwy. Burleigh Hd 60 B3
bwy. Burleigh Wtr 60 B3
la. Tweed Hd W 82 A8
rd. Coomera 7 F1
rd. Coomera 327 F20
rd. Springbrook 66 P16
st. Tweed Hd W 81 R8
tce. Coomera 327 G15
BANKSIADALE
cl. Elanora 70 G5
BANKSIA LAKES
dr. Hope Island 8 A5
BANNOCKBURN
rd. Bannockburn 283 P17
rd. Windaroo 283 Q17
BANORA
bvd. Banora Pt 92 K1
tce. Bilambil Ht 91 F1
BANORA HILLS
dr. Banora Pt 92 H7
BANROCK
st. Pimpama 327 B9
BANTRY
ct. Eagleby 264 F18
BANYAN
ct. Ashmore 38 N3
st. Crestmead 261 D7
BANYULA
dr. Gaven 27 J6
dr. Nerang 27 L16
BANZAI
st. Kingscliff 103 F11
BARADINE
st. Mt Warren Pk 284 G6
BARAH
st. Loganholme 263 N4
BARAK
st. Pimpama 327 F10
BARAKA
ct. Mudgeeraba 57 Q13
BARAKEE
st. Crestmead 261 D5
st. Pimpama 326 J3
BARAKULA
ct. Cedar Creek 304 G14
BARATA
ct. Russell I 268 N9
BARATTA
st. Southport 28 P11
BARBARA
wy. Benowa 38 P15
BARBER
ct. Waterford 263 A15
BARBERRY
ct. Palm Beach 60 H19
BARBET
pl. Burleigh Wtr 59 Q1
BARBIE
av. Varsity Lakes 59 F7
BARBOSSA
st. Park Ridge 281 D2
BARCELONA
tce. Russell I 268 M4
wy. Burleigh Wtr 49 N17
BARCLAY
dr. Casuarina 103 J14
BARCOO
ct. Clagiraba 35 K8
ct. Mt Nathan 35 K8
dr. Logan Res 261 P12
st. Holmview 283 F4
st. Pacific Pines 26 L3
BARCREST
ct. Crestmead 261 M9
BARDEN RIDGE
rd. Bonogin 58 N17
rd. Reedy Creek 58 N17
rd. Reedy Creek 68 N1
BARDON
av. Miami 49 L17
BARDS
ct. Nerang 37 B8
BARDWELL
dr. Willow Vale 5 N4
BARDYN HALLIDAY
dr. Mt Warren Pk 284 H8
BARELLAN
cr. Banora Pt 92 M6
BARIA
av. Witheren 45 G1
BARINA
ct. Cornubia 264 E4
ct. Tugun 71 D13
BARK
ct. Maudsland 16 H15
BARKER
la. Coomera 327 K16
st. Currumbin 71 C4
BARKLEY
st. Pacific Pines 26 R3
BARKLYA
pl. Marsden 262 A4
pl. Palm Beach 60 H17
BARLEE
ct. Elanora 70 F5
pl. Maudsland 26 A8
BARLEY
st. Park Ridge 261 F17
BARMARK
st. Tallebudgera Vy 68 N14
BARNARD
st. Biggera Wtr 18 Q14
BARNETT
pl. Molendinar 28 A11
BARNEY
st. Southport 29 J16
BARNEYS POINT
rd. Banora Pt 92 N5
BARNEYS POINT BRIDGE
Banora Pt 92 P7
BARNHILL
tce. Edens Landing 263 E17
BARNYARD
dr. Park Ridge 261 F18
BAROKEE
dr. Tanah Merah 263 G1
BARON
ct. Tallai 47 J17
BAROSSA
st. Highland Pk 37 M13
BAROW
ct. Ashmore 38 F3
BARRA
ct. Merrimac 48 C7
BARRACK
st. Loganholme 263 L8
BARRACUDA
ct. Palm Beach 60 J15
BARRADEEN
cct. Pacific Pines 26 K4
BARRADINE
cr. Helensvale 17 E4
BARRANBALI
st. Surfers Pdse 39 J5
BARRATT
st. Coomera 7 H1
st. Coomera 327 H20
BARREL
st. Kingscliff 103 F10
BARRENJOEY
dr. Ormeau Hills 304 R11
dr. Ormeau Hills 305 A20
dr. Ormeau Hills 325 A1
BARRETT
av. Southport 29 A8
st. Tweed Hd W 82 B10
BARRI
la. Up Coomera 6 A13
BARRIER REEF
dr. Mermaid Wtr 49 E8
dr. Mermaid Wtr 49 F10
BARRINE
cr. Coombabah 18 L1
dr. Worongary 37 N16
BARRINGTON
cct. Waterford 282 Q1
st. Pacific Pines 16 K20
st. Up Coomera 6 B18
BARRON
ct. Pimpama 326 H13
BARRS
av. Oxenford 16 C7
ct. Oxenford 16 E7
BARRY
rd. Tamborine 3 A19
st. Pimpama 326 G6
BARTLE
rd. Tamborine Mtn 23 N7
BARTLE FREE
cl. Terranora 92 C8
BARTLETT
av. Nerang 37 C4
BARTLETTS
rd. Eviron 101 A17
BARTON
av. Southport 29 A9
rd. Terranora 91 H9
st. Reedy Creek 58 P16
BARUCH
st. Varsity Lakes 59 K3
BARWON
la. Pimpama 327 C9
st. Burleigh Wtr 60 A3
BASALT
dr. Yarrabilba 294 C20
dr. Yarrabilba 300 C1
la. Tweed Hd S 82 J15
BASHFULL
la. Coomera 328 D16
BASKET BEACH
rd. Russell I 268 M7
BASPA
st. Holmview 263 E20
BASS
av. Molendinar 28 E18
ct. Oxenford 16 J10
pl. Paradise Pt 8 M13
st. Russell I 268 N8
BASSWOOD
cct. Park Ridge 261 E17
ct. Bonogin 67 L11
BATCHWORTH
rd. Molendinar 28 C14
BATEHAVEN
st. Loganholme 263 M8
BATEKE
rd. Tamborine Mtn 24 B17
BATH
st. Labrador 19 D20
BATHURST
ct. Helensvale 17 D8
BATLOW
ct. Helensvale 17 F8
BATTEN
st. Nerang 37 J7
BAUER
dr. Mundoolun 1 D7
st. Southport 29 H16
BAUHINIA
dr. Russell I 268 P11
la. Nerang 37 M5
BAUM
ct. Windaroo 283 R14
BAUMANN
st. Up Coomera 6 B20
BAUMEA
ct. Elanora 70 C6
BAW BAW
la. Pimpama 326 M5
BAXTER
ct. Arundel 28 K1
BAY
dr. Jacobs Well 308 C8
st. Southport 29 E12
st. Tweed Heads 82 J2
BAYBERRY
la. Robina 48 H18
BAYES
rd. Logan Res 261 N12
BAY HILL
tce. Hope Island 7 R1
tce. Hope Island 327 R20
BAYMILL
ct. Merrimac 48 B12
BAYNTON
av. Helensvale 17 G10
ct. Russell I 268 P4
BAYRICK
st. Pacific Pines 26 M6
BAYSIDE
av. Jacobs Well 308 B11
cl. Hope Island 8 F2
BAYSWATER
av. Varsity Lakes 59 B9
av. Varsity Lakes 59 C7
rd. Russell I 268 N3
st. Mt Warren Pk 284 G6
BAYVIEW
dr. Tanah Merah 263 H2
st. Hollywell 8 R17
st. Paradise Pt 8 R17
st. Runaway Bay 19 C13
wk. Hope Island 8 E3
BAYWOOD
ct. Ormeau 305 N8
BAZA
st. Bahrs Scrub 283 E6
BAZAAR
st. Robina 58 M2
BEACH
la. Pimpama 326 Q7
pde. Surfers Pdse 39 N14
rd. Surfers Pdse 39 M7
rd. Surfers Pdse 40 L11
st. Kingscliff 93 B17
BEACHCOMBER
cov. Casuarina 103 J18
ct. Burleigh Wtr 60 A8
BEACHSTAR
av. Up Coomera 326 J18
BEACON
ct. Elanora 60 H20
dr. Cornubia 264 D3
dr. Russell I 268 N7
la. Hope Island 7 Q9
rd. Tamborine Mtn 13 D11
BEACONSFIELD
dr. Burleigh Wtr 49 K18
dr. Miami 49 K18
BEACROFT
st. Coomera 327 H19
BEAL
wy. Up Coomera 6 E8
BEALE
st. Southport 29 B11
BEARDMORE
st. Marsden 261 L3
BEARDSLEY
ct. Paradise Pt 8 P12
BEARS
ct. Arundel 28 L1
BEASLEY
wy. Canungra 33 C11
BEASON
ct. Casuarina 103 J19
BEATON
ct. Ormeau 305 G13
BEATTIE
rd. Coomera 7 A7
rd. Mundoolun 11 A15
BEATTY
st. Loganlea 262 F1
st. Southport 29 B10
BEAU
ct. Highland Pk 37 K14
pde. Bonogin 68 G4
BEAUDESERT
st. Tamborine Mtn 23 Q14
BEAUDESERT-BEENLEIGH
rd. Bahrs Scrub 283 N19
rd. Bannockburn 304 E9
rd. Beenleigh 283 N19
rd. Belivah 283 N19
rd. Belivah 304 E9
rd. Birnam 11 C18
rd. Cedar Creek 304 E20
rd. Luscombe 304 E9
rd. Mt Warren Pk 283 N19
rd. Mundoolun 11 C18
rd. Tabragalba 21 A15
rd. Tamborine 2 H12
rd. Tamborine 11 M6
rd. Tamborine 304 E20
rd. Windaroo 283 N19
rd. Wolffdene 304 E9
BEAUDESERT-NERANG
rd. Benobble 23 E20
rd. Biddaddaba 22 H10
rd. Birnam 21 A7
rd. Boyland 21 K10
rd. Boyland 22 H10
rd. Canungra 33 A9
rd. Clagiraba 25 E19
rd. Maudsland 26 A12
rd. Mt Nathan 25 E19
rd. Mt Nathan 36 C1
rd. Nerang 36 C1
rd. Nerang 36 L6
rd. Tabragalba 21 B16
rd. Witheren 33 K17
rd. Wonglepong 23 E20
BEAUFORT
cr. Ormeau Hills 305 F19
ct. Highland Pk 37 F13
wy. Hope Island 7 K9
BEAU GESTE
pl. Coomera 328 B15
BEAUMARIS
ct. Robina 48 R11
BEAUMONT
cr. Pacific Pines 16 P16
ct. Currumbin Wtr 70 G12
dr. Pimpama 327 C9
dr. Russell I 268 N5
rd. Park Ridge 261 A20
BEAUSANG
pl. Ormeau 305 E7
BEAUTY POINT
dr. Robina 49 E13
BEAUVALE
pl. Currumbin Wtr 70 K19
BECCA
ct. Arundel 28 L5
BECK
st. Park Ridge 261 G18
BECKINGTON
tce. Mudgeeraba 58 M9
BEDARA
ct. Mermaid Wtr 49 H9
BEDFORD
cr. Eagleby 264 M15
cr. Mudgeeraba 58 L9
rd. Pimpama 326 G6
BEDIVERE
dr. Ormeau 305 L12
BEDMAN
st. Willow Vale 326 B9
BEDROFF
st. Up Coomera 6 J12
BEE
ct. Burleigh Hd 59 H12
BEECH
ct. Elanora 60 F19
la. Casuarina 103 E17
st. Marsden 261 R3
st. Park Ridge 281 E1
BEECHMONT
av. Tamborine Mtn 14 F11
rd. Advancetown 35 L17
rd. Beechmont 45 G18
rd. Beechmont 45 K19
rd. Clagiraba 35 L17
rd. Flying Fox 45 G18
rd. Lr Beechmont 45 R8
rd. Numinbah Vy 45 K19
rd. Witheren 33 K18
BEECHWOOD
dr. Hope Island 7 M5
BEECROFT
pl. Robina 49 F16
BEEKA
st. Labrador 28 R6
BEELONG
st. Crestmead 261 E6

Map Ref

BEELYU
st. Burleigh Hd 60 G10
BEENLEIGH CONNECTION
rd. Beenleigh 264 A18
rd. Beenleigh 284 C3
BEENLEIGH-REDLAND BAY
rd. Carbrook 265 B3
rd. Cornubia 264 G1
rd. Loganholme 263 N1
BEERWAH
st. Pacific Pines 16 P20
BEETHAM
ct. Logan Res 261 M13
BEETSON
ct. Eagleby 264 H12
BEGONIA
st. Ormeau 305 L9
BEHMS
rd. Jacobs Well 307 J9
rd. Norwell 307 J9
BEHMS CREEK
rd. Jacobs Well 307 M4
rd. Norwell 307 M4
BEILBY
cr. Pimpama 327 F10
BEITZ
av. Labrador 19 A20
rd. Alberton 266 B13
BELAH
ct. Banora Pt 92 A3
st. Ashmore 38 G2
st. Crestmead 261 K6
BELAIR
dr. Yatala 284 D17
BELALIE
ct. Ormeau 305 D4
BELAROMA
st. Ormeau 306 B10
BELCONNEN
dr. Pimpama 326 N6
BELGRAVE
pl. Helensvale 17 C2
BELHAVEN
av. Yarrabilba 300 G11
av. Yarrabilba 300 G9
BELIVAH
rd. Bahrs Scrub 283 M16
rd. Belivah 283 M16
BELL
ct. Maudsland 16 G11
la. Logan Res 261 P20
pl. Mudgeeraba 58 D2
BELLA
bvd.Pimpama 326 D8
bvd.Willow Vale 326 C10
ct. Eagleby 264 J10
BELLA DONNA
pl. Robina 58 Q2
BELLAGIO
cr. Coomera 327 F18
BELLARA
st. Ashmore 27 Q20
BELLARINE
cct. Coomera 7 K1
BELLATRIX
st. Reedy Creek 68 Q1
BELLATTA
dr. Ashmore 38 H1
BELLA VISTA
cct. Edens Landing 263 J14
BELLAVISTA
cl. Highland Pk 37 E13
BELLBIRD
av. Burleigh Wtr 60 A6
cr. Coomera 327 M17
dr. Kingscliff 93 B20
pl. Gilston 36 Q16
BELLBROOK
cl. Robina 49 B16
BELLERIVE
pl. Banora Pt 92 F7
BELLEVUE
pde.Labrador 28 R5
st. Kingscliff, off Danielle St 93 A20
BELLEW
st. Beenleigh 284 D1
BELLFIELD
pl. Robina, off Windemere Cr 59 D3
BELLFINCH
rd. Eagleby 264 C13
BELLINGER
key,Pacific Pines 26 L6
la. Waterford 282 R1

Map Ref

BELLISS
rd. Mt Nathan 35 N8
BELLONA
ct. Pacific Pines 17 B14
BELLS
bvd.Kingscliff 103 F9
BELLTHORPE
cr. Waterford 262 P19
rd. Ormeau 305 N8
BELLTOP
ct. Helensvale 7 F17
BELLVIEW
cr. Nerang 27 P19
BELLVUE
dr. Varsity Lakes 59 E2
BELLWOOD
pl. Molendinar 28 F13
BELMONT
ct.e,Hope Island 7 L8
ct.w,Hope Island 7 K8
dr. Varsity Lakes 59 D2
BELMONT PARK
dr. Mudgeeraba 57 D14
BELMORE
cl. Robina 49 B16
BELONGIL
st. Pacific Pines 16 Q20
BELROSE
bvd.Varsity Lakes 59 F6
BELTANA
dr. Bilambil 91 B10
wy. Nerang 37 B6
BELVEDERE
ct. Chambers Ft 281 B10
dr. Park Ridge 261 B14
BELYANDO
st. Holmview 283 C2
BEN
ct. Mudgeeraba 58 L5
BENALLA
ct. Parkwood 28 A2
BENARKIN
cl. Waterford 262 R19
cl. Waterford 263 A19
BENAROON
ct. Tallebudgera 69 E9
BEN BUCKLER
ct. Robina 49 E12
BEN DALLEY
dr. Helensvale 7 Q17
BENDIGO
cr. Tallai 57 N1
BENECIA
av. Coomera 328 G13
BENETTI
cr. Hope Island 8 D10
BENEVIS
pl. Terranora 91 C10
BENGAL
rd. Tallebudgera Vy 69 K1
st. Yarrabilba 294 A18
BEN HOGAN
cr. Parkwood 28 F5
BENJAMIN
rd. Logan Vill 293 Q10
st. Pimpama 326 G6
wy. Windaroo 283 Q12
BENJUL
dr. Beenleigh 283 M3
BENJY
la. Coomera 327 E19
BEN LEXCEN
ct. Mt Warren Pk 284 D6
pl. Robina 49 H16
BEN LOMOND
dr. Highland Pk 37 E11
BENNELONG
ct. Beenleigh 283 L3
BENNETT
wy. Up Coomera 6 L2
BEN NEVIS
st. Tamborine Mtn 24 C13
BENOWA
rd. Ashmore 38 P7
rd. Benowa 38 N13
rd. Benowa 38 P7
rd. Southport 38 R3
st. Tamborine Mtn 23 R14
BENSON
st. Ormeau 305 M6
st. Tweed Hd W 81 F12
BENT
st. Nerang 36 M9
BENTINCK
st. Waterford W 262 E8
BENTLEIGH
ct. Robina 49 A11

Map Ref

BENTLEY
wy. Banora Pt 92 N1
BENWERRIN
rd. Loganholme 263 M4
st. Pimpama 326 P10
BENZ
lk. Up Coomera 6 G1
BERENDT
ct. Meadowbrook 262 P1
BERGAMO
dr. Varsity Lakes 59 B7
BERGAMONT
st. Elanora 70 D2
BERGOMI
ct. Eagleby 264 F14
BERKLEY
ct. Highland Pk 37 F13
BERKSHIRE
cr. Hope Island 8 C5
BERMUDA
st. Broadbeach Wtr 39 E20
st. Burleigh Hd 59 H16
st. Burleigh Wtr 59 L10
st. Clear I Wtr 49 D7
st. Mermaid Wtr 49 D7
st. Robina 49 D8
st. Varsity Lakes 59 K1
BERNADETTE
pl. Highland Pk 37 K14
BERNARD
cct. Yarrabilba 293 Q20
cct. Yarrabilba 299 Q1
ct. Arundel 18 C18
BERNARDINO
ct. Mermaid Wtr 49 H10
BERNBOROUGH
pl. Mudgeeraba 58 D9
BERNDT
rd. Steiglitz 287 E10
BERNICE
st. Loganlea 262 L1
BERNINI
dr. Coombabah 18 K8
pl. Coombabah 18 J8
BERNOTH
st. Currumbin Wtr 70 Q16
BERRI
pl. Helensvale 17 D3
BERRIGAN
st. Southport 28 R18
BERRIGANS
rd. Mudgeeraba 57 E5
rd. Mudgeeraba 57 K5
BERRIMILLA
la. Coomera 328 D13
BERRINGA
ct. Ashmore 28 J17
BERRY
la. Bonogin 67 H2
BERTANA
dr. Mudgeeraba 57 M9
BERTHA
rd. Logan Res 282 B1
BERT HOOD
st. Hope Island 8 H10
BERWICK
ct. Arundel 18 K20
BERYL
st. Southport 29 D17
st. Tweed Heads 82 J4
BERZINS
ct. Bahrs Scrub 283 C6
BETHANY
pl. Up Coomera 6 N5
BETONY
ct. Elanora 70 F3
BETTONG
pl. Nerang 36 G5
BETTY
st. Up Coomera 6 K5
BETULA
pl. Elanora 70 E5
BEULAH
la. Main Beach 29 N17
BEUTEL
st. Logan Res 262 A9
st. Waterford W 262 E10
BEVERLEY
cr. Broadbeach Wtr 39 J17
st. Beenleigh 264 B17
BEXLEY
pl. Helensvale 17 J4
BIANCA
st. Loganlea 262 F3
BIANO
rd. Tamborine Mtn 24 B15

Map Ref

BIBARINGA
cl. Beechmont 65 G10
BIBBA
ct. Mudgeeraba 57 N7
BIBY
pl. Banora Pt 92 J7
st. Tugun 71 D11
BICTON
ct. Elanora 70 H5
BIDDADDABA
rd. Boyland 22 G8
BIDDADDABA CREEK
rd. Biddaddaba 21 R19
BIDMEAD
cct. Pimpama 326 G6
BIDWILL
ct. Elanora 70 B10
BIELBY
st. Tugun 71 F10
BIENVENUE
dr. Currumbin Wtr 70 N15
BIGAL
av. Stockleigh 293 G5
BIGGLES
la. Up Coomera 6 P7
BIGGS
pl. Southport 29 H17
BIGHT
ct. Mermaid Wtr 49 N11
BIGNELLS
rd. Maudsland 15 Q13
BILAMBIL
dr. Russell I 268 K2
rd. Bilambil 90 M5
rd. Bilambil 90 M7
rd. Bilambil Ht 91 A3
rd. Bungalora 91 C11
rd. Terranora 91 C11
BILBOROUGH
ct. Springbrook 66 R18
BILBUNGRA
st. Russell I 268 F11
BILBY
cl. Nerang 36 F4
BILGOLA
pl. Robina 49 F16
BILINGA
st. Currumbin 71 C6
BILK
st. Crestmead 261 M7
BILKURRA
ct. Elanora 70 C8
BILL
ct. Parkwood 28 B8
BILLABIRRA
cr. Nerang 36 Q1
BILLABONG
cr. Bethania 263 A5
ct. Currumbin Wtr 70 H13
ct. Gilston 36 P18
dr. Crestmead 261 G12
pl. Burleigh Wtr 59 R11
BILLEROY
pl. Nerang 37 B6
BILLET
ct. Ormeau 305 L2
BILLIAU
rd. Guanaba 14 R15
BILLINGHURST
cr. Up Coomera 6 H5
BILLINGTON
st. Labrador 19 B20
BIMBAD
cr. Russell I 268 K9
BIMBADEEN
av. Banora Pt 92 L7
dr. Loganholme 263 M3
BIMBI
ct. Surfers Pdse 39 K12
BIMBUL
ct. Benobble 33 D9
BIMINI
ct. Clear I Wtr 48 Q3
BINALONG
dr. Ashmore 38 J5
BINARY
st. Yatala 284 R19
BINBURRA
st. Russell I 268 E12
st. Russell I 268 F12
BINDA
pl. Bundall 39 E13
st. Palm Beach 60 J14
BINDARIN
la. Up Coomera 6 B14
BINDARRI
cl. Waterford 263 B16

Map Ref

BINDOON
cl. Elanora 70 J3
BINDRA
st. Holmview 283 E1
BINGARA
la. Pimpama 326 C4
BINGO
st. Holmview 263 L16
BINKAR
bvd.Robina 58 R3
BINNA BURRA
rd. Beechmont 65 H2
rd. Binna Burra 65 G15
rd. Natural Br 65 G15
rd. Numinbah Vy 65 G15
BINNACLE
ct. Mermaid Wtr 49 P13
BINNOWEE
wy. Pimpama 306 A16
BINSTEAD
dr. Southport 28 Q14
esp.Coomera 7 B10
wy. Oxenford 16 L14
wy. Pacific Pines 16 L14
BINYA
av. Coolangatta 82 B3
BIONE
av. Banora Pt 92 M3
BIOTA
ct. Palm Beach 60 F17
BIOTITE
st. Bethania 262 Q5
BIRAL
cl. Bilambil 90 N8
BIRCH
ct. Oxenford 16 Q2
ct. Palm Beach 60 F17
st. Marsden 261 P6
BIRCHWOOD
cl. Stapylton 284 Q6
st. Park Ridge 281 D2
BIRDIE
ct. Arundel 28 H3
BIRDLIFE
ct. Nerang 36 H4
BIRDS
rd. Guanaba 15 K11
rd. Guanaba 15 K15
rd. Maudsland 15 K15
BIRDS BAY
dr. Tweed Hd W 81 K14
BIRDSVILLE
st. Mudgeeraba 57 P1
BIRDWOOD
rd. Molendinar 27 P11
BIRIGUN
st. Mermaid Wtr 49 Q12
BIRINBURRA
cct. Benobble 33 D6
BIRKDALE
ct. Banora Pt 92 D1
st. Robina 49 B16
tce. Hope Island 8 E4
BIRLEY
lk. Up Coomera 326 F19
BIRMINGHAM
rd. Carrara 38 E13
BIRNAM
av. Banora Pt 92 H8
st. Waterford W 262 C6
BIRON
st. Yarrabilba 294 B20
BIRRIBI
av. Nerang 37 E4
BIRT
av. Surfers Pdse 39 L3
BIRTWISTLE
st. Southport 39 D1
BISCAY
wy. Coombabah 18 M8
BISHAMPTON
cct. Logan Res 261 N12
BISHOP
ct. Loganlea 262 E3
st. Eagleby 264 G15
BISHOPP
ct. Tamborine Mtn 23 N7
BISHOPWOOD
ct. Up Coomera 326 L17
BITTENBINDER
av. Logan Res 262 B19
BITTERN
av. Burleigh Wtr 60 A3
BIX
ct. Crestmead 261 M8
BIXA
st. Southport 38 R3

Map Ref

BIZET
ct. Oxenford 16 J13
BLACKALL
st. Coomera 327 L18
BLACKBEAN
ct. Elanora 70 D2
st. Marsden 261 P5
BLACKBIRD
st. Beenleigh 264 B14
BLACKBURN
rd. Russell I 268 H14
BLACKBUTT
st. Crestmead 261 K6
BLACK CHERRY
st. Park Ridge 261 E18
BLACKCOMB
ri. Ormeau Hills 305 F15
BLACK DIAMOND
cr. Edens Landing 263 D12
BLACKFEN
ct. Arundel 18 E18
BLACKHEATH
tce. Pacific Pines 16 N19
BLACK MYRTLE
ct. Terranora 91 M14
BLACKS
rd. Willow Vale 325 F18
BLACKSTUMP
dr. Gilston 36 R18
BLACK WATTLE
cct. Casuarina 103 D18
BLACKWATTLE
cct. Arundel 17 Q12
BLACKWOOD
pl. Palm Beach 60 K20
BLADENSBURG
dr. Waterford 262 M18
BLAIR ATHOL
cr. Bundall 38 R13
BLAIRS
bvd.Southport 28 N7
BLAKE
st. Southport 29 A16
BLAKEHURST
pl. Robina 49 G14
BLAMEY
dr. Currumbin 71 B10
dr. Tugun 71 B10
BLANCK
st. Ormeau 305 H9
BLANFORD
st. Arundel 18 M19
BLAXLAND
av. Molendinar 28 E18
av. Paradise Pt 8 N17
st. Russell I 268 N9
BLEADON
pl. Mudgeeraba 58 P8
BLENCOE
st. Yarrabilba 300 G2
BLIGH
ct. Benowa 38 M7
BLISSETTS
rd. Carool 89 G5
BLONDELL
av. Surfers Pdse 39 L3
BLOODWOOD
cr. Molendinar 28 G16
ct. Molendinar 28 F17
st. Crestmead 261 K6
BLOOM
av. Coomera 327 C18
BLOOMFIELD
av. Park Ridge 261 J14
ct. Ormeau 306 A8
BLOOMVALE
wy. Currumbin Wtr 80 G2
BLOSSOM
st. Pimpama 326 C9
st. Yarrabilba 293 Q16
BLOSSOMTREE
mw. Robina, off Riverwalk Av 58 K1
BLUEASH
cr. Oxenford 6 J17
BLUE BAY
st. Jacobs Well 308 B10
BLUEBELL
ct. Nerang 37 M5
BLUEBELLE
dr. Nerang 36 K3
BLUEBERRY
ct. Banora Pt 82 M19
BLUEBIRD
ct. Ashmore 28 D20
la. Reedy Creek 58 L14

Map Ref

BLUEFEN
ct. Up Coomera 6 K8
BLUE GUM
av. Russell I.......... 268 M2
ct. Gilston 46 R1
BLUE-GUM
dr. Marsden 261 Q5
BLUEGUM
av. Hollywell 9 A20
bvd. Banora Pt 92 B5
dr. Wonglepong 23 F13
BLUE HAZE
cr. Banora Pt 92 H9
BLUE HILL
ct. Nerang 36 H1
BLUE HORIZON
dr. Casuarina 103 D19
BLUE JAY
cct. Kingscliff...... 93 C19
BLUEJAY
st. Burleigh Wtr 60 A4
BLUE LAGOON
ct. Nerang 37 B4
BLUEMOON
cl. Burleigh Wtr 59 K5
BLUE RIDGE
cr. Varsity Lakes .. 59 B3
BLUESTONE
dr. Carrara 37 R12
dr. Logan Res 261 R17
BLUETAIL
cr. Up Coomera 6 G10
BLUE WATERS
cr. Tweed Hd W.. 82 B10
BLUE WREN
ct. Currumbin Vy .. 79 N3
BLUFF
ct. Beenleigh 283 Q4
BLUNDELL
bvd. Tweed Hd S.. 82 H15
BLY
st. Logan Res 261 L16
BOAB
st. Elanora 70 F3
BOAMBEE
ct. Reedy Creek .. 58 P15
BOAMBILLEE
dr. Coomera 327 N16
BOAT
ct. Mt Warren Pk .. 284 D9
BOATWORKS
dr. Coomera 7 G9
BOB BARNARD
dr. Tugun 71 C13
BOBERMIEN
rd. Logan Vill...... 293 F13
rd. Stockleigh 293 F13
BOBSLED
la. Coomera 328 H14
BODA
st. Runaway Bay .. 19 B3
BODACIOUS
tce. Pimpama 326 C8
BODALLA
pl. Tallebudgera .. 69 D15
BODE
ct. Witheren 45 E2
BOEA
st. Arundel........ 28 L5
BOEING
st. Loganholme 263 L6
BOEING RIDGE
rd. Russell I........ 268 M3
BOGART
ct. Oxenford 17 B11
BOICE
st. Yarrabilba 293 N20
BOIKE
rd. Witheren 33 L17
BOISE
ct. Tamborine Mtn . 13 H12
BOLAN
ct. Crestmead 261 F9
BOLGART
ct. Elanora 70 H4
BOLLARD
cct. Clear I Wtr 48 R8
BOLSENA
cct. Hope Island 7 N10
BOLT
ct. Parkwood 28 D8
BOLTON
st. Coolangatta .. 82 B2
BOLTON ABBEY
cl. Arundel........ 18 A16
BOLWARRA
pl. Bilambil Ht.... 81 G13

BOMBALA
st. Broadbeach Wtr .. 39 G20
BOMPA
rd. Waterford W 262 L9
BON AIRE
ct. Clear I Wtr 49 C4
BONANZA
pl. Buccan 282 N20
BONDI
av. Mermaid Bch .. 49 P7
pl. Kingscliff 103 F10
BONGAREE
rd. Terranora 91 F13
BONIN
cl. Pacific Pines.. 17 D18
BONITA
ct. Mudgeeraba .. 58 G6
BONNER
ct. Pacific Pines.. 16 P14
BONNIE
ct. Bonogin 58 B17
BONNIE BRAE
dr. Maudsland 25 N2
BONNY GLEN
pl. Banora Pt 92 C9
BONOGIN
rd. Austinville 67 F19
rd. Bonogin 58 B20
rd. Bonogin 67 G12
rd. Mudgeeraba .. 58 D7
rd.e, Bonogin 67 M5
BOODERA
st. Palm Beach........ 60 G13
BOOGAERDT
ri. Bonogin 58 H14
BOOGARD
pl. Clagiraba 25 A10
BOOLAMA
pl. Mudgeeraba........ 58 L6
BOOLONG
st. Logan Vill.... 294 M14
BOOM
ct. Currumbin Wtr..... 70 L14
BOOMERANG
ct. Bundall 39 D14
rd. Mudgeeraba .. 57 C12
rd. Tamborine 3 C2
rd. Tamborine 3 F1
rd. Tamborine 304 B20
st. Kingscliff 103 F1
BOONAH
st. Helensvale 17 E2
BOONEEN BURROW
Currumbin Vy .. 79 Q5
BOONGALA
rd. Beechmont 65 H11
rd. Broadbeach Wtr .. 39 L16
BOORALA
ct. Tugun 71 D14
BOORAN
st. Hope Island 7 Q3
BOOWAGGAN
ct. Merrimac 48 J5
BOOYONG
ct. Ormeau 305 E4
BOPPLE NUT
ct. Cobaki 80 M15
BORAX
ct. Bethania 262 M4
BORDEAUX
pde. Mermaid Wtr .. 49 L4
st. Tweed Hd S.... 81 Q20
BORDER
dr. Currumbin Wtr..... 70 Q16
dr.n, Currumbin Wtr .. 70 R15
BOREE
ct. Ormeau 305 D5
st. Ashmore........ 38 K6
BOREEN
ct. Helensvale 17 L5
BORGER
pl. Edens Landing .. 263 G15
BORMAN
ct. Worongary 37 J15
BORNEO
ct. Tamborine Mtn . 24 L9
st. Witheren 33 L19
BORONIA
av. Russell I........ 268 H10
ct. Ormeau 305 E2
dr. Eagleby 264 J6
dr. Southport 39 C1
st. Coomera 327 C16
BORROWDALE
ct. Mundoolun 1 C9

BORUMBA
ct. Marsden 261 L2
BOS
dr. Coomera 7 D7
BOSTON
ct. Varsity Lakes .. 59 E1
pl. Burleigh Wtr .. 49 K18
BOSUN
bvd. Banora Pt 92 J11
pde. Ashmore...... 37 R1
BOTANICAL
cct. Banora Pt 91 N2
cct. Banora Pt 91 P1
dr. Labrador 28 M5
BOTANIQUE
tce. Robina 48 P16
BOTANY
cr. Tweed Heads .. 82 K6
BOTHWELL
st. Loganholme 263 Q8
st. Robina 49 B17
BOTTLE BRUSH
cct. Coomera 327 G15
BOTTLEBRUSH
la. Wongawallan .. 4 Q12
BOTTLETREE
ct. Coomera 327 K16
la. Lr Beechmont .. 35 H20
BOTTLEWOOD
ct. Burleigh Wtr .. 59 L9
BOU
st. Edens Landing .. 263 J15
BOUGAINVILLE
st. Beenleigh 264 B19
BOULTON
dr. Nerang 37 Q4
BOUNDARY
la. Tweed Heads .. 72 M20
st. Beenleigh 264 A19
st. Coolangatta .. 82 K1
st. Currumbin Wtr.. 70 P9
st. Tweed Heads .. 82 K1
BOUNTY
wy. Pacific Pines.. 17 D18
BOURKE
st. Waterford W .. 262 B5
BOURKE LODGE
dr. Currumbin Vy .. 80 C1
BOURTON
rd. Merrimac 48 B8
BOW
st. Waterford W .. 262 Q13
BOWDEN
cl. Tallebudgera .. 69 A19
st. Nerang 37 N3
BOWEN
av. Russell I........ 268 J6
ct. Helensvale 17 G11
lp. Cudgen 102 Q2
BOWER
rd. Eagleby 264 D12
BOWERBIRD
la. Maudsland 16 G14
pl. Burleigh Wtr .. 49 L20
BOWLEY
st. Pacific Pines.. 26 N1
BOWLINE
rd. Mermaid Wtr .. 49 M12
BOWMAN
la. Waterford W .. 262 M15
BOWMORE
ct. Merrimac 48 A7
BOWOOD
ct. Berrinba 261 D2
BOWRAL
ct. Ashmore 38 F3
BOXTHORN
ct. Ashmore........ 38 N3
BOXTON
ct. Mt Warren Pk .. 284 G7
BOYA
ct. Elanora 70 K4
BOYD
st. Bilinga 71 F15
st. Cobaki L........ 71 B20
st. Eagleby 264 H19
st. Tugun 71 F15
st. Tweed Heads .. 82 H6
BOYDAW
rd. Ormeau 306 B10
BOYDS BAY BRIDGE
Tweed Heads .. 82 H8
BOYER
st. Pacific Pines.. 26 Q2
BOYKAMBIL
esp.n, Hope Island .. 8 J9
esp.s, Hope Island .. 8 J13

BOYLAND
rd. Boyland 21 K9
BOYLE
av. Banora Pt 82 P20
BOYNE
ct. Holmview 263 D19
BOY-ULL
rd. Springbrook .. 66 P17
BOZIER
ct. Casuarina 103 J19
BRABANT
st. Loganlea 262 H3
BRABHAM
cct. Robina 58 N3
st. Crestmead 261 C10
BRACKEN
ct. Witheren 45 E4
la. Hope Island 8 F4
BRACKENFIELD
ct. Bonogin 68 J9
BRADBROOK
st. Southport 39 F4
BRADFORD
st. Labrador 29 D5
BRADLEY
av. Miami 49 Q18
BRADMAN
ct. Clear I Wtr 48 Q1
dr. Currumbin Vy .. 70 A20
BRADSHAW
dr. Currumbin Wtr.. 70 L12
pl. Kingscliff 93 A12
BRADSTONE
rd. Carrara 38 A19
BRADY
ct. Ormeau 305 Q10
dr. Coombabah .. 8 M20
BRAE
ct. Carrara 38 B20
BRAEMER
ct. Benowa 38 P13
BRAESIDE
cr. Maudsland 25 M2
BRAEWOOD
dr. Currumbin Vy .. 78 L20
BRAHMAN
ct. Tallebudgera .. 69 P16
rd. Tamborine 13 D2
BRAKE
st. Burleigh Hd .. 60 F7
BRAKES
cr. Miami 50 C18
BRAMLEY
ct. Mt Warren Pk .. 284 G4
dr. Tallebudgera Vy .. 78 H6
BRAMPTON
ct. Mermaid Wtr .. 49 J10
ct. Pimpama 327 E6
BRANCH
cr. Reedy Creek .. 59 A14
BRANDON
ct. Beenleigh 283 R4
BRANSTON
ct. Nerang 36 P9
BRASSIE
st. Arundel........ 28 G2
BRAUER
ct. Mt Warren Pk .. 284 F10
BRAVO
ct. Waterford W .. 262 A7
BRAY
ct. Eagleby 264 G19
BRAYSIDE
av. Russell I........ 268 G14
BRAZEL
ct. Cornubia 264 D3
BREAKER
st. Main Beach .. 29 L18
BREAKSPEAR
rd. Molendinar .. 28 D15
BREAKWATER
rd. Robina 48 C17
BREAMLEA
tce. Up Coomera .. 5 R14
BREASLEY
st. Willow Vale .. 326 D11
BRECCIA
st. Yarrabilba 294 C19
BRECKENRIDGE
rd. Logan Res 281 P5
BREDALBANE
st. Mundoolun 1 A6
BREDBO
st. Ormeau Hills .. 305 G19
BREEANA
ct. Mudgeeraba .. 58 H5

BREEZE
ct. Mt Warren Pk 284 D9
la. Elanora 70 F6
BREEZEWAY
dr. Bahrs Scrub .. 283 N15
BRENDA
ct. Coomera 327 F20
BRENDAN
dr. Nerang 37 K6
BRENNAN
cl. Maudsland 16 J18
BRENTFORD
rd. Bethania 263 A10
BRENTWOOD
tce. Oxenford 6 M19
BRETT
av. Labrador 29 D5
st. Pimpama 326 R10
st. Tweed Heads .. 82 H5
st. Tweed Heads .. 82 J5
BRETTON
ct. Carrara 37 Q17
BREWER
ct. Parkwood 28 D7
BREYNIA
ct. Elanora 70 C10
BRIBIE
ct. Mermaid Wtr .. 49 J9
BRIDGE
la. Southport 28 K11
BRIDGET
st. Pimpama 327 A11
BRIDGEWATER
dr. Varsity Lakes .. 59 E5
pl. Mt Nathan 25 P14
BRIDGMAN
dr. Reedy Creek .. 58 Q12
BRIDIE
dr. Up Coomera .. 6 F1
dr. Up Coomera .. 326 F19
BRIDLE
cl. Kingsholme 325 H3
la. Molendinar .. 28 C16
BRIER
cr. Varsity Lakes .. 59 F10
BRIGADE
dr. Eagleby 264 C14
BRIGALOW
st. Marsden 261 Q5
BRIGANTINE
ct. Currumbin Wtr.. 70 H14
BRIGHT
av. Labrador 29 D3
st. Yarrabilba 293 N16
BRIGHTLANDS
ct. Mermaid Bch.. 49 P4
BRIGHTON
cr. Robina 49 C11
pde. Southport 29 G17
st. Banora Pt 92 C2
st. Biggera Wtr .. 19 C16
BRIGHTSTAR
st. Ormeau 305 L3
BRILLIANT
la. Coomera 328 D14
BRIM
ct. Edens Landing .. 263 J15
BRINDABELLA
cl. Coomera 328 E18
st. Cornubia 264 H1
BRINDISI
av. Surfers Pdse .. 39 L12
BRINSMEAD
rd. Duranbah 101 R19
BRISBANE
rd. Arundel........ 18 H16
rd. Biggera Wtr .. 18 H16
rd. Labrador 18 H16
BRISBANE-BEENLEIGH
rd. Beenleigh 263 P19
rd. Beenleigh 264 C20
rd. Bethania 262 N10
rd. Bethania 263 C15
rd. Edens Landing .. 263 C15
rd. Holmview 263 C15
rd. Loganlea 262 D6
rd. Loganlea 262 N10
rd. Waterford 262 N10
rd. Waterford W .. 262 D6
rd. Waterford W .. 262 N10
BRISSENDON
st. Maudsland 16 K17
BRISTOL
pl. Arundel........ 17 Q15
BRITANNIA
av. Broadbeach .. 39 N17

BRITTANIC
cr. Paradise Pt 9 B14
BRITTANY
dr. Oxenford 6 F19
BRITTNEY
ct. Ashmore...... 28 E19
BRIXTON
ct. Tallai 47 B9
BROAD
st. Labrador 19 B20
BROADBEACH
bvd. Broadbeach .. 39 P15
BROADOAK
ct. Bonogin 67 F15
BROADVIEW
pl. Robina 48 P20
BROADWATER
av. Hope Island .. 8 E12
esp. Bilambil Ht.... 91 F1
st. Runaway Bay .. 19 A12
BROADWAY
av. Marsden 261 E2
dr. Oxenford 16 R11
BROCKET
ct. Up Coomera .. 6 N11
BROCKMAN
wy. Pacific Pines.. 26 N2
BROCKS
rd. Currumbin Vy .. 79 K12
BROCKWELL
wy. Yarrabilba 300 G10
BROKEN HILLS
dr. Hope Island .. 8 G3
BROLGA
av. Southport 29 D18
BROMFIELD
dr. Bonogin 67 F1
BRON
ct. Loganlea 262 G4
BRONBERG
ct. Southport 39 B4
BRONHILL
st. Currumbin Wtr.. 70 G8
BRONTE
ct. Robina 49 H14
pl. Kingscliff 103 E8
BRONZEWING
cct. Bahrs Scrub .. 283 E7
cl. Elanora 70 H7
BROOK
ct. Nerang 36 P8
la. Ormeau 305 F5
BROOKE
av. Palm Beach .. 60 K15
av. Southport 29 B9
cl. Edens Landing .. 263 H13
ct. Crestmead 261 E10
BROOKFIELD
ct. Nerang 26 Q18
st. Pimpama 326 Q13
BROOKHAVEN
bvd. Bahrs Scrub .. 283 F7
BROOKLAND
ct. Molendinar .. 28 F14
BROOKLYN
cl. Park Ridge 261 K14
cr. Robina 58 L3
ct. Pimpama 327 C10
BROOKONG
ct. Buccan 282 K15
BROOKSIDE
cct. Ormeau 305 D1
rd. Labrador 19 A19
BROOKTON
ct. Helensvale 17 E10
BROOKVALE
st. Chambers Ft .. 281 G7
BROOKVIEW
pl. Bahrs Scrub .. 283 B9
BROOME
st. Currumbin Wtr.. 70 R15
BRORA
ct. Merrimac 48 B6
BROSNAHAN
ct. Belivah 283 J20
BROUGHAM
pde. Up Coomera .. 6 J1
pde. Up Coomera .. 326 J20
BROWN
st. Labrador 28 Q3
BROWNLIE
ct. Beenleigh 283 M3
BROWNS PLAINS
rd. Berrinba 261 B2
rd. Browns Pl 261 B2
rd. Crestmead 261 B2
rd. Crestmead 261 C2

CONCORDE

Map Ref

CONCORDE
dr. Loganholme ... 263 M6
CONCOURSE
dr. Mermaid Wtr ... 49 G3
CONDAMINE
cr. Helensvale ... 7 F15
dr. Logan Vill ... 294 M15
pl. Loganlea ... 262 G6
st. Holmview ... 283 F4
CONDOR
av. Russell I ... 268 N3
ct. Burleigh Wtr ... 60 A1
dr. Coomera ... 328 E15
CONEBUSH
cct. Ormeau ... 305 D4
st. Ashmore ... 38 Q3
CONESTOGA
wy. Up Coomera ... 6 H1
wy. Up Coomera ... 326 H20
CONGREVE
cl. Mudgeeraba ... 57 P2
CONICA
pl. Ormeau ... 305 F5
CONIFER
cr. Broadbeach Wtr .. 39 A19
ct. Logan Vill ... 294 G18
CONIMBLA
cr. Waterford ... 282 P1
st. Pimpama ... 326 J3
CONJOLA
cr. Up Coomera ... 6 C14
la. Waterford ... 282 Q1
CONLAN
ct. Oxenford ... 16 K12
CONNECTION
rd. Tallai ... 47 F17
CONNELLY
ct. Mudgeeraba ... 58 G9
CONNEMARA
rd. Gaven ... 17 G19
CONNOR
st. Burleigh Hd ... 60 E7
CONOBLE
ct. Eagleby ... 264 H18
CONOCHIE
pl. Pimpama ... 326 H13
CONONDALE
wy. Waterford ... 262 N19
CONRADI
av. Crestmead ... 261 L12
CONSERVATION
dr. Pimpama ... 326 K12
CONSTANCE
av. Mermaid Wtr ... 49 Q11
esp.Runaway Bay ... 19 D4
CONSTELLATION
cr. Mudgeeraba ... 58 A1
dr. Loganholme ... 263 M6
CONTOUR
rd. Tamborine Mtn ... 14 B6
CONVERY
cr. Highland Pk ... 37 L14
CONWAY
ct. Nerang ... 27 B17
st. Waterford ... 262 R18
st. Waterford ... 263 A18
COOBAH
ct. Ashmore ... 38 L3
COOBOWIE
st. Broadbeach Wtr .. 49 G1
COOCHIN
la. Pacific Pines ... 16 P20
COOGEE
ct. Elanora ... 70 G7
COOGEEN
st. Bundall ... 39 E11
COOGERA
la. Casuarina ... 103 E15
COOINDA
av. Currumbin ... 71 D7
COOINGIE VIEW
rd. Logan Vill ... 294 M8
COOK
av. Russell I ... 268 M11
cl. Southport ... 28 K13
cr. Tweed Hd S ... 82 B19
la. Logan Res ... 261 Q14
rd. Tamborine Mtn ... 14 B12
COOKS
rd. Woongoolba ... 286 M7
COOLABAH
ct. Banora Pt ... 92 C4
ct. Gilston ... 36 R19
st. Russell I ... 268 F11
st. Russell I ... 268 F12

COOLAMON
ct. Tugun ... 71 C14
vw. Currumbin Vy ... 79 N5
COOLANGATTA
rd. Bilinga ... 71 K14
rd. Coolangatta ... 82 B1
rd. Tugun ... 71 G11
COOLARA
st. Tugun ... 71 F13
COOLATAI
la. Pimpama, off
Christopher St ... 326 G5
COOLAWIN
pl. Nerang ... 37 B5
COOLEROO
cr. Southport ... 28 Q18
COOLGARDIE
st. Elanora ... 70 M7
COOLIBAH
cr. Varsity Lakes ... 59 F10
dr. Palm Beach ... 60 H17
rd. Gaven ... 27 J14
st. Southport ... 28 R20
COOLMUNDA
st. Marsden ... 261 K2
st. Marsden ... 261 L3
COOLONG
cr. Carrara ... 38 M15
ct. Ashmore ... 38 L3
COOLOON
cr. Tweed Hd S ... 82 K14
COOLRIDGE
cct. Yarrabilba ... 293 R19
COOMBABAH
rd. Biggera Wtr ... 18 M12
rd. Biggera Wtr ... 18 Q14
rd. Runaway Bay ... 18 M12
rd. Runaway Bay ... 18 Q14
COOMBAH
dr. Russell I ... 268 L5
COOMBE
av. Hope Island ... 8 H11
av. Hope Island ... 8 H13
COOMERA
ct. Helensvale ... 7 B13
COOMERA BRIDGE
Oxenford ... 6 Q12
COOMERA GORGE
dr. Tamborine Mtn ... 24 H15
COOMERA GRAND
dr. Up Coomera ... 326 J20
COOMERA HEIGHTS
dr. Pimpama ... 326 L15
COOMERA SPRINGS
bvd.Up Coomera ... 326 G18
COOMERA VALLEY
dr. Clagiraba ... 25 D4
dr. Guanaba ... 25 D4
COOMERONG
cr. Up Coomera ... 6 A17
COOMVILLE
cr. Nerang ... 27 E19
COONARDOO
ct. Wongawallan ... 5 A12
COONDA
av. Russell I ... 268 L10
COONEANA
ct. Tamborine ... 1 L2
COONOWRIN
st. Pacific Pines ... 16 P19
COOPER
pde.Southport ... 39 F1
COORABELLE
cr. Ormeau ... 305 Q7
COORABIN
ct. Tallebudgera ... 69 D10
COORAN
st. Beenleigh ... 263 Q17
COORONG
st. Coomera ... 7 K2
st. Yarrabilba ... 300 J11
COOROO
la. Pimpama ... 326 M5
COORUMBENE
ct. Tallai ... 47 E12
COOTE
ct. Currumbin Wtr ... 70 F11
COOTHARABA
dr. Helensvale ... 17 L5
COPAL
dr. Logan Res ... 261 R17
COPE
pl. Pacific Pines ... 16 Q15
COPELAND
st. Pimpama ... 326 E5
COPETON
st. Marsden ... 261 K4

COPLICK
cr. Buccan ... 282 G6
COPLICKS
la. Tallebudgera ... 69 M7
COPPER
dr. Bethania ... 262 P5
pde.Pimpama ... 326 N10
COPPERFIELD
dr. Eagleby ... 264 D11
COPPING
st. Loganholme ... 263 N9
COQUILLE
pl. Tweed Hd S ... 82 L18
CORAI
cl. Pacific Pines ... 17 D19
CORAL
av. Labrador ... 29 C1
ct. Witheren ... 45 D5
st. Beenleigh ... 284 A1
st. Bilambil Ht ... 91 D1
st. Loganlea ... 262 J2
st. Pimpama ... 326 E3
st. Russell I ... 268 N11
st. Steiglitz ... 287 R9
st. Tweed Heads ... 82 L1
CORALCOAST
dr. Tallai ... 47 B14
CORAL GABLES
key,Broadbeach Wtr .. 39 K20
CORALINA
cr. Logan Res ... 261 R17
CORAL SEA
ct. Burleigh Wtr ... 59 Q8
CORAL TREE
ct. Robina ... 48 N16
CORBOULD
ct. Jacobs Well ... 307 Q7
CORCORAN
ct. Witheren ... 45 F1
CORDATA
ct. Robina ... 58 Q6
CORDEAUX
pl. Pacific Pines ... 16 Q18
CORDYLINE
dr. Reedy Creek ... 59 D18
CORELLA
av. Burleigh Wtr ... 60 A4
av. Eagleby ... 264 H9
ct. Marsden ... 261 L1
CORINA
cl. Robina ... 58 Q3
CORINDA
ct. Helensvale ... 17 K9
CORIO
ct. Robina ... 49 F16
CORKWOOD
ct. Coomera ... 327 M17
pl. Beenleigh ... 283 L5
CORLETTE
st. Loganholme ... 263 P8
CORMACK
pl. Currumbin Wtr ... 70 M15
CORMORANT
cr. Jacobs Well ... 308 B7
pl. Kingscliff ... 93 B19
st. Worongary ... 37 L19
CORNDALE
st. Loganholme ... 263 P9
CORNELIUS
st. Up Coomera ... 6 E18
CORNELL
ct. Varsity Lakes ... 59 F3
CORNET
la. Casuarina ... 103 J14
CORNWALL
dr. Elanora ... 70 A15
COROMANDEL
la. Varsity Lakes ... 58 R8
CORONADO
ct. Currumbin Wtr ... 70 K20
CORONATA
pl. Reedy Creek ... 59 D18
CORONET
cr. Burleigh Wtr ... 49 L20
cr. Burleigh Wtr ... 49 M20
CORPORATE
ct. Bundall ... 39 G6
CORPORATION
cct. Tweed Hd S ... 82 G17
rd. Ashmore ... 28 L18
CORREA
ct. Elanora ... 70 D5
CORRIGIN
ct. Elanora ... 70 G3
CORRINE
av. Southport ... 29 A8

CORRINGLE
cl. Helensvale ... 17 M4
CORUNNA
cr. Ashmore ... 28 M20
CORVUS
ct. Bahrs Scrub ... 283 G7
wy. Robina ... 49 C20
CORYMBIA
st. Coomera ... 327 D17
wy. Molendinar ... 28 E16
CORYPHA
ct. Tamborine Mtn ... 23 R2
COSMOS
ct. Elanora ... 70 B4
COSSINGTON
cct. Maudsland ... 16 K16
COSTA
ct. Broadbeach Wtr .. 39 G15
COSTA DEL SOL
av. Coombabah ... 18 L7
COSTELLO
ct. Ormeau ... 305 B5
COSTELLOE
st. Tugun ... 71 C12
COSTIGAN
tce. Edens Landing .. 263 G14
COTINGA
cr. Burleigh Wtr ... 59 Q2
COTLEW
st. Ashmore ... 28 F20
st. Southport ... 39 A1
st.e,Southport ... 39 B2
st.w,Ashmore ... 28 E19
COTMAN
wy. Pimpama ... 327 D12
COTSWOLD
st. Mt Warren Pk ... 284 G7
COTTAGE
pl. Coomera ... 7 D1
pl. Coomera ... 327 E20
COTTEE
cct. Park Ridge ... 281 F2
COTTESLOE
dr. Mermaid Wtr ... 49 J15
dr. Robina ... 49 D16
COTTON
st. Burleigh Hd ... 60 F8
st. Nerang ... 37 H2
COTTON PALM
dr. Ormeau ... 305 H7
COTTONWOOD
la. Casuarina ... 103 D20
la. Casuarina ... 103 J13
pl. Marsden ... 261 R4
pl. Oxenford ... 6 Q18
st. Marsden ... 261 R4
COTTRELL
dr. Pimpama ... 327 C13
COUCAL
ct. Bahrs Scrub ... 283 E7
COUGAL
cl. Loganholme ... 263 P13
dr. Russell I ... 268 K4
dr. Russell I ... 268 L3
rd. Carool ... 89 H11
st. Southport ... 29 E13
COULTER
rd. Willow Vale ... 325 R17
COUNTRY
cr. Nerang ... 36 H2
ct. Park Ridge ... 261 C14
COUNTRY CLUB
dr. Helensvale ... 17 K15
COUNTRY MEADOWS
cct. Loganholme ... 263 P10
COUNTRY VIEW
dr. Nerang ... 36 G1
COUNTRYVIEW
st. Kingsholme ... 325 G3
COUNTY
cl. Parkwood ... 27 Q4
la. Merrimac ... 48 F8
COURSER
ct. Burleigh Wtr ... 59 Q3
COURTNEY
dr. Up Coomera ... 6 B7
COVA
bvd.Hope Island ... 7 R9
COVE
ct. Merrimac ... 48 A11
st. Marsden ... 261 H4
COVEDEN
cr. Russell I ... 268 M4
COVENT GARDENS
wy. Banora Pt ... 92 B3

COVENTRY
ct. Labrador ... 28 P1
COVESIDE
la. Hope Island ... 8 F4
COWAL
ct. Elanora ... 70 E4
COWDEROY
dr. Russell I ... 268 M7
st. Labrador ... 29 B7
COWELL
dr. Burleigh Hd ... 59 K20
dr. Burleigh Hd ... 59 M18
COWLEY
rd. Norwell ... 306 N5
COWPER
av. Eagleby ... 264 F15
COWRA
st. Tanah Merah ... 263 K2
COWRIE
la. Casuarina ... 103 E18
COWRY
pl. Helensvale ... 17 G7
COX
dr. Tweed Hd S ... 82 H11
rd. Pimpama ... 326 L8
COYNE
st. Coolangatta ... 82 B1
COZENS
wy. Highland Pk ... 37 J14
wy. Worongary ... 37 J14
CRADLE
la. Pimpama ... 326 M6
CRAFT
ct. Miami ... 49 R18
CRAGIN
la. Pimpama ... 326 C4
CRAIG
av. Carrara ... 38 M18
st. Crestmead ... 261 F11
CRAIGS
wy. Maudsland ... 16 J14
CRAMER
bvd.Mt Warren Pk ... 284 F9
CRAMPTON
ct. Parkwood ... 28 D4
CRAN
st. Ashmore ... 28 J18
CRANBERRIE
cr. Pimpama ... 326 D8
CRANBOURNE
ct. Robina ... 49 A11
CRANE
cr. Nerang ... 36 N3
CRANNEYS
rd. Duroby ... 90 D19
rd. N Tumbulgum ... 90 D19
rd. Upper Duroby ... 90 D19
CREAGHE
st. Park Ridge ... 281 F2
CREAL
ct. Currumbin Wtr ... 70 K15
CREAMER
rd. Tamborine ... 2 P10
CREEK
ct. Tamborine ... 3 D17
pl. Pacific Pines ... 27 H1
pl. Park Ridge ... 261 J15
rd. Coomera ... 6 Q1
rd. Coomera ... 326 P19
st. Bilinga ... 82 A1
st. Coolangatta ... 82 A1
st. Kingsholme ... 305 K12
st. Ormeau ... 305 J12
st. Ormeau ... 305 K12
st. Pimpama ... 305 L16
st. Pimpama ... 325 R1
wy. Currumbin Vy ... 79 P5
CREEK FLAT
rd. Mt Nathan ... 25 P11
CREEKSIDE
ct. Worongary ... 47 M13
CREEKVIEW
st. Helensvale ... 7 H15
CREEKWOOD
pl. Helensvale ... 7 G15
CRELGA
ct. Merrimac ... 48 B8
CREMORNE
ct. Robina ... 49 D16
CRENSHAW
ct. Parkwood ... 28 E5
CRESCENDO
pl. Crestmead ... 261 E11
CRESCENT
av. Hope Island ... 8 F14
av. Mermaid Bch ... 49 P5
av. Mermaid Wtr ... 49 P5

dr. Russell I ... 268 M16
st. Cudgen ... 102 Q3
CRESS
ct. Pimpama ... 327 F13
CRESSBROOK
dr. Hope Island ... 7 K9
CREST
dr. Currumbin ... 71 A8
dr. Currumbin ... 71 A9
dr. Elanora ... 70 J2
st. Beenleigh ... 283 Q1
tce. Beenleigh ... 283 Q1
CRESTA
ct. Broadbeach Wtr .. 39 H16
CRESTBROOK
gln. Molendinar ... 28 G13
CRESTGARDEN
ct. Molendinar ... 28 E15
CREST HILL
dr. Wongawallan ... 5 C11
CRESTMORE
ct. Mermaid Wtr ... 49 H11
CRESTRIDGE
cr. Oxenford ... 16 Q10
CREST VIEW
key,Broadbeach Wtr .. 39 K20
CRESTVIEW
st. Loganlea ... 262 J5
CRESTWOOD
dr. Molendinar ... 28 E15
st. Bahrs Scrub ... 283 M15
CRETE
st. Beenleigh ... 284 C1
CRIMSON
ct. Miami ... 49 Q19
CRIMSON ROSELLA
cl. Gilston ... 37 B16
CRINKLE
ct. Southport ... 39 B1
CRINUM
cct. Coomera ... 327 H15
cr. Southport ... 38 Q2
st. Crestmead ... 261 G9
CRISCI
st. Marsden ... 261 G4
CRISP
ct. Miami ... 49 R18
st. Ormeau ... 305 M14
CRISTOBEL
ct. Broadbeach Wtr .. 39 H16
CROCKER
st. Worongary ... 47 Q10
CROCUS
wy. Gaven ... 27 F6
CROFT
ct. Tugun ... 71 B14
CROFTERS
wy. Bilambil ... 91 C8
CROMBIE
av. Bundall ... 39 D7
av. Surfers Pdse ... 39 E7
CROMER
ct. Banora Pt ... 92 F1
ct. Loganholme ... 263 P9
CROMWELL
ct. Tallai ... 47 L19
CRONIN
av. Main Beach ... 29 L18
CRONK
la. Currumbin Wtr ... 70 F16
CRONULLA
av. Mermaid Bch ... 49 Q4
ct. Kingscliff ... 103 E10
CROSBY
av. Pacific Pines ... 26 Q2
CROTON
gr. Bundall ... 39 B5
CROWN
ct. Varsity Lakes ... 59 D11
st. Fingal Head ... 92 R4
CROWS ASH
ct. Oxenford ... 16 Q2
CROWSNEST
cl. Parkwood ... 27 P4
CROZET
ct. Burleigh Wtr ... 59 R9
CRUISER
ct. Mermaid Wtr ... 49 M12
pl. Bannockburn ... 283 P18
CRUMP
st. Loganholme ... 263 K11
CRUSADE
ct. Coomera ... 328 C14
CRUSADER
wy. Nerang ... 37 C6
CRUSOE
st. Coomera ... 327 K19

DIETER

Map Ref

CRYSTAL
ct. Up Coomera 6 E6
CRYSTAL CREEK
rd. Willow Vale 325 N19
CRYSTAL REEF
dr. Coombabah 18 L4
CRYSTAL SPRINGS
ct. Maudsland 26 A11
CRYSTAL VALE
rd. Currumbin Wtr 70 K19
CRYSTAL WATERS
dr. Tweed Heads 82 D11
CUBA
av. Palm Beach 70 M4
CUCKOO
cr. Burleigh Wtr 59 N5
CUDGEN
rd. Cudgen 102 K7
rd. Duranbah 102 A10
rd. Kingscliff 103 D3
rd. Stotts Ck 101 M8
CUDGERIE
ct. Casuarina 103 E15
CUDMORE
st. Pimpama 327 F8
CULGOA
cr. Logan Vill 293 R13
st. Palm Beach 60 K14
CULGOORA
cr. Reedy Creek 58 N15
CULLEN
st. Pimpama 327 D12
CULLODEN
ct. Highland Pk 37 G10
CUMBERLAND
dr. Varsity Lakes 59 G6
CUMMINGS
cct. Willow Vale 326 C10
CUMULUS
cct. Coomera 327 F15
CUNNINGHAM
av. Main Beach 29 M15
av. Russell I 268 M11
dr.n,Coomera 327 C14
dr.n,Pimpama 327 C14
st. Tweed Hd S 82 G12
st. Waterford W 262 B6
CUPANIA
ct. Tweed Hd W 81 J13
pl. Elanora 70 D5
CURACAO
pl. Clear I Wtr 49 D4
CURIO
ct. Tamborine 12 P4
CURLEW
cr. Burleigh Wtr 60 B4
cr. Eagleby 264 C11
ct. Tamborine 299 L8
wy. Tweed Hd W 81 L14
CURRAGH
ct. Worongary 47 N1
CURRANT
st. Elanora 70 G1
CURRAWONG
cct. Hope Island 8 D14
cct. Worongary 37 K18
cr. Up Coomera 6 G8
ct. Tamborine 299 H13
pl. Tweed Hd S 82 H13
CURREY
rd. Wongawallan 5 E18
CURRICULUM
wy. Up Coomera 6 L9
CURRINGA
ct. Carbrook 266 A6
ct. Tallebudgera 69 D12
CURRONG
cr. Mudgeeraba 57 N7
CURRUMBIN
ch. Currumbin 70 R9
CURRUMBIN CREEK
rd. Currumbin 70 M15
rd. Currumbin Vy 79 B16
rd. Currumbin Vy 79 J6
rd. Currumbin Wtr 70 M15
CURRUMBIN CREEK-TOMEWIN
rd. Currumbin Vy 79 F19
CURRUMBIN CREST
dr. Currumbin 71 A9
CURRUMBURRA
rd. Ashmore 28 K17
CURTAWILLA
st. Banora Pt 92 H9
CURTIN
av. Southport 29 A9
st. Bethania 263 A8

Map Ref

CURTIS
ct. Mudgeeraba 58 G10
rd. Cedar Creek 304 D12
rd. Tamborine Mtn 13 Q15
rd. Tamborine Mtn 14 C16
st. Labrador 29 B2
st. Pimpama 326 D5
CURVE
av. Loganholme 263 L11
CUSTODIAN
cr. Ormeau 305 M14
CUTANA
ct. Ashmore 38 G1
CUTHBERT
dr. Ormeau 305 E1
dr. Yatala 285 B17
CUTHERO
ct. Highland Pk 37 B11
CUTLER
dr. Russell I 268 M6
CUTTER
ct. Helensvale 7 A18
CUTTS
st. Loganholme 263 L10
CUTWATER
cl. Clear I Wtr 48 R10
CYAN
st. Helensvale 17 K16
CYCAD
cl. Beenleigh 283 K4
ct. Bundall 39 C6
ct. Varsity Lakes 59 E10
pl. Terranora 91 M7
CYCLADES
cr. Currumbin Wtr 70 K10
cr. Currumbin Wtr 70 L9
CYGNUS
cr. Coomera 327 D15
CYLINDERS
dr. Kingscliff 103 F13
CYMBIDIUM
ct. Southport 29 A20
CYPRESS
av. Russell I 268 M7
av. Surfers Pdse 39 M5
av. Surfers Pdse 40 K6
cct. Coomera 327 G17
cr. Stapylton 284 Q7
ct. Beechmont 45 J20
dr. Broadbeach Wtr 39 C20
dr. Marsden 261 Q5
dr.w,Broadbeach Wtr 38 Q20
tce. Palm Beach 60 M17
tce.n,Palm Beach 60 J13
CYPRESS PINE
st. Maudsland 16 H15
CYPRESS POINT
tce. Hope Island 8 A1
tce. Hope Island 328 A20

D

DABCHICK
dr. Burleigh Wtr 60 A7
DAFFODIL
st. Tallebudgera 69 R1
DAHLIA
cr. Ormeau 305 L9
ct. Logan Res 261 P13
DAIMLER
dr. Bundall 39 D7
DAINTREE
cl. Banora Pt 91 N2
ct. Austinville 66 P2
ct. Austinville 67 A5
ct. Neranwood 66 P2
ct. Park Ridge 261 J15
dr. Coomera 327 J17
dr. Logan Vill 294 G13
dr. Parkwood 27 N4
DAIRY CREEK
rd. Buccan 282 H1
rd. Waterford 262 G20
rd. Waterford 282 H1
rd. Waterford 283 A2
DAISY
la. Robina 48 N16
st. Elanora 70 F1
DAKARA
dr. Southport 28 N15
DAKOTA
pl. Oxenford 16 N4
DALBY
ct. Helensvale 17 E12
st. Holmview 283 D4
DALE
ct. Bundall 39 B12
ct. Tallebudgera Vy 77 K20

Map Ref

DALES
wy. Coomera 7 L1
wy. Coomera 327 L20
DALEY
st. Oxenford 16 J12
DALGLEISH
rd. Ormeau Hills 304 R11
DALLEY PARK
dr. Helensvale 7 M15
DALLOW
cr. Helensvale 7 Q15
DALLOWAY
ct. Arundel 18 B16
DALMA
st. Ormeau Hills 305 K15
DALPURA
st. Surfers Pdse 39 J5
DALRYMPLE
cl. Waterford 263 A18
DALTON
rd. Tallebudgera Vy 77 R1
st. Southport 28 Q15
st. Terranora 91 G14
st. Up Coomera 6 M1
DALWOOD
ct. Tallebudgera 69 Q14
DALY
la. Ormeau Hills 305 F19
wy. Worongary 47 N7
DAME PATTI
av. Mermaid Wtr 49 Q9
DAMIAN LEEDING
wy. Up Coomera 326 H19
DAMPIER
av. Eagleby 264 E15
ct. Molendinar 28 F17
DAMSON
pl. Elanora 70 E3
DA NANG
rd. Witheren 33 M20
DANBULLA
st. Pimpama 327 C9
st. Yarrabilba 300 H6
DANDALOO
ct. Pimpama 305 P19
dr. Currumbin 71 A5
DANDALUP
av. Ormeau Hills 305 E16
DANDAR
dr. Southport 28 R18
DANDENONG
tce. Robina 49 A16
DANE
ct. Coombabah 18 M6
DANIEL
cr. Ashmore 28 J20
st. Kingscliff 93 A20
DANIELLA
dr. Marsden 261 H1
DANIELLE
st. Chinderah 93 A20
st. Oxenford 6 G20
DANIELLS
ct. Ormeau 305 M13
DANIELS
la. Yarrabilba 293 N20
ri. Benobble 33 D6
DANJELLA
st. Reedy Creek 58 R11
DANTE
ct. Arundel 28 L3
DANYENAH
st. Loganholme 263 J10
DAPHNE
ct. Elanora 70 C5
st. Loganholme 263 L10
DAPPLES
ct. Burleigh Hd 59 J19
DAPPURA
dr. Russell I 268 K10
DAPSANG
dr. Tamborine Mtn 14 A13
DARCEY
st. Pimpama 326 R12
DAREL
dr. Ashmore 38 H3
DARGO
st. Nerang 36 M7
DARLEY
st. Coomera 7 H7
DARLING
cl. Pacific Pines 16 L14
cr. Molendinar 28 G18
st. Russell I 268 N9
DARLINGTON
dr. Banora Pt 92 E2
dr. Banora Pt 92 H7

Map Ref

dr. Yarrabilba 293 N19
dr. Yarrabilba 299 P1
dr. Yatala 284 K16
dr. Yatala 284 L16
ri. Tamborine Mtn 14 B15
DARLINGTON RANGE
rd. Canungra 33 E20
rd. Witheren 45 A4
DARNAY
rd. Broadbeach Wtr 39 E19
DARNEL
st. Elanora 60 F19
DARNELL
st. Yarrabilba 294 A20
st. Yarrabilba 300 A1
st. Yarrabilba 300 A2
DARRAMBAL
st. Surfers Pdse 39 K5
DARRAU
av. Yarrabilba 294 B20
DARRO
rd. Terranora 92 B9
DARRYL
st. Loganlea 262 G4
DARTER
ct. Burleigh Wtr 59 Q4
DARTMOUTH
ct. Varsity Lakes 59 G3
DARU
av. Runaway Bay 19 C6
DARWALLA
av. Currumbin 71 E7
rd. Mt Nathan 25 P9
DARWALLAH
av. Russell I 268 H7
DARWIN
st. Beenleigh 264 A19
DARYL
dr. Varsity Lakes 59 G8
DAUPHIN
cr. Merrimac 48 D9
DAVALL
st. Currumbin Wtr 70 N11
DAVEBILL
ct. Labrador 28 N2
DAVENPORT
dr. Bonogin 67 J3
pl. Pimpama 326 L6
st. Southport 29 F11
DAVES CREEK
rd. Natural Br 65 Q20
DAVEY
st. Tweed Hd S 82 M16
DAVID
av. Pimpama 326 Q7
ct. Miami 49 Q20
st. Up Coomera 16 E3
DAVIDSON
pl. Carrara 38 C15
rd. Jimboomba 299 A13
rd. Russell I 268 M1
DAVIES
st. Pacific Pines 16 N15
DAVIS
ct. Parkwood 28 D7
st. Coomera 7 N1
DAVIS CUP
ct. Oxenford 16 L9
DAVISON
la. Southport, off Davenport St 29 G12
DAVO
ct. Burleigh Hd 59 H13
DAVY GOODING BRIDGE
Beenleigh 264 A18
DAWE
st. Maudsland 16 H18
DAWES
av. Kingscliff 103 E3
DAWN
pde.Miami 49 Q18
DAWNANN
ct. Carrara 37 P9
DAWNRIDGE
pl. Currumbin Wtr 70 K20
DAWSON
ct. Helensvale 7 D16
DAYANA
st. Marsden 261 N4
DAYBREAK
bvd.Casuarina 103 J17
pde.Currumbin Wtr 70 M18
st. Yarrabilba 293 N16
DAYFLOWER
st. Up Coomera 326 J18

Map Ref

DAYLESFORD
cct. Ormeau 306 B8
DAYS
rd. Up Coomera 6 D1
rd. Up Coomera 6 M3
rd. Up Coomera 326 D20
DEAGON
dr. Runaway Bay 18 R13
DEAKIN
av. Southport 29 A9
dr. Terranora 91 J11
DEAL
cov.Arundel 17 R16
DEAN
ct. Up Coomera 6 L9
st. Marsden 261 N6
DEARNE
pl. Carrara 37 Q12
DEAUVILLE
dr. Southport 39 F1
DEBANIE
ct. Marsden 261 E2
DE BARNETT
st. Coomera 6 R10
DEBBIE
wy. Nerang 36 R10
DEBORAH
av. Benowa 38 N14
DE BORTOLI
st. Stapylton 285 A7
DECLAN
dr. Oxenford 16 J11
DEE
la. Coomera 327 J15
DEEDEE
la. Currumbin Vy 79 N5
DEEPAK
dr. Pimpama 326 B8
dr. Willow Vale 326 C9
DEEPWATER
av. Russell I 268 P14
DEER
la. Waterford 262 G14
DE HAVILAND
av. Benowa 38 P12
DEHLIA
st. Marsden 261 N3
DEL
ct. Wongawallan 15 A1
DELANTY
ct. Edens Landing 263 F13
DELAWAY
st. Chambers Ft 281 F6
DELL
ct. Coombabah 8 N20
ct. Nerang 37 D3
DELLAMERE
ct. Eagleby 264 N15
DELLCAL
pl. Tamborine 299 L14
DELLWOOD
cct. Molendinar 28 G14
DELMAR
pde.Russell I 268 N5
DELNOTE
ct. Varsity Lakes 59 J6
DELONIX
ct. Arundel 18 C19
DELORAINE
ct. Mermaid Wtr 49 G10
DELTA
ct. Crestmead 261 J11
DELTA COVE
dr. Worongary 37 K16
DELUNGRA
st. Broadbeach Wtr 49 G1
DEMAND
av. Arundel 18 H20
DEMARR
ct. Meadowbrook 262 R1
DEMAVEND
dr. Tamborine Mtn 14 D2
DENALI
st. Holmview 283 C1
DENAWEN
st. Palm Beach 60 L19
DENDY
pl. Edens Landing 263 K16
DENHAM
cct. Willow Vale 326 C9
rd. Logan Res 282 A3
DENIKA
ct. Mudgeeraba 58 J4
DENISE
dr. Up Coomera 6 G7

Map Ref

DENISON
av. Eagleby 264 F11
ct. Robina 49 E13
st. Meadowbrook 262 R1
DENKMANN
ct. Windaroo 283 Q13
DENMAN
dr. Cudgen 102 P2
DENNING
rd. Currumbin Vy 78 L18
DENT
la. Pimpama 326 Q7
DENTON
st. Up Coomera 6 J4
DEODAR
dr. Burleigh Hd 60 B3
dr. Burleigh Wtr 60 B3
DEPOT
ct. Molendinar 27 R17
rd. Kings Forest 102 P15
rd. Pimpama 326 F4
DERBY
pl. Mudgeeraba 58 M9
rd. Logan Res 281 H4
DERMOTT
pl. Tallebudgera 69 G10
DERRIN
la. Currumbin Vy 79 P4
DERWENT
av. Helensvale 7 F16
cl. Holmview 283 E2
DESCHAMPS
cl. Loganlea 262 E5
DESERT FALLS
cr. Parkwood 28 F9
DESIGN
pl. Highland Pk 37 K15
DESLEY
st. Marsden 261 M4
DES QUINLAN
cr. Tallebudgera 79 A4
DEVANEY
ct. Maudsland 16 K16
DEVCO
pl. Ashmore 38 R5
DEVINE
st. Marsden 261 E1
DEVLIN
st. Parkwood 28 E3
DEVON
dr. Tamborine 12 R1
DEVRON
ct. Eagleby 264 K9
DEW
st. Yarrabilba 293 M17
DEWAR
ct. Highland Pk 37 F14
dr. Loganholme 263 L10
dr. Loganholme 263 N13
DEWBERRY
wy. Gaven 27 H7
DEWRANG
dr. Pimpama 306 A20
dr. Pimpama 326 A1
DEXTER
cl. Robina 58 P3
DIAMANTINA
cct. Pacific Pines 26 K3
ct. Clagiraba 35 J7
st. Holmview 283 F4
DIAMENTINA
dr. Logan Vill 294 H12
DIAMOND
dr. Yarrabilba 300 F10
pl. Tweed Heads 82 C10
DIAMOND SAND
dr. Up Coomera 6 J14
DIANA
av. Burleigh Hd 60 D4
pl. Russell I 268 L2
DIANE
cr. Bilambil Ht 81 F20
DIANELLA
cr. Maudsland 15 N5
ct. Elanora 70 K3
dr. Casuarina 103 D17
DIANNE
st. Loganlea 262 G1
DICKENSON
dr. Russell I 268 L5
DICKINSON
st. Up Coomera 6 L6
DIDDAMS
st. Loganholme 263 M11
DIETER
ct. Edens Landing 263 F17

Map Ref

DIETRICH
ct. Maudsland 26 A3
DILGARA
st. Tugun 71 D13
DILKERA
av. Russell I. 268 L14
DILLER
dr. Crestmead 261 K10
DILLON
ct. Mudgeeraba 58 L4
DILTAR
st. Loganlea 262 G4
DIMITRI
av. Biggera Wtr 19 B15
DINE
ct. Up Coomera 6 M7
DINJIRRA
ct. Tugun 71 C14
DINSEY
st. Kingscliff 103 E3
DION
dr. Eagleby 264 G11
DIPLACUS
dr. Palm Beach 60 D17
DIPLOMA
rd. Up Coomera 6 K10
DIPPER
dr. Burleigh Wtr 59 M3
DIRK HARTOG
pl. Hollywell 9 A19
DISCOVERY
bvd. Bahrs Scrub 283 C8
cov. Tweed Heads 82 H7
dr. Helensvale 17 E1
DISTILLERY
rd. Eagleby 284 H1
DISTRIBUTION
av. Molendinar 28 A16
ct. Arundel 18 H19
DIXON
cct. Yarrabilba 300 E4
dr. Pimpama 327 A11
dr. Southport 29 G19
st. Coolangatta 82 G4
st. Yatala 284 R15
DJERRAL
av. Burleigh Hd 60 E9
DOBBYS
cr. Terranora 92 B10
DOBELL
av. Banora Pt 92 P2
av. Paradise Pt 8 N13
DOBSON
av. Pimpama 327 E10
DODDS
ct. Crestmead 261 M8
rd. Chinderah 92 D16
DOGGETT
dr. Miami 49 R19
DOGWOOD
dr. Palm Beach 60 E17
DOHERTY
ct. Ormeau 305 F13
dr. Pimpama 326 J11
DOLAN
ct. Currumbin Wtr 70 M16
DOLLAR BIRD
ct. Gilston 36 R14
DOLLARBIRD
dr. Tamborine 299 H7
DOLOSTONE
st. Yarrabilba 294 E20
DOLPHIN
av. Mermaid Bch 49 R10
ct. Palm Beach 60 J16
pl. Banora Pt 92 P2
DOMAIN
rd. Currumbin 71 B9
DOMBEYAH
st. Crestmead 261 G9
DOMES
la. Yarrabilba 294 A18
DOMINIC
dr. Logan Res 282 C2
DOMINIONS
rd. Ashmore 28 L17
DOMINIQUE
cr. Merrimac 48 E7
DONALD
av. Paradise Pt 8 R12
ct. Tamborine 12 L4
st. Cornubia 264 C1
DONCASTER
ct. Robina 49 A13
dr. Beechmont 45 G19
DONEGAL
cr. Bundall 39 A17
ct. Banora Pt 92 H9
ct. Eagleby 264 F19
DONGARA
cl. Elanora 70 J4
DONGARVEN
dr. Eagleby 264 G18
DONILLA
pl. Nerang 37 D3
DONINGTON
dr. Oxenford 16 G10
DON MURPHY
la. Mudgeeraba, off Railway St 58 D1
DOOLAN
st. Ormeau 305 C3
DOOLEE
ct. Currumbin Vy 79 Q4
DOOLOOM
dr. Currumbin Vy 79 Q6
DOOMBEN
ct. Beechmont 45 G18
wy. Logan Res 261 N16
DOONBUR
dr. Broadbeach Wtr 39 E20
DORA
ct. Logan Res 262 A14
DORADO
st. Yarrabilba 294 C19
DORCHESTER
cl. Pimpama 326 G2
ct. Oxenford 16 J1
DORE
ct. Bonogin 58 H13
DOREEN
dr. Coombabah 18 M1
DORIS GIBBS
ct. Oxenford 6 Q19
DORMELLO
dr. Worongary 47 P1
DOROTHY
pl. Varsity Lakes 59 F6
DORRETTI
cct. Up Coomera 6 E1
DORRIGO
dr. Worongary 37 M17
st. Yarrabilba 300 J7
DORSET
pl. Elanora 70 A13
st. Pimpama 326 E5
DORSEY
st. Crestmead 261 L9
DOTTEREL
dr. Burleigh Wtr 60 A6
DOUBLE CROSSING
rd. Canungra 33 A20
DOUBLE ISLAND
out. Russell I. 268 P7
DOUBLEVIEW
dr. Elanora 70 G6
DOUG BRUHN
wy. Coombabah 18 G12
DOUGLAS
st. Coolangatta 82 C1
st. Loganlea 262 E1
DOUMA
dr. Mudgeeraba 57 P4
DOVE
cl. Kingscliff 93 B20
ct. Ashmore 28 E20
ct. Gilston 36 R18
rd. Tallebudgera Vy 77 R5
st. Eagleby 264 D13
DOVER
dr. Burleigh Hd 59 L14
DOVETAIL
ct. Up Coomera 6 H9
DOVETON
cr. Mt Warren Pk 284 H6
DOWLING
cr. Eagleby 264 K11
dr. Southport 29 A10
DOWSON
esp. Mudgeeraba 57 Q4
DOYALSON
pl. Helensvale 17 G12
DOYLE
ct. Ormeau Hills 305 H16
dr. Banora Pt 82 F20
DRAFTERS
cr. Maudsland 16 A7
DRAKE
av. Paradise Pt 8 R12
rd. Logan Res 261 Q14
DRAMA
st. Oxenford 16 R12
DRAYTON
tce. Mermaid Wtr 49 F7
DREAMWORLD
pky. Coomera 6 R5
DREW
ct. Ormeau 305 M14
DREWE
ct. Carrara 38 C15
DREWS
rd. Loganholme 263 K11
rd. Tanah Merah 263 L6
DREYER
rd. Eagleby 265 A9
DRIFT
ct. Kingscliff 93 D19
DRIFT AWAY
ct. Robina 48 D17
DRIFTWOOD
cct. Kingsholme 325 N3
dr. Merrimac 48 C16
dr. Robina 48 C16
pl. Parkwood 27 R5
st. Crestmead 261 L7
st. Marsden 261 L7
DRISCOLL
la. Tamborine Mtn 14 E11
DRIVER
ct. Mermaid Wtr 49 P11
DROMANA
cr. Helensvale 17 D4
DROMARA
ct. Banora Pt 92 G9
DROME
st. Biggera Wtr 19 A14
st. Runaway Bay 19 A14
DROVERS
av. Gilston 36 Q18
DRUMBEAT
pl. Coomera 328 B16
DRUMFISH
dr. Currumbin Wtr 70 L16
DRUMMOYNE
ct. Robina 49 C16
DRURY
av. Southport 29 D20
la. Bethania 262 R8
DRYANDER
st. Yarrabilba 300 H5
DRYANDRA
dr. Eagleby 264 E15
DRYANDRAS
ct. Casuarina 103 J16
DRY DOCK
rd. Tweed Hd S 82 B12
rd. Tweed Hd S 82 D12
DRYSDALE
av. Tamborine 299 D17
la. Parkwood 27 P8
pl. Paradise Pt 8 P14
DUBBO
ct. Helensvale 17 H8
DUBLIN
dr. Eagleby 264 F18
DUBUJI
la. Coomera 327 J18
DUCAT
dr. Russell I. 268 K8
st. Tweed Heads 82 C7
DUCATS
rd. Tallebudgera 79 B2
DUCE
ct. Up Coomera 6 H6
DUCHESS
ct. Loganlea 262 E2
ct. Tallai 47 F19
DUDGEON
dr. Tallebudgera 69 P13
DUDLEY
ct. Crestmead 261 E11
st. Mermaid Bch 49 Q6
DUESBURY
cr. Edens Landing 263 F15
DUET
dr. Mermaid Wtr 49 L6
DUFFY
st. Tweed Hd S 82 L14
DUGANDAN
st. Nerang 36 L7
DUICE
ct. Oxenford 16 N12
DUKE
ct. Tallai 47 F18
st. Fingal Head 83 A13
DUKES
ct. Logan Vill 294 N8
DULCIE
dr. Burleigh Hd 59 N16
DULGUIGAN
rd. Bungalora 90 Q20
rd. N Tumbulgum 90 B20
rd. N Tumbulgum 101 A6
DULHUNTY
wy. Tallai 47 N20
DULKARRA
av. Bilinga 71 M17
DULWICH
pl. Robina 48 Q16
st. Loganholme 264 A5
DUMARESQ
ct. Pacific Pines 16 M16
DUMOSA
ct. Beenleigh 283 R4
DUNADEN
st. Logan Res 261 M16
DUNBAR
rd. Bonogin 67 J2
DUNBARTON
av. Bundall 39 B14
la. Bethania 262 R8
DUNCAN
rd. Advancetown 46 M4
rd. Gilston 46 M4
st. Canungra 33 F15
DUNDEE
ct. Robina 48 R18
dr. Banora Pt 92 D7
DUNE
st. Fingal Head 83 C17
st. Tugun 71 G11
DUNEDIN
cl. Merrimac 48 E10
DUNGOGIE
dr. Tallebudgera 69 L14
DUNHILL
ct. Carrara 37 P11
DUNKEITH
av. Benowa 38 P11
DUNKIRK
cl. Arundel 18 K19
DUNLIN
dr. Burleigh Wtr 59 Q2
dr. Burleigh Wtr 60 A9
DUNLOP
ct. Mermaid Wtr 49 G4
DUNLOY
ct. Banora Pt 92 E8
DUNN
cl. Maudsland 16 J15
DUNNES
av. Hope Island 8 H9
DUNNS
rd. Wolffdene 304 E4
DUNOON
st. Tanah Merah 263 K1
DUNRAVEN
dr. Pimpama 326 F8
DUNSBY
dr. Carrara 38 A17
DUNSTAN
dr. Robina 59 A2
DURACK
la. Ormeau Hills, off River Run Cct 305 F19
DURANBAH
rd. Duranbah 101 Q15
DURANG
pl. Reedy Creek 58 P13
DURANTA
ct. Crestmead 261 D6
st. Ormeau 305 L8
DURBAR
rd. Illinbah 65 B6
DURHAM
st. Southport 39 G2
DURI
pl. Ashmore 38 K4
DURIGAN
pl. Banora Pt 92 J6
DURINGAN
st. Currumbin 70 R7
st. Currumbin 71 B4
st. Russell I. 268 M10
DUROBBY
dr. Currumbin Vy 79 L3
DUROBY CREEK
rd. Bungalora 90 L13
rd. Duroby 90 L13
DUROR
st. Pacific Pines 27 A3
DURRAN
st. Tugun 71 E10
DURRANT
ct. Tamborine 2 Q7
DUSK
pl. Crestmead 261 K10
DUSSEK
rd. Numinbah Vy 65 M3
DUTTON
st. Coolangatta 82 F4
st. Coolangatta 82 G1
DUXTON
dr. Varsity Lakes 59 D2
DWYER
cl. Tallebudgera 69 K12
DYLAN
st. Arundel 27 Q1
DYSART
dr. Holmview 283 F4
DYWER
st. Pimpama 327 F10

E

EACHAM
av. Coombabah 18 L1
EADIE
st. Park Ridge 261 H19
EADY
av. Broadbeach Wtr 39 L18
EAGLE
av. Burleigh Wtr 60 C5
av. Waterford W 262 K8
dr. Eagleby 264 C11
EAGLEBY
rd. Eagleby 264 F7
EAGLE HEIGHTS
rd. Tamborine Mtn 13 R14
rd. Tamborine Mtn 14 D13
EAGLEMONT
dr. Terranora 91 K11
EAGLES
cl. Tamborine Mtn 14 H12
EAGLES RETREAT
pl. Tamborine Mtn 14 H12
EAGLEVIEW
ct. Bonogin 68 M3
EALING
ct. Nerang 36 P8
EAMONN
ct. Highland Pk 37 K12
EARLE
ct. Tallai 47 G17
EARLEHAM
ct. Pimpama 326 E8
EARLWOOD
ct. Robina 49 D14
EAST
la. Robina 48 K17
st. Burleigh Hd 60 D7
EASTBANK
tce. Helensvale 7 M16
EAST BEAUMONT
rd. Park Ridge 261 D20
rd. Park Ridge 281 D1
EASTBOURNE
ch. Arundel 18 A15
rd. Bethania 263 A9
EAST CARNIVAL
st. Loganlea 262 K1
EASTER
cr. Pacific Pines 27 A3
EASTERLY
st. Waterford 262 P17
EASTERN
av. Bilinga 71 M18
ct. Helensvale 7 G19
EASTERN SERVICE
rd. Ormeau 285 A13
rd. Ormeau 285 A15
rd. Stapylton 284 Q10
EASTHILL
dr. Robina 58 H2
EASTLAKE
st. Carrara 47 Q2
EASTLAKES
dr. Tweed Hd S 82 M18
EAST LYNNE
Benowa 38 Q12
EASTPARK
dr. Helensvale 7 N15
EASTPARK WATERS
Helensvale 7 N15
EAST QUAY
dr. Biggera Wtr 18 M12
EASTRIDGE
st. Stapylton 285 A8
EASTSIDE
esp. Helensvale 7 Q13
EASTWELL
ct. Mt Warren Pk 284 G9
EASTWOOD
dr. Robina 49 C13
EASY
st. Loganholme 263 K8
EBELING
ct. Worongary 47 J8
EBONY
ct. Casuarina 103 E16
pl. Palm Beach 60 H18
st. Marsden 261 R3
ECHIDNA
ct. Coombabah 18 M4
ECHLIN
st. Labrador 29 C5
ECHO
la. Casuarina 103 E20
ECHUCA
cr. Banora Pt 92 M5
ECLIPSE
ct. Mudgeeraba 48 A20
la. Casuarina 103 E20
EDDIES
la. Tugun 71 E12
EDDY
av. Edens Landing 263 G13
av. Kingscliff 93 A14
EDELSTEN
ct. Carrara 38 B15
EDELWEISS
wy. Gaven 27 G6
EDEN
av. Coolangatta 72 K20
cct. Reedy Creek 58 N12
cl. Edens Landing 263 G14
cl. Pimpama 326 G2
ct. Nerang 37 L2
ct. Tamborine Mtn 14 C5
la. Marsden 261 K5
st. Tweed Heads 82 M1
EDENLEA
dr. Meadowbrook 262 P1
EDEN PARK
ct. Mt Nathan 25 R16
EDEN VIEW
dr. Reedy Creek 58 P12
EDGECLIFF
dr. Hope Island 8 E8
dr. Hope Island 8 H5
EDGEHILL
dr. Nerang 36 R7
EDGEMOUNT
ct. Oxenford 16 Q12
EDGEWARE
rd. Pimpama 326 F8
rd. Pimpama 326 F9
EDGEWATER
ct. Robina 48 K20
la. Kingscliff 103 F12
pl. Helensvale 8 C17
EDGEWORTH
pl. Helensvale 17 H4
EDINBURGH
dr. Bethania 262 P6
rd. Benowa 38 P13
EDITHVALE
ct. Robina 49 B14
EDMOND
st. Coomera 7 M1
EDMUND RICE
dr. Southport 28 L13
EDWARD
st. Labrador 29 A5
EDWARDS
pl. Ormeau 305 H13
EDWARDSON
dr. Coomera 327 G15
EE-JUNG
rd. Springbrook 66 N16
EGERTON
st. Southport 29 F17
EGGERSDORF
rd. Norwell 306 B9
rd. Ormeau 305 K11
rd. Ormeau 306 B9
EGRET
av. Burleigh Wtr 60 B3
ct. Cornubia 264 C2
la. Coomera 327 F16
EIDER
av. Paradise Pt 8 R13
EIGER
st. Holmview 283 C1
EIGHTH
av. Palm Beach 60 N19
EILDON
pl. Helensvale 17 E5

FEATHERTAIL

GOLDEN BEAR

Map Ref

FULHAM
ct. Robina 48 K16
FULLBROOK
st. Pimpama 327 E13
FULLERTON
st. Benowa 38 R11
FULMAR
pl. Burleigh Wtr 59 M3
FULMER
st. Yarrabilba 293 N20
FURLONG
st. Broadbeach Wtr 39 J14
FYFES
rd. Gilston 36 N11
FYSHWICK
st. Loganholme 263 P8

G

GABLE
st. Oxenford 17 B11
GABOR
ct. Maudsland 26 B1
GABRIELLE
gr. Burleigh Hd 60 C11
GABRIELS
ct. Robina 48 R14
GAGGIN
wy. Kingscliff 103 F3
GAILES
rd. Cornubia 264 F1
st. Beenleigh 264 C17
GAINSBOROUGH
dr. Pimpama 326 K6
dr. Pimpama 327 A8
dr. Varsity Lakes 59 G8
GALA
gr. Coolangatta 82 B3
GALAH
st. Maudsland 16 H13
GALAHAD
ct. Nerang 37 C6
st. Marsden 261 N2
GALAPAGOS
wy. Pacific Pines 27 F1
GALAXY
ct. Labrador 28 N4
dr. Coomera 327 L19
GALEEN
dr. Burleigh Wtr 59 N2
GALENA
ct. Bethania 262 N5
GALFIN
rd. Russell I 268 K8
GALLAGHER
st. Yarrabilba 300 H3
GALLEON
wy. Currumbin Wtr 70 H11
GALLERIA
ct. Highland Pk 37 D14
GALLEY
rd. Hope Island 8 A10
GALLI
cr. Carrara 37 R11
GALLILEO
pl. Mermaid Wtr 49 M9
GALLOWAY
dr. Ashmore 38 D1
GALT
rd. Willow Vale 5 N2
GALVIN
st. Loganholme 263 N8
GALWAY
ct. Banora Pt 92 G8
st. Eagleby 264 G18
GAMBIER
cr. Pacific Pines 27 F1
GAMMON
dr. Varsity Lakes 59 B2
la. Yarrabilba 300 H12
GANGSTON
av. Russell I 268 H14
GANNET
pl. Up Coomera 326 H16
st. Burleigh Wtr 59 M3
GANNON
wy. Up Coomera 6 H6
GANTON
ct. Parkwood 28 H5
GARAGUL
st. Jacobs Well 308 C10
GARAWARRA
cr. Up Coomera 6 B16
GARDA
av. Hope Island 7 L11
GARDEN
ct. Currumbin Wtr 70 J20
gr. Bahrs Scrub 283 P12

Map Ref

gr. Carrara 38 L12
rd. Cedar Creek 304 D13
rd. Coomera 7 F1
rd. Coomera 327 F20
row.Currumbin Vy 79 P4
st. Coomera 7 J7
st. Southport 29 F13
GARDENDALE
cr. Burleigh Wtr 59 N7
GARDENIA
dr. Bonogin 67 H11
gr. Burleigh Hd 60 C1
GARDEN VIEW
ct. Merrimac 48 D8
GARDINER
rd. Holmview 263 C20
rd. Waterford 263 C20
rd. Waterford 283 B1
GARDINERS
pl. Southport 29 F16
GARFIELD
tce. Surfers Pdse 39 P11
tce. Surfers Pdse 40 P17
GARIGAL
ct. Up Coomera 6 B16
GARISWOOD
ct. Edens Landing 263 G14
GARLINGE
ct. Bonogin 67 E15
GARNET
ct. Carrara 37 R10
GARRAGULL
dr. Yarrabilba 293 R20
dr. Yarrabilba 299 R1
GARRAN
ct. Loganholme 263 N8
GARRARD
st. Up Coomera 6 C20
GARRICK
la. Coolangatta, off Garrick St 82 F1
st. Coolangatta 82 E4
st. Coolangatta 82 F1
st. Park Ridge 281 D1
GARRIMA
dr. Loganholme 263 N3
GARRY
pl. Crestmead 261 G12
GARSON
st. Eagleby 264 K12
GARTSIDE
av. Maudsland 16 A6
GARVIE
pl. Highland Pk 37 H13
GARY
ct. Carrara 38 C16
GARY PLAYER
cr. Parkwood 28 C8
GASCOYNE
st. Pacific Pines 26 M5
GASSMAN
dr. Yatala 284 M9
GATEWAY
ct. Coomera 7 E8
dr. Biggera Wtr 18 L16
GATINA
cr. Coomera 327 D14
GATSBY
pl. Maudsland 16 A20
GATTON
ct. Helensvale 17 F11
GAVEN
cr. Mermaid Bch 49 P5
wy. Gaven 17 H16
wy. Gaven 27 M9
wy. Helensvale 17 H16
wy. Molendinar 27 M9
wy. Nerang 27 J18
wy. Nerang 27 M9
GAVEN ARTERIAL
rd. Maudsland 16 D10
rd. Oxenford 16 D10
GAW
tce. Bonogin 67 M2
GAWAIN
dr. Ormeau 305 L12
dr. Ormeau 305 M13
GAWLER
pl. Up Coomera 16 E1
GAWTHERN
dr. Pimpama 326 N8
GAY
tce. Russell I 268 M6
GAYE
pde.Miami 49 Q17
GAYLE
ct. Logan Vill 293 L12
st. Southport 29 C20

Map Ref

GAYNOR
ct. Mt Warren Pk 284 C8
GEANEY
bvd.Crestmead 261 F12
GEARY
cr. Molendinar 28 B19
GECKO
cr. Up Coomera 326 G19
GEEBUNG
ct. Coomera 328 B18
GEELONG
ct. Eagleby 264 H12
GEIGER
rd. Canungra 33 A18
GEISSMANN
dr. Tamborine Mtn 13 N15
dr. Tamborine Mtn 13 Q10
st. Tamborine Mtn 13 M12
GELLERT
cl. Maudsland 16 H18
GEM
ct. Alberton 265 F19
GEMBROOK
ct. Parkwood 27 R3
GEMINI
cct. Coomera 327 F13
cct. Molendinar 28 D14
GEMMA
gld. Labrador 28 R1
GEMSTONE
ct. Bethania 262 R13
ct. Bethania 263 A13
ct. Carrara 37 R12
GEMVALE
rd. Mudgeeraba 58 K6
rd. Reedy Creek 58 Q9
GENE KELLY
ct. Maudsland 16 A19
GENOA
st. Surfers Pdse 39 M14
GENOVESE
av. Ormeau 306 B9
GENTIAN
dr. Arundel 17 Q13
GEOFFERY MILLER
av. Pimpama 327 B15
GEOFF PHILP
dr. Logan Vill 293 H4
dr. Stockleigh 293 H4
GEOFF PHILP BRIDGE
Chambers Ft 293 M3
GEOFFREY
av. Southport 28 R9
GEOFF WOLTER
dr. Molendinar 28 B13
dr.w,Molendinar 28 A13
GEORGE
av. Broadbeach 49 P1
la. Hope Island 8 G12
st. Beenleigh 264 A20
st. Beenleigh 264 B20
st. Beenleigh 284 F1
st. Bilinga 71 N17
st. Eagleby 264 L18
st. Southport 29 D12
st.c,Burleigh Hd 60 D8
st.e,Burleigh Hd 60 G8
st.w,Burleigh Hd 60 C7
GEORGE ALEXANDER
wy. Coomera 7 C1
wy. Coomera 327 B20
GEORGES
rd. Russell I 268 J16
GEORGETOWN
st. Varsity Lakes 59 K4
GEORGIA
st. Coombabah 18 F1
st. Varsity Lakes 59 G3
GEORGIE
la. Yatala 304 R1
GEORGINA
dr. Logan Vill 293 R12
st. Oxenford 6 H20
GERALDTON
dr. Robina 59 B1
dr. Varsity Lakes 59 B1
GERANIUM
st. Ormeau 305 L9
GERARA
ct. Clagiraba 35 F1
GERARD
st. Pacific Pines 16 P17
GERONA
cct. Varsity Lakes 59 B8
GERRALE
dr. Willow Vale 325 J11

Map Ref

GERRAND
st. Loganlea 262 J3
GERRARD
st. Coolangatta 82 H2
GERSHWIN
ct. Nerang 36 K9
GERTRUDE
pl. Windaroo 283 Q12
GET A
wy. Currumbin Vy 79 Q4
GETUP
cl. Currumbin Vy 79 N6
GHILGAI
rd. Merrimac 48 D7
GHOSTGUM
gr. Up Coomera 6 H14
GIACCO
st. Pimpama 327 F13
GIARDINO
la. Varsity Lakes 59 D8
GIBB
la. Ormeau Hills 305 G17
GIBBS
st. Arundel 18 L18
st. Southport 29 F15
GIBOSA
la. Coomera 327 E19
GIBRALTAR
dr. Surfers Pdse 39 H9
GIBSON
st. Bilinga 71 M16
st. Kingscliff 103 F3
GIBSONS
rd. Woongoolba 286 N7
rd. Woongoolba 287 A7
GIBSONVILLE
st. Tallebudgera Vy 78 G2
GIDEON
gdn.Pimpama 327 A12
GIDGEE
ct. Molendinar 28 G17
GIDYA
rd. Mudgeeraba 57 P11
GILBERT
st. Eagleby 264 F11
GILCHRIST
dr. Currumbin Wtr 70 R14
GILCREST
ct. Molendinar 28 H12
rd. Russell I 268 H5
GILES
gr. Worongary 37 P18
GILGANDRA
cl. Reedy Creek 58 Q17
GILL
ct. Mudgeeraba 58 G11
st. Pimpama 326 H6
GILLESPIE
cl. Edens Landing 263 H14
GILLIAN
dr. Coomera 327 K14
la. Southport 29 F15
GILLIN
pl. Ormeau 305 N13
GILMOUR
la. Southport 29 E7
GILPIN
ct. Up Coomera 16 D1
GILRUTH
st. Pacific Pines 16 N14
GILSTON
rd. Gilston 46 L3
rd. Nerang 37 B9
GILWARD
dr. Mudgeeraba 57 A7
GIMLET
st. Crestmead 261 H8
GINGER
st. Bahrs Scrub 283 H7
GINGER ROGERS
rd. Maudsland 16 A20
rd. Maudsland 25 R1
GINNINDERRA
ct. Loganholme 263 N8
GIPPSLAND
dr. Helensvale 17 L6
GIRO
pl. Ashmore 38 G4
GIRRAL
av. Ashmore 38 F2
GIRRALONG
st. Eagleby 264 H16
GIRRAMAY
st. Yarrabilba 300 G4
GIRRAWEEN
gr. Ashmore 38 G5
pl. Waterford 263 B16
st. Pimpama 326 K6

Map Ref

GIRTIN
cr. Pimpama 327 D11
GIRUA
av. Runaway Bay 19 A4
GIRVAN
la. Belivah 283 N17
GLADE
dr. Gaven 17 F14
dr. Pacific Pines 17 F19
GLADES
dr. Robina 48 D19
dr. Robina 48 D20
GLADFUL
ct. Varsity Lakes 59 J7
GLADIOLI
av. Terranora 91 C14
GLADIOLUS
ct. Hollywell 19 A3
GLADROSE
cr. Wongawallan 15 G6
GLADYS
st. Labrador 28 M2
GLASS
st. Ashmore 38 E1
GLASSHOUSE
dr. Varsity Lakes 59 B3
GLASSON
dr. Bethania 263 B14
GLASSWING
dr. Up Coomera 6 J13
GLASTONBURY
dr. Bethania 263 C10
dr. Mudgeeraba 58 M8
GLAUCA
st. Burleigh Hd 69 L1
GLEBE
pl. Banora Pt 92 A3
GLEN
cct. Clagiraba 35 D4
cl. Ormeau 305 F6
rd. Logan Res 282 A4
GLENAFTON
ct. Ormeau 305 P7
GLENALTA
pl. Robina 48 K16
GLENAURA
dr. Tallai 46 R4
dr. Tallai 47 A8
GLEN AYR
dr. Banora Pt 92 C8
GLENBRAE
dr. Terranora 91 E12
GLENBROOK
av. Benowa 38 Q12
GLENCOE
ct. Bonogin 58 A17
GLENDA
st. Waterford W 262 J9
GLENDALE
pl. Helensvale 17 H3
rd. Russell I 268 E12
rd. Russell I 268 F12
rd. Russell I 268 K13
st. Marsden 261 Q1
GLENDEVON
cr. Mt Warren Pk 284 G5
GLENEAGLE
ct. Bonogin 67 P7
GLEN EAGLES
dr. Robina 48 Q19
GLENEAGLES
av. Cornubia 264 H2
dr. Hope Island 8 B4
pl. Banora Pt 92 J3
GLENELG
av. Mermaid Bch 49 P6
GLENFERN
pl. Bonogin 67 P6
GLENFERRIE
dr. Robina 49 B15
GLENFIELD
av. Russell I 268 K6
GLENGALLON
wy. Hope Island 7 M9
GLENGARRIE
rd. Carool 89 A6
rd. Glengarrie 89 A11
rd. Glengarrie 89 A4
rd. Glengarrie 89 A8
GLENGARRY
cl. Highland Pk 37 H11
GLENGATE
st. Helensvale 7 K16
GLENHAVEN
ct. Merrimac 48 F9
GLENHILL
ct. Up Coomera 6 K11

Map Ref

GLENHOPE
st. Up Coomera 6 J4
GLEN IRIS
pl. Robina 48 R16
GLENLYON
st. Marsden 261 K3
GLENMORE
dr. Ashmore 38 B3
dr. Bonogin 67 N3
GLENN
ct. Worongary 37 K17
GLEN NATHAN
ct. Mt Nathan 25 H13
GLENNY
st. Mudgeeraba 58 H9
GLEN OSMOND
rd. Yatala 284 C18
GLENRIDGE
st. Up Coomera 6 J4
GLENROWAN
dr. Tallai 47 A9
GLENSHEE
st. Up Coomera 6 K4
GLENSIDE
dr. Robina 48 Q16
GLENTREE
av. Up Coomera 6 J12
GLENTREES
gr. Currumbin Wtr 70 F11
GLENVIEW
rd. Up Coomera 15 Q2
GLENWATER
cr. Helensvale 7 J17
GLENWOOD GREEN
ct. Mudgeeraba 58 F5
GLENYS
st. Tweed Hd S 81 Q18
GLIDER
ct. Bonogin 68 H16
GLOBAL
plz. Oxenford 6 Q17
GLOUCESTER
ct. Highland Pk 37 G13
pl. Up Coomera 6 F6
st. Waterford 263 A19
GLYN
st. Benowa 38 Q11
GODDARD
st. Logan Res 261 P14
GODDEN
dr. Up Coomera 6 K7
GOLD
av. Yarrabilba 300 C1
GOLD COAST
hwy.Arundel 17 H13
hwy.Arundel 18 L16
hwy.Biggera Wtr 18 L16
hwy.Bilinga 71 G11
hwy.Broadbeach 39 N17
hwy.Burleigh Hd 60 C1
hwy.Coombabah 17 H13
hwy.Coombabah 18 L16
hwy.Currumbin 71 A4
hwy.Gaven 17 H13
hwy.Helensvale 17 H13
hwy.Labrador 18 L17
hwy.Labrador 29 E2
hwy.Main Beach 29 H12
hwy.Mermaid Bch 49 P2
hwy.Miami 49 R14
hwy.Palm Beach 60 L15
hwy.Southport 29 H12
hwy.Surfers Pdse 39 M1
hwy.Tugun 71 A4
hwy.Tugun 71 G11
hwy.Tweed Heads 81 R1
hwy.Tweed Hd W 81 R1
GOLD COAST BRIDGE
Southport 29 J16
GOLD COAST-SPRINGBROOK
rd. Advancetown 46 M20
rd. Carrara 48 B7
rd. Clear I Wtr 48 B7
rd. Merrimac 48 B7
rd. Mudgeeraba 57 B16
rd. Neranwood 46 M20
rd. Numinbah Vy 46 D18
rd. Numinbah Vy 66 H6
rd. Springbrook 66 H6
GOLDCREST
dr. Up Coomera 6 H9
GOLDEN
cr. Southport 39 C2
GOLDEN BEAR
dr. Arundel 17 P19

Map Ref

GOLDEN FOUR
dr. Bilinga ... 71 M16
dr. Tugun ... 71 F10
GOLDEN GROVE
bvd.Reedy Creek ... 58 Q18
bvd.Reedy Creek ... 68 Q1
ct. Mundoolun ... 1 B10
GOLDEN PALM
dr. Ormeau ... 305 K6
GOLDEN PALMS
ct. Ashmore ... 28 E20
GOLDEN VALLEY
rd. Tallebudgera Vy ... 68 Q9
GOLDFINCH
av. Burleigh Wtr ... 49 M20
GOLD MARKET
dr. Bundall ... 39 B7
GOLDMINE
ct. Advancetown ... 36 E12
rd. Ormeau ... 285 M20
rd. Ormeau ... 305 H7
rd. Ormeau ... 305 M6
GOLDSBOROUGH
pde.Waterford ... 262 P19
GOLDVILLA
dr. Elanora ... 70 G4
GOLDWATER
dr. Robina ... 58 P5
GOLDWYN
wy. Oxenford ... 17 C12
GOLF COURSE
rd. Tamborine Mtn ... 24 E13
GOLFERS
cr. Tamborine Mtn ... 14 E12
GOLF VIEW
ct. Banora Pt ... 92 E3
tce. Robina ... 48 D16
GOLFVIEW
ct. Arundel ... 28 C1
GOLINE
ct. Tallebudgera ... 69 G13
GOLLAN
dr. Tweed Hd W ... 81 L12
dr. Tweed Hd W ... 81 L13
GONA
st. Beenleigh ... 284 E3
GOODING
dr. Carrara ... 38 N20
dr. Carrara ... 48 A8
dr. Clear I Wtr ... 38 N20
dr. Coombabah ... 18 M2
dr. Merrimac ... 48 A8
GOODING DRIVE VILLAGE ACCESS
Merrimac ... 48 F6
GOODMAN
cl. Highland Pk ... 37 M14
GOODOOGA
dr. Bethania ... 262 Q13
dr. Bethania ... 263 A12
dr. Waterford ... 262 Q13
GOODRICK
ct. Mt Warren Pk ... 284 B7
GOODSELL
cr. Tamborine ... 3 B1
cr. Tamborine ... 304 A20
GOODWIN
cl. Park Ridge ... 261 G14
tce. Burleigh Hd ... 60 G6
GOODWOOD
wy. Arundel ... 18 D20
GOODYEAR
st. Southport ... 28 P13
GOOLABAH
dr. Tallebudgera ... 69 F10
GOOLAGONG
ct. Broadbeach Wtr .. 38 P20
GOOLWA
ct. Pimpama ... 327 D10
GOONAL
pl. Banora Pt ... 92 J10
GOORA
st. Nerang ... 36 Q4
GOORAWIN
st. Runaway Bay ... 18 Q13
GORBASH
cr. Russell I ... 268 H14
GORDON
dr. Up Coomera ... 6 B10
la. Coolangatta ... 82 E2
st. Beenleigh ... 264 B20
st. Labrador ... 29 B1
st. Ormeau Hills ... 305 E19
GORDONIA
dr. Reedy Creek ... 59 C17
GORDONVALE
pl. Helensvale ... 17 K8

GOROKA
ct. Clear I Wtr ... 49 D2
pl. Runaway Bay ... 19 C8
GOSFORD
ct. Helensvale ... 17 J6
GOSHAWK
ct. Bahrs Scrub ... 283 E8
GOSS
av. Labrador ... 29 B5
GOSSAN
cct. Yarrabilba ... 294 C19
GOTHORPE
pl. Varsity Lakes ... 59 J7
GOTTSFREID
pl. Windaroo ... 283 Q13
GOUGH
pl. Currumbin Wtr ... 70 F11
GOULBURN
cl. Arundel ... 28 K2
cl. Helensvale ... 17 J6
st. Yarrabilba ... 300 K10
GOULD
ct. Bahrs Scrub ... 283 C7
pl. Pacific Pines ... 26 R4
GOUNDRY
dr. Holmview ... 283 H3
GOVERNMENT
rd. Labrador ... 28 M5
rd. Labrador ... 28 R4
GOVETT
ct. Pacific Pines ... 16 N19
GOW
ct. Crestmead ... 261 K13
GOWER
la. Pimpama ... 327 D11
st. Terranora ... 91 R7
GOWRIE
wy. Hope Island ... 7 L8
GRACE
av. Labrador ... 29 C3
st. Bethania ... 263 A10
GRACEMERE
cct.e,Hope Island ... 7 L8
cct.n,Hope Island ... 7 L7
cct.w,Hope Island ... 7 K8
dr. Hope Island ... 7 L8
GRACEMERE GARDENS
cct. Hope Island ... 7 L10
GRACILIS
ct. Elanora ... 70 E10
GRADUATE
cl. Mudgeeraba ... 58 E7
GRAHAM
st. Bilinga ... 71 P18
st. Pimpama ... 326 R13
st. Southport ... 29 E16
GRAHAMS DIP
rd. Biddaddaba ... 22 F11
GRAMMAR
st. Up Coomera ... 6 L10
GRAMPIAN
ct. Reedy Creek ... 58 R19
GRAMPIANS
cct. Yarrabilba ... 300 J9
cct. Yarrabilba ... 300 K10
GRAND
pde.Casuarina ... 103 D18
pde.Eagleby ... 264 H8
tce. Waterford ... 262 P20
tce. Waterford ... 283 A1
GRAND CANAL
wy. Runaway Bay ... 18 P12
GRANDE
ent. Helensvale ... 7 Q15
tce. Helensvale ... 7 Q16
GRANDIS
ct. Elanora ... 69 R5
GRANDVIEW
rd. Crestmead ... 261 E8
tce. Tallai ... 57 E2
GRANGE
av. Miami ... 50 B15
bvd.n,Up Coomera ... 6 H10
bvd.s,Up Coomera ... 6 H11
GRANITE
st. Yarrabilba ... 294 E20
st. Yarrabilba ... 300 E1
GRANT
av. Hope Island ... 8 D11
pl. Broadbeach Wtr .. 39 J17
GRANTHAM
rd. Pimpama ... 326 F8
GRANYA
ct. Pacific Pines ... 16 Q14
GRASSDALE
st. Buccan ... 282 Q11

GRASSLANDS
cr. Reedy Creek ... 58 N19
st. Yarrabilba ... 293 P18
GRASSMERE
ct. Banora Pt ... 92 F7
ct. Robina ... 49 H15
GRASSTREE
ct. Molendinar ... 28 G13
GRAVESEND
la. Pimpama, off Bundy Ct ... 326 F5
GRAY
st. Beenleigh ... 264 A20
st. Beenleigh ... 284 A1
st. Southport ... 29 E10
st. Tallebudgera ... 69 M11
st. Tweed Hd W ... 81 R9
GRAYSON
st. Yarrabilba ... 299 R2
GRAYWILLOW
bvd.Oxenford ... 6 J17
GREAT HALL
dr. Miami ... 49 R13
GREAT SANDY
cct. Pimpama ... 326 H3
cct. Pimpama ... 326 J4
GREAT SOUTHERN
dr. Robina ... 49 C18
GREAVES
ct. Carrara ... 38 A19
GREBE
pl. Burleigh Wtr ... 49 M19
GREEN
ct. Maudsland ... 16 F12
ct. Reedy Creek ... 58 P13
la. Tallebudgera ... 69 N13
rd. Crestmead ... 261 A10
rd. Park Ridge ... 261 A10
GREENACRE
dr. Arundel ... 27 M2
dr. Parkwood ... 27 P7
dr. Parkwood ... 27 R4
wy. Maudsland ... 16 C11
GREENBANK
cct. Carrara ... 37 R13
GREENCASTLE
pde.Maudsland ... 16 F11
GREENDALE
pl. Banora Pt ... 92 F2
pl. Burleigh Wtr ... 59 P7
pl. Currumbin Wtr ... 70 L18
GREENDRAGON
cr. Up Coomera ... 326 J17
GREENFIELD
st. Eagleby ... 264 L18
GREENFINCH
ct. Jacobs Well ... 307 R6
GREENGATE
st. Helensvale ... 7 J15
GREEN GLEN
rd. Ashmore ... 28 K16
GREENHAVEN
pl. Currumbin Wtr ... 80 F3
GREENLANDS
dr. Varsity Lakes ... 59 G8
GREENLEAF
cl. Burleigh Wtr ... 59 K7
st. Up Coomera ... 6 E15
GREEN MEADOWS
rd. Pimpama ... 307 K20
rd. Pimpama ... 327 L1
GREENMOUNT
st. Pimpama ... 326 M7
GREENPARK
dr. Crestmead ... 261 J10
GREENRIDGE
st. Oxenford ... 16 Q11
GREENSBOROUGH
cr. Parkwood ... 27 P4
GREENSHANK
dr. Bahrs Scrub ... 283 E7
GREENSTONE
st. Yarrabilba ... 294 B19
GREENSWARD
rd. Tamborine ... 299 F18
rd. Tamborine ... 299 N19
GREENVALE
cr. Maudsland ... 15 N8
GREEN VALLEY
wy. Piggabeen ... 79 R12
GREENVIEW
cct. Arundel ... 17 M20
dr. Up Coomera ... 15 N1
pl. Reedy Creek ... 58 P11
GREENWAY
bvd.Maudsland ... 16 K14
dr. Banora Pt ... 82 F20
dr. Tweed Hd S ... 82 G16

GREENWICH
av. Pimpama ... 326 P10
ct. Robina ... 49 C9
ct. Runaway Bay ... 19 B11
GREENWOOD
ct. Helensvale ... 7 H15
ct. Parkwood ... 27 R5
GREER
tce. Southport ... 29 G18
GREG
lk. Up Coomera ... 6 K2
GREG CHAPPELL
dr. Burleigh Hd ... 59 F12
GREG NORMAN
cr. Parkwood ... 28 E7
GREGOR
cr. Coomera ... 327 L15
GREGORY
dr. Carrara ... 38 M17
GREHAN
cr. Mt Warren Pk ... 284 G8
GREISEN
ct. Bethania ... 262 R5
GRENADA
ct. Varsity Lakes ... 59 C6
GRENASIDE
ct. Robina ... 49 D17
GRENFELL
st. Nerang ... 37 K5
GRESSWELL
ct. Up Coomera ... 6 B13
GRETEL
dr. Mermaid Wtr ... 49 M6
pl. Hollywell ... 8 Q18
GRETTY
la. Lr Beechmont ... 46 C3
GREVILLEA
dr. Jacobs Well ... 308 G16
dr. Varsity Lakes ... 59 H10
GREVILLIA
av. Eagleby ... 264 J9
av. Southport ... 39 D1
cr. Maudsland ... 15 N6
GREY GUM
rd. Chambers Ft ... 281 A8
rd. Helensvale ... 17 A3
GREYHOUND
rd. Gilberton ... 285 K16
rd. Ormeau ... 285 K16
GREY JACK
ct. Worongary ... 47 P5
GRICE
av. Paradise Pt ... 8 Q16
GRIFFEN
pl. Crestmead ... 261 L12
GRIFFITH
st. Coolangatta ... 82 G1
st. Tamborine Mtn ... 13 M14
st. Tweed Heads ... 82 G1
st. Yarrabilba ... 300 H10
st. Southport ... 28 H13
GRIFFITH UNIVERSITY BRIDGE
Southport ... 28 K10
GRIFFON
st. Merrimac ... 48 E9
GRIMSDYKE
ct. Molendinar ... 28 C14
GRISSOM
ct. Worongary ... 37 K16
GRIX
ct. Crestmead ... 261 F7
GROSS
rd. Woongoolba ... 287 H20
rd. Woongoolba ... 307 H1
GROSVENOR
ct. Worongary ... 47 M9
GROVE
rd. Edens Landing ... 263 J15
rd. Holmview ... 263 J15
rd. Russell I ... 268 H9
GROVE CREEK
cl. Reedy Creek ... 58 Q16
GROVEDALE
ct. Parkwood ... 27 Q5
GROZIER
dr. Russell I ... 268 L16
GUAM
pl. Pacific Pines ... 27 E1
GUANABA
rd. Up Coomera ... 15 N1
rd. Tamborine Mtn ... 24 H11
rd. Tamborine Mtn ... 24 L5
GUANABA CREEK
rd. Guanaba ... 14 N19
rd. Maudsland ... 25 L6

GUARA
gr. Pimpama ... 306 B20
gr. Pimpama ... 306 D20
gr. Pimpama ... 326 B1
gr.e,Pimpama ... 306 C18
GUAVA
ct. Bonogin ... 67 K10
GUILFOYLE
la. Cudgen ... 102 R3
GUILLEMOT
st. Up Coomera ... 6 H10
GUINEAS CREEK
rd. Currumbin Wtr ... 70 G7
rd. Elanora ... 69 N8
rd. Tallebudgera ... 69 N8
GUINEVERE
ct. Bethania ... 263 B11
GULAI
st. Palm Beach ... 60 K17
GULL
pl. Tweed Hd W ... 81 K13
GULLIVER
cr. Logan Res ... 262 A13
GULLWING
dr. Up Coomera ... 6 D1
GUM
ct. Burleigh Wtr ... 59 K7
GUMBEEL
ct. Highland Pk ... 37 K12
GUMBLETON
rd. Upper Duroby ... 90 B14
GUMLEAF
ct. Nerang ... 37 B6
dr. Molendinar ... 28 F14
GUMNUT
gr. Banora Pt ... 92 C5
la. Nerang ... 37 M4
GUMTREE
cr. Up Coomera ... 6 G10
ct. Beechmont ... 45 G20
ct. Gilston ... 37 A18
GUMVIEW
st. Molendinar ... 28 F13
GUNNAMATTA
av. Kingscliff ... 103 F10
GUNSYND
dr. Mudgeeraba ... 58 B11
GUNTHER
av. Coomera ... 7 F1
GUNYAH
gr. Ashmore ... 38 H4
GURLEY
st. Eagleby ... 264 J9
GURNEY
st. Waterford W ... 262 H8
wy. Russell I ... 268 P14
GURRAH
av. Southport ... 28 Q17
GUSTAV
wy. Windaroo ... 283 R12
GUTHRIE
pde.Carrara ... 37 Q13
GUY
la. Oxenford ... 16 M10
GUYRA
av. Burleigh Hd ... 60 F10
cl. Mt Warren Pk ... 284 H5
GWINGANA
cr. Beechmont ... 65 H11
GWONGORELLA
pde.Springbrook ... 66 F15
GWYDIR
ct. Helensvale ... 7 B18
GYMEA
cr. Varsity Lakes ... 59 F8
GYMPIE
ct. Parkwood ... 27 R4
GYPSUM
pl. Pimpama ... 326 P9

H

HAASE
cr. Ormeau ... 305 B4
HABANA
st. Helensvale ... 17 H17
HABITAT
dr. Casuarina ... 103 E19
wy. Pimpama ... 326 K15
HACKING RIDGE
rd. Russell I ... 268 K7
HACKNEY
ct. Up Coomera ... 6 J1
ct. Up Coomera ... 326 J20
HACKWORTH
ct. Worongary ... 47 P7

HADDON
ct. Carrara ... 38 B17
HADLOW
st. Waterford W ... 262 H8
HADRIAN
ct. Pacific Pines ... 16 K20
HAIG
rd. Loganlea ... 262 H2
rd. Loganlea ... 262 H3
st. Coolangatta ... 82 C1
HAKARI
st. Crestmead ... 261 F6
HAKEA
ct. Palm Beach ... 60 F13
dr. Tweed Hd W ... 81 Q8
st. Crestmead ... 261 H6
HALBORNE
dr. Mermaid Wtr ... 49 F10
HALBURY
ct. Helensvale ... 17 J9
HALCYON
dr. Pimpama ... 326 Q6
wy. Hope Island ... 8 C13
wy. Logan Res ... 262 C16
HALE
st. Pacific Pines ... 16 N14
HALFWAY
dr. Ormeau ... 305 E2
HALIFAX
cct. Pimpama ... 327 D8
pl. Browns Pl ... 261 D1
HALL
ct. Mudgeeraba ... 58 H5
HALLAM
lk. Pimpama ... 327 B13
HALLIDAY
st. Eagleby ... 264 K9
HALLMARK
ct. Ashmore ... 37 R2
HALLS
rd. Luscombe ... 304 E9
HALO
pl. Tamborine ... 1 J4
HALYARD
cr. Hope Island ... 7 Q9
HAMERSLEY
st. Pimpama ... 326 F2
wy. Worongary ... 37 M15
HAMILTON
av. Surfers Pdse ... 39 N9
av. Surfers Pdse ... 40 N15
rd. Logan Vill ... 294 H3
HAMMEL
st. Beenleigh ... 263 R20
st. Beenleigh ... 284 A1
HAMMERSFORD
dr. Currumbin Wtr ... 70 P13
HAMMOCK
pl. Hope Island ... 8 G10
HAMMOND
st. Gaven ... 27 G5
HAMPSHIRE
cl. Highland Pk ... 37 G12
HAMPSTEAD
ct. Highland Pk ... 37 F13
HAMPTON
ct. Currumbin Wtr ... 80 H1
ct. Paradise Pt ... 9 C9
dr. Russell I ... 268 J12
la. Pimpama ... 327 C12
rd. Burleigh Hd ... 59 K12
st. Loganholme ... 263 L9
HANA
st. Park Ridge ... 281 E1
HANBY
ct. Edens Landing .. 263 K16
HANCOX
pl. Robina ... 48 D16
HANDEL
av. Worongary ... 47 L6
HANLAN
st. Surfers Pdse ... 39 N8
st. Surfers Pdse ... 40 N11
HANLINK
wy. Pimpama ... 326 Q12
HANLON
st. Tanah Merah ... 263 H5
HANNAFORD
ct. Helensvale ... 7 D20
HANNAH
ct. Worongary ... 47 P9
HANOVER
dr. Pimpama ... 326 F7
dr. Pimpama ... 326 F8
st. Beenleigh ... 264 C17
HANOVERIAN
wy. Up Coomera ... 6 L7

Map Ref

JACINTA
ct. Crestmead 261 L12
JACKAROO
cr. Gilston 36 Q18
JACKEY
st. Park Ridge 281 G1
JACKLIN
ct. Parkwood 28 E7
JACKMAN
st. Southport 29 C12
JACKMANS
rd. Bonogin 67 N7
JACK NICKLAUS
wy. Parkwood 28 D6
JACKSON
ch. Logan Res 262 B20
la. Yatala 284 D13
st. Coomera 327 H16
st. Eagleby 264 F15
JACKSON RIDGE
rd. Up Coomera 5 P19
JACOB
ct. Up Coomera 6 H6
dr. Labrador 18 P18
st. Reedy Creek 58 R11
JACOBS
rd. Molendinar 27 Q18
JACOBS RIDGE
rd. Ormeau 305 M10
JACOBS WELL
rd. Alberton 285 M2
rd. Gilberton 286 C6
rd. Jacobs Well 307 M5
rd. Jacobs Well 308 C9
rd. Norwell 307 M1
rd. Stapylton 284 Q8
rd. Stapylton 285 M2
rd. Steiglitz 287 H16
rd. Woongoolba 286 J11
JACOSA
rd. Gilberton 285 P7
JACQUELINE
av. Labrador 28 P4
rd. Buccan 282 L13
JACQUELINE BAY
Ormeau 305 P12
JADE
dr. Molendinar 28 A18
wy. Helensvale 17 L15
JADE STONE
ct. Carrara 37 R12
JAEGER
wy. Benowa 38 P15
JAGER
pl. Edens Landing 263 E13
JAGERA
dr. Up Coomera 326 E20
JAGUAR
dr. Bundall 39 D6
JAIDEN
wy. Coomera 327 C17
JAKE
ct. Bonogin 68 G4
JAKES
wy. Worongary 47 M6
JALAN
st. Tanah Merah 263 L1
JALIBAH
av. Tweed Heads 82 B8
JALINDA
ct. Currumbin Vy 80 D1
JAMBEROO
ct. Tallebudgera 69 Q12
JAMBI
ct. Tanah Merah 263 J6
JAMEKA
st. Logan Res 261 K16
JAMES
cl. Ormeau 305 L15
pl. Maudsland 16 H20
rd. Tweed Hd S 81 Q14
st. Beenleigh 284 A2
st. Burleigh Hd 60 E6
st. Chinderah 92 R20
st. Crestmead 261 J12
st. Currumbin 71 C4
st. Kingscliff 92 R20
st. Pimpama 326 F6
JAMES CAGNEY
cl. Parkwood 27 Q8
JAMES COOK
dr. Banora Pt 92 M5
esp. Hollywell 9 A18
JAMES MILE
Cedar Creek 4 E8
Wongawallan 4 E8

Map Ref

JAMIE NICOLSON
av. Edens Landing 263 G15
JAMIESON
ct. Waterford W 262 B6
dr. Parkwood 27 Q8
JAMISON
st. Up Coomera 5 Q19
JAN
ct. Bethania 263 A11
JANAL
pl. Currumbin Wtr 70 P16
JANCOON
ct. Carrara 37 Q9
JANDAKOT
ct. Elanora 70 H5
JANE
la. Oxenford 16 N9
st. Southport 29 B18
JANELLE
st. Pimpama 326 E6
JANINE
dr. Bahrs Scrub 283 Q8
JANNALI
pl. Robina 49 E11
JANNIE
ct. Labrador 18 Q20
JAPONICA
dr. Palm Beach 60 D17
st. Eagleby 264 H17
JARAMAN
pl. Boyland 23 D1
JARDINE
ct. Logan Vill 294 A13
rd. Lr Beechmont 45 Q11
st. Pacific Pines 26 L5
JAREMA
dr. Mudgeeraba 58 K6
JARMO
cr. Southport 28 Q20
JARRAH
pl. Ashmore 38 J6
pl. Banora Pt 92 A4
st. Russell I 268 E12
JARRAHDALE
dr. Elanora 70 G2
J A R THOMPSON
pl. Arundel 18 L20
JARVIS
la. Coolangatta 82 G2
pl. Arundel 18 A20
rd. Waterford 262 P20
rd. Waterford 282 N1
st. Holmview 263 L16
JASMARIN
dr. Tallebudgera 69 M14
JASMINA
pde. Waterford 263 A17
JASMINE
av. Hollywell 19 B1
cct. Ormeau 305 P10
pl. Banora Pt 91 Q1
pl. Beenleigh 283 N5
JASNAR
la. Coomera 328 F13
JASPER
ct. Currumbin Wtr 70 H9
JAVA
ct. Tamborine Mtn 24 L8
la. Palm Beach 70 N2
JAX
ct. Up Coomera 5 N20
JAXSON
tce. Pimpama 326 D7
JAY
ct. Mt Warren Pk 284 C5
JAYDEN
pl. Molendinar 28 A13
JAYGEE
ct. Nerang 37 L9
JEAN
st. Labrador 28 N2
st. Loganlea 262 H2
JEANNE
st. Russell I 268 J12
JEDDA
st. Tallebudgera 69 E14
JEDINAK
ct. Clagiraba 25 C10
JEETHO
st. Holmview 263 L17
JEFFERSON
ct. Up Coomera 6 N8
la. Palm Beach 60 M16
JEFFREY
ct. Mt Warren Pk 284 E8
JELLICOE
st. Loganlea 262 E1

Map Ref

JEMIMA
pl. Up Coomera 16 C2
JEMPAL
ct. Tanah Merah 263 J4
JENAYA
pl. Labrador 28 R1
JENDI
ct. Tugun 71 D13
JENKINS
ct. Up Coomera 6 D5
JENLEY
ct. Up Coomera 6 H12
JENNIFER
av. Runaway Bay 19 C9
ct. Mt Warren Pk 284 G9
JENSEN
la. Yarrabilba 293 R20
JENYNS
rd. Tamborine Mtn 24 G14
JEREMY
ct. Worongary 47 P8
st. Coomera 327 L14
JERILDERIE
ct. Nerang 37 H8
JEROME
st. Canungra 33 G15
JERRAWA
st. Nerang 37 J8
JERROB
ct. Carrara 37 Q16
JERSEY
ct. Tallebudgera 69 P16
rd. Tamborine 13 D1
JERVIS
pl. Beechmont 45 G20
JESMOND
rd. Helensvale 17 D6
JESSICA
ct. Arundel 28 L4
dr. Up Coomera 6 J7
JESSIE
cr. Bethania 263 C12
JESSY
st. Crestmead 261 K11
JET
st. Up Coomera 6 P7
JEWEL
ct. Tweed Heads 82 D10
st. Currumbin Wtr 70 P9
J G CAMPBELL
la. Tamborine 2 H17
JIB
ct. Mermaid Wtr 49 L12
JILLIAN
ct. Logan Vill 293 Q9
JILPANGI
cr. Ashmore 28 J19
JIM
pl. Mt Warren Pk 284 A5
JIM DAVIDSON
bvd. Belivah 283 M17
JIMMIESON
av. Labrador 28 R6
JIMMY
rd. Coomera 327 E19
JINDABYNE
ct. Highland Pk 37 H14
JINDALBA
dr. Coomera 327 J18
JINDIVICK
st. Worongary 37 N17
JINGELLA
av. Russell I 268 L14
st. Hope Island 7 Q3
JINGREE PERCH
Currumbin Vy 79 P5
JINKER
wy. Nerang 36 M9
JIPPI
av. Southport 28 Q16
JIREH
ct. Beenleigh 264 D17
JITRA
pl. Tanah Merah 263 H4
JMcD SHARP BRIDGE
Witheren 34 J13
JOAN
st. Burleigh Wtr 50 A20
st. Park Ridge 261 H19
st. Southport 29 D17
JOANNE
ct. Currumbin Vy 79 Q1
JOBSON
pl. Crestmead 261 F12
JOCELYNA
st. Reedy Creek 58 R11

Map Ref

JODEN
pl. Southport 29 C20
JODIE
ct. Mermaid Wtr 49 L7
st. Tugun 71 E12
JODRELL
ct. Reedy Creek 58 P20
JOEITH
ct. Miami 49 P19
JOEL
ct. Helensvale 7 N15
JOH
ct. Bethania 263 B13
JOHANNA
pl. Windaroo 284 B12
JOHN
cr. Pimpama 327 B11
la. Beenleigh 264 D20
st. Bilinga 71 K14
st. Waterford W 262 H9
JOHNATHON
cl. Jacobs Well 308 C10
JOHN COLLINS
dr. Mundoolun 1 A10
JOHN DALLEY
dr. Helensvale 7 P16
JOHN DAVISON
pl. Crestmead 261 L12
JOHN DUNCAN
ct. Varsity Lakes 59 E11
JOHN FRANCIS
dr. Carrara 37 M10
JOHN KEMP
st. Main Beach 29 M17
JOHN LUND
dr. Hope Island 8 F9
JOHN MUNRO
ct. Carrara 38 A16
JOHN MUNTZ CAUSEWAY
Oxenford 16 E5
Up Coomera 16 G3
JOHN NIELSEN
ct. Worongary 47 J9
JOHN ROBB
wy. Cudgen 102 R3
JOHN ROGERS
rd. Mudgeeraba 57 D11
JOHNS
rd. Mudgeeraba 57 C12
JOHNSON
av. Russell I 268 H13
pde. Ormeau Hills 305 G15
st. Banora Pt 92 K5
JOHNSTON
st. Bilinga 71 Q19
st. Southport 28 R10
JOHNSTONE
rd. Alberton 265 C18
rd. Stapylton 265 C18
JOHN WAYNE
cl. Maudsland 15 Q20
JONAS
cct. Holmview 283 C2
JONATH
ct. Edens Landing 263 F16
JONATHON
st. Up Coomera 6 G5
JONDARYAN
st. Ormeau 305 N7
JONDIQUE
av. Merrimac 48 D6
JONES
pl. Beenleigh 263 Q17
st. Coomera 327 H20
JONNY FOX
rd. Coomera 327 C20
JONQUIL
st. Ormeau 305 K8
JOOLIM NEST
Currumbin Vy 79 P4
JORDAN
st. Waterford 262 N12
JORDANA
st. Arundel 27 Q1
JOSEPH
st. Runaway Bay 19 C4
JOSEPHFINA
ct. Logan Res 282 A11
JOSEPHINE
rd. Coomera 328 H14
st. Loganholme 264 A5
tce. Highland Pk 37 C11
JOSH
ct. Ashmore 27 M19
st. Logan Res 282 C1

Map Ref

JOSHUA
ct. Arundel 27 M3
pl. Oxenford 16 J13
st. Park Ridge 261 J14
JOSLIN
ct. Eagleby 264 L12
JOTOWN
dr. Coomera 7 G1
JOURAMA
ct. Waterford 263 A19
JOURDANA
dr. Cedar Creek 4 G10
dr. Wongawallan 4 G10
JOWETT
st. Coomera 6 R10
JOY
av. Burleigh Wtr 60 C3
av. Paradise Pt 8 Q17
JOYCE
ct. Tallebudgera 69 H6
JOYDON
la. N Tumbulgum 101 J3
JUBERA
cl. Yarrabilba 293 R20
cl. Yarrabilba 299 R1
JUBILEE
av. Broadbeach 39 N18
ct. Bahrs Scrub 283 N15
JUCARA
av. Robina 58 R3
JUDELLER
rd. Currumbin Wtr 70 Q10
JUDITH
av. Southport 28 R9
st. Crestmead 261 H11
JULAH
ct. Ashmore 38 H5
JULATTEN
dr. Robina 49 F12
JULIA
st. Burleigh Hd 60 G8
st.n, Burleigh Hd 60 H7
JULIE
ct. Oxenford 6 J18
st. Beenleigh 283 Q3
st. Crestmead 261 D11
wy. Mudgeeraba 57 E6
JULIUS
ct. Marsden 261 K4
pl. Kingscliff 103 F3
JULLIAN
rd. Up Coomera 6 A20
JULNDOR
pl. Wongawallan 15 A1
JUMBUCK
cr. Terranora 91 H12
rd. Gaven 27 L14
JUNCTION
dr. Park Ridge 261 H17
rd. Burleigh Hd 59 K15
JUNE
ct. Miami 49 Q17
JUNIPER
ct. Beenleigh 264 E18
st. Logan Res 261 N14
JUPITER
cl. Labrador 28 P4
JURA
ct. Tamborine Mtn 14 E3
pde. Merrimac 48 A7
JURIEN
cr. Varsity Lakes 59 D5
JUST
st. Currumbin Wtr 70 P15
JUSTIN
av. Tamborine Mtn 24 B4
la. Burleigh Hd 60 E6
pl. Crestmead 261 H12
st. Pimpama 326 P12
JUTLAND
pl. Currumbin Wtr 70 K17

K

KABANG
ct. Tanah Merah 263 K3
KABI
pl. Pacific Pines 16 P20
KABOOL
rd. Burleigh Hd 60 B14
KABRA
ct. Worongary 47 N4
KABUT
ct. Tanah Merah 263 G3
KADIE
pl. Pacific Pines 26 M4

Map Ref

KADINA
ct. Helensvale 17 E10
KAELAH
la. Mudgeeraba 58 D6
KAFFIA
ct. Elanora 70 F2
KAGI
ct. Runaway Bay 19 A5
KAGOOLA
dr. Mudgeeraba 57 B4
KAHAN
ct. Pimpama 327 E12
KAHLUA
ct. Highland Pk 37 L13
KAI
ct. Waterford 263 A17
KAILAS
ct. Tamborine Mtn 14 F3
KAIRA
la. Currumbin Vy 79 N5
KAISER
ct. Waterford W 262 G8
dr. Windaroo 283 P13
dr. Windaroo 283 P14
rd. Tamborine Mtn 24 C10
KAIZLEE
cr. Up Coomera 6 L8
KAKADU
ct. Banora Pt 91 Q2
st. Pimpama 327 B8
KALAMUNDA
cl. Elanora 70 J2
KALANG
st. Palm Beach 60 L19
KALBARI
ct. Worongary 37 M17
KALBARRI
st. Yarrabilba 300 L9
KALEENA
st. Tugun 71 F12
KALGOORLIE
st. Pimpama 326 M5
KALGUN
cr. Ashmore 38 G4
KALIMNA
dr. Broadbeach Wtr 39 G18
st. Loganholme 263 P10
st. Loganholme 263 Q10
KALKADOON
ct. Cobaki 80 J14
KALLARA
st. Tugun 71 E12
KALLAROO
ct. Ashmore 38 G1
KALLAY
st. Miami 49 P14
KALLISTA
cl. Robina 48 R16
KALMIA
ct. Elanora 70 C5
ct. Tamborine Mtn 14 D3
KALYAN
st. Surfers Pdse 39 K4
KAMALA
cr. Casuarina 103 E16
ct. Bonogin 67 L10
KAMBAH
pl. Reedy Creek 58 N16
KAMBALDA
ct. Worongary 37 N15
KAMET
ct. Tamborine Mtn 14 D7
KAMHOLTZ
ct. Molendinar 28 A20
KAMO
ct. Ashmore 38 K5
KANANGRA
cr. Pacific Pines 16 P18
KANDRA
av. Currumbin 71 C5
KANGAROO
av. Coombabah 18 L4
KANIMBLA
st. Holmview 263 C20
KANNI
ct. Ashmore 38 J2
KANSAS
ct. Oxenford 16 P4
KANTON
pl. Pacific Pines 27 B3
KAO
st. Marsden 261 E1
KAPALA
st. Southport 39 G3
KAPLAN
st. Oxenford 16 M12

Map Ref

LAVAZZA
st. Ormeau 306 B10
LAVELLE
dr. Logan Vill 282 B20
dr. Logan Vill 294 E1
st. Nerang 37 G1
LAVENDER
st. Waterford W 262 C8
LAVER
dr. Robina 48 J19
LAVERS
st. Mundoolun 1 D7
LAVERTON
st. Ormeau 305 L3
LAVINA
rd. Marsden 261 F2
LAVINIA
st. Southport 38 R2
wy. Coomera 7 K2
LAWLER
ct. Belivah 283 M20
LAWLER PARK EASEMENT
Southport 29 D10
LAWLEY
cr. Pacific Pines 26 N1
LAWLOR
pl. Terranora 91 J12
LAWNHILL
dr. Nerang 27 A20
LAWRENCE
dr. Nerang 37 L7
LAWSON
ct. Canungra 33 D17
st. Nerang 27 G20
st. Russell I 268 N9
st. Southport 29 F14
st. Up Coomera 6 D9
LAWTON
la. Canungra 33 E14
LAXON
la. Willow Vale 326 E10
LAYCOCK
st. Surfers Pdse 39 N9
st. Surfers Pdse 40 M13
LAYSAN
cr. Oxenford 16 P11
LAZY
wy. Guanaba 24 N1
LEABROOK
cr. Robina 48 N17
pl. Pimpama 327 B12
LEACH
rd. Boyland 12 K1
rd. Tamborine 2 G14
LEAFY
cl. Burleigh Wtr 59 K9
LEAGUES CLUB
dr. Nerang 37 N5
LEAH
dr. Belivah 283 L20
LEAMONTH
dr. Belivah 283 N18
LEANDER
cct. Oxenford 6 N16
LEANNE
ct. Mt Warren Pk 284 D7
st. Marsden 261 N1
st. Marsden 261 N2
LEARMONTH
pl. Reedy Creek 58 N17
LEARNING
st. Coomera 327 J18
LEAVER
ct. Ormeau 304 R3
LEAWARRA
dr. Loganholme 263 N5
la. Loganholme 263 P5
LEAWOOD
pl. Helensvale 17 F8
LEAZA
st. Marsden 261 M6
LEDA
dr. Burleigh Hd 59 N13
LEDDAYS CREEK
rd. Stotts Ck 101 F14
LEE
ct. Bahrs Scrub 283 N13
rd. Runaway Bay 19 C12
st. Pimpama 326 R9
LEE ANNE
cr. Helensvale 7 N15
LEEDS
cl. Arundel 17 Q15
LEESA
ct. Highland Pk 37 K13
LEESIDE
pl. Hope Island 7 R9
LEET
ct. Arundel 18 B18
LEEWARD
tce. Tweed Heads 82 F6
LEEWAY
pl. Clear I Wtr 48 R10
LEE-WEENA
av. Russell I 268 L14
LEFROY
ct. Carrara 38 C16
dr. Coombabah 8 L20
LEGEND
trl. Robina 48 E19
LEHMANS
rd. Beenleigh 283 P2
LEHVILLE
st. Beenleigh 264 C18
LEICA
ct. Mudgeeraba 58 A10
LEICESTER
tce. Mudgeeraba 58 M9
LEICHHARDT
cl. Park Ridge 281 H2
st. Coomera 327 H16
tce. Russell I 268 P9
LEIDEN
st. Reedy Creek 58 L16
LEIGH
pl. Edens Landing 263 K13
LEIGHANNE
cr. Arundel 27 Q1
LEIGHTON
dr. Edens Landing 263 D14
LEILA
ct. Mudgeeraba 58 G6
LEISEL
cl. Up Coomera 6 N5
LEISHA
ct. Elanora 70 J6
LEISURE
dr. Banora Pt 92 B1
la. Worongary 47 K12
LELAND
st. Yarrabilba 299 Q1
LEMANA
la. Burleigh Hd 50 B20
la. Miami 50 B20
LE MANS
dr. Mermaid Wtr 49 N4
LEMONGROVE
st. Eagleby 264 J18
LEMONTREE
ct. Nerang 37 M5
la. Currumbin Vy 79 P9
LENA
pl. Windaroo 283 P13
LEN DICKFOS
rd. Tallebudgera Vy 77 F20
LENNA
ct. Mt Warren Pk 284 C8
LENNEBERG
st. Southport 29 G16
LENNIE
av. Main Beach 29 L16
LENNON
dr. Windaroo 283 P16
LENNOX
st. Pacific Pines 16 Q19
LENSGATE
rd. Coombabah 18 G15
LENTON
st. Coomera 327 H20
LEONA
ct. Tamborine Mtn 24 M7
LEONARD
av. Surfers Pdse 39 K9
pde.Currumbin Wtr 70 P11
LEONARDO
cct. Coombabah 18 J8
LEONIE
ct. Logan Vill 293 L7
LEOPARD
av. Elanora 70 B10
LEOPARD TREE
pl. Molendinar 28 F14
LEOPARDWOOD
cct. Robina 58 R6
dr. Beenleigh 283 K5
LERGESSNER
st. Biggera Wtr 18 R16
LESLEY
av. Miami 49 Q17
LESLEY-ANNE
ct. Maudsland 26 A12
LES NOBLE
pde.Chinderah 92 R20
LETITIA
av. Russell I 268 J5
rd. Fingal Head 82 P4
LEURA
pl. Helensvale 17 C3
LEVEN
pl. Up Coomera 5 Q18
LEVESTAM
ct. Carrara 37 P13
LEVIATHAN
dr. Mudgeeraba 58 K4
LEWIS
dr. Biggera Wtr 18 M17
st. Elanora 70 H7
LEXHAM
st. Waterford W 262 D9
LEXINGTON
dr. Worongary 47 M1
LEYSHON
ct. Bonogin 57 P19
LEYTE
av. Palm Beach 70 P5
LIAM
ct. Labrador 18 P19
LIANA
ct. Banora Pt 92 A3
LIAO
ct. Crestmead 261 E12
LIBERTY
pl. Banora Pt 82 H20
ri. Coomera 7 G1
ri. Coomera 327 G20
LICUALA
dr. Tamborine Mtn 23 R1
LIDO
la. Russell I 268 L3
prm.Robina 48 L20
LIFESTYLE
cl. Waterford W 262 H8
LIGHTBODY
ct. Ormeau 305 B3
LIGHTHOUSE
pde.Fingal Head 83 C16
LIGNUM
st. Ormeau 305 E4
LILAC
st. Park Ridge 281 D1
wy. Gaven 27 J4
LILAC TREE
ct. Beechmont 45 H20
LILLE
st. Burleigh Wtr 49 N17
LILLEE
ct. Currumbin Vy 69 Q19
LILLIAN
cr. Ashmore 38 J1
la. Austinville 57 F20
la. Bonogin 57 F20
LILLI PILLI
dr. Southport 28 Q19
LILLY
la. Logan Res 282 C1
LILLY MUNTZ
dr. Willow Vale 325 P11
LILLY PILLY
av. Eagleby 264 J8
dr. Banora Pt 82 M20
dr. Coomera 327 E19
st. Crestmead 261 K8
st. Crestmead 261 K9
LILLYPILLY
ct. Helensvale 7 A19
LILLYWOOD
cct. Molendinar 28 G12
LILY
av. Coomera 327 E17
cr. Nerang 36 J4
la. Jacobs Well 308 F15
LILYDALE
pl. Molendinar 28 E13
LILYPILLY
st. Bahrs Scrub 283 H6
LILYVALE
cr. Ormeau 305 P6
LIM
ct. Up Coomera 6 G6
LIMA
st. Edens Landing 263 H17
st. Holmview 263 H17
LIME
st. Helensvale 17 K18
LIMERICK
dr. Crestmead 261 F6
dr. Witheren 45 D4
st. Banora Pt 82 C20
LIMESTONE
ct. Yarrabilba 300 E1
LIMETREE
pde.Runaway Bay 18 N12
LIMEWOOD
cr. Ormeau Hills 305 G16
LIMKIN
st. Burleigh Wtr 59 P5
LIMMEN
st. Pimpama 327 D8
LIMOSA
ct. Crestmead 261 D7
rd. Tweed Hd W 81 P9
st. Ashmore 38 N3
LIMOUSIN
pl. Waterford W 262 D8
LINCOLN
st. Beenleigh 264 B17
st. Mudgeeraba 58 L8
LIND
av. Palm Beach 60 K15
av. Southport 29 A9
LINDA
wy. Up Coomera 6 M6
LINDAL
st. Ashmore 28 M20
LINDAU
st. Edens Landing 263 D15
LINDEMAN
cct. Pimpama 326 N5
ct. Mermaid Wtr 49 F8
LINDEN
ct. Palm Beach 60 E16
LINDENTHAL
rd. Park Ridge 261 B18
rd. Park Ridge 281 B1
LINDFIELD
rd. Helensvale 17 F11
LINDNER
cl. Eagleby 264 J10
LINDSAY
la. Pimpama 327 A12
pde.Paradise Pt 8 P14
st. Loganholme 263 L12
LINDWALL
pl. Currumbin Vy 70 B19
LINDY
st. Beenleigh 283 Q3
LING
pl. Palm Beach 60 D17
LINGA
ct. Ashmore 28 J19
LINK
dr. Yatala 284 N15
la. Southport 28 K9
rd. Guanaba 15 J14
LINKS
st. Banora Pt 92 E3
LINKSVIEW
ct. Helensvale 17 H5
LINNING
st. Mt Warren Pk 284 E7
st. Mt Warren Pk 284 F7
LINTON
st. Loganlea 262 H4
LINTROSE
ct. Edens Landing 263 E12
LINUM
st. Palm Beach 60 D16
LIONEL
av. Southport 29 B8
LIONS PARK
dr. Yatala 284 P13
LIQUIDAMBER
cl. Tallai 47 A8
LIRIOPE
st. Casuarina 103 C17
LISA
cr. Coomera 327 D17
ct. Arundel 27 R1
LISMORE
dr. Helensvale 17 H5
LISTER
st. Oxenford 16 M12
LITA
ct. Tallebudgera 69 G5
LITCHFIELD
st. Yarrabilba 300 H8
LITHFIELD
pl. Loganholme 263 P12
LITHGOW
st. Loganholme 263 M8
LITSEA
ct. Reedy Creek 59 C17
LITTABELLA
st. Pimpama 326 N5
LITTLE BLUE
la. Varsity Lakes 59 E2
LITTLE COVE
rd. Russell I 268 M4
LITTLE FLYING FOX
rd. Flying Fox 45 B15
LITTLE HAMPTON
ct. Arundel 17 R16
LITTLE HIGH
st. Southport 29 E13
LITTLE HILL
st. Tweed Heads 82 L1
LITTLE LORIKEET
ct. Gilston 37 A16
LITTLE NERANG
rd. Advancetown 46 Q18
rd. Mudgeeraba 46 Q18
rd. Mudgeeraba 57 A8
LITTLE NERANG DAM
rd. Austinville 66 L5
rd. Neranwood 66 L4
rd. Springbrook 66 L5
LITTLE NORMAN
st. Southport 29 E8
LITTLE USHER
av. Labrador 28 N1
LIVINGSTONE
st. Logan Res 261 K16
st. Up Coomera 6 J5
st. Yarrabilba 300 L9
LIZDA
st. Marsden 261 D3
LLAMA
vst. Willow Vale 5 P6
LLANDOVERY
la. Maudsland 16 D12
LLOYD
st. Southport 29 D11
st. Tweed Hd S 82 G12
LLOYDS
la. Yatala 284 P10
rd. Springbrook 66 G16
LOADERS
la. Alberton 265 D13
LOANE
dr. Edens Landing 263 G13
LOBB
ct. Arundel 28 K2
LOBBAN
ct. Highland Pk 37 N14
LOBELIA
cr. Casuarina 103 D14
LOBSTER POT
pl. Runaway Bay 18 Q11
LOCHERN
st. Yarrabilba 300 J6
LOCHINVAR
ct. Ashmore 38 B2
ct. Highland Pk 37 F16
LOCHLARNEY
st. Beenleigh 263 M19
LOCHLOMOND
dr. Banora Pt 92 D9
LOCHORE
ct. Crestmead 261 L7
ct. Crestmead 261 M7
LOCHRIDGE
st. Logan Res 261 R14
LOCHVIEW
ct. Tamborine 2 D13
LOCKE
st. Southport 29 B10
LOCKHART
pl. Helensvale 17 H6
LOCKWOOD
pl. Molendinar 28 G13
LOCKYER
pl. Crestmead 261 K11
LODER
st. Biggera Wtr 19 C17
LODERS
rd. Duranbah 102 A20
LOFFS
rd. Loganholme 263 K12
LOFT
cr. Pimpama 326 J12
LOFTUS
cr. Russell I 268 L6
st. Merrimac 48 B7
st. Ormeau 305 L15
LOFTY
la. Coomera 327 H18
LOGAN
av. Miami 49 Q18
cr. Oxenford 16 J10
mwy.Loganholme 263 F2
mwy.Tanah Merah 263 F2
pde.Logan Res 262 E13
st. Beenleigh 264 B17
st. Eagleby 264 F17
st. Logan Vill 293 P4
LOGAN BOATRAMP
la. Eagleby 264 B12
LOGANDALE
bvd.Cornubia 264 G1
LOGANLEA
rd. Loganlea 262 K9
rd. Waterford W 262 K9
LOGAN RESERVE
rd. Logan Res 262 B20
rd. Logan Res 281 H8
rd. Logan Res 281 M5
rd. Waterford W 262 C12
LOGAN RIVER
rd. Beenleigh 263 A12
rd. Bethania 263 B12
rd. Edens Landing 263 B12
rd. Holmview 263 B12
rd. Waterford 263 A12
LOGANVIEW
rd. Logan Res 281 N10
rd.n,Logan Res 261 P20
rd.n,Logan Res 281 P3
LOG CREEK
rd. Logan Vill 282 E19
LOGISTICS
pl. Arundel 18 G18
st. Yatala 284 N13
LOHMANN
ct. Canungra 33 C17
LOK-EVYN
ct. Wongawallan 5 E19
LOKI
rd. Coomera 327 Q15
LOLITA
ct. Varsity Lakes 59 G4
LOMAN
la. Burleigh Hd 59 R15
LOMANDRA
ct. Oxenford 6 K17
LOMATIA
ct. Bonogin 67 M9
LOMBOK
ct. Tamborine Mtn 24 M10
LOMIC
ct. Eagleby 264 G12
LOMOND
ct. Varsity Lakes 59 J5
LONDON
ch. Arundel 18 A15
LONDY
st. Eagleby 264 N16
LONE PINE
cct. Up Coomera 5 N19
LONG
rd. Tamborine Mtn 14 C11
rd. Tamborine Mtn 23 Q2
LONGBOARD
cct. Kingscliff 103 E9
LONGBOAT
pl. Biggera Wtr 18 Q15
LONGCOVE
pl. Parkwood 28 E10
LONGHILL
rd. Gilston 36 P18
LONG ISLAND
ct. Mermaid Wtr 49 E9
dr. Windaroo 283 R12
LONGLAND
rd. Redland Bay 266 G7
LONGMORN
cr. Merrimac 48 A5
LONGREEF
cr. Parkwood 28 F10
LONGSTAFF
cr. Pimpama 327 F13
LONGUEVILLE
ct. Robina 49 D13
LONGVIEW
ct. Nerang 27 D20
LONSDALE
pl. Varsity Lakes 59 F2
LOOBY
cr. Pimpama 327 F11
LOOKOUT
pde.Tamborine Mtn 24 H14
pl. Mt Nathan 25 Q12
LOONGANA
av. Bilinga 71 K15
LOOP
rd. Lr Beechmont 46 C4
LOOWA
av. Russell I 268 M14

MOONSTONE

Map Ref

MELASTOMA
wy. Arundel 17 Q13
MELBA
ct. Crestmead 261 D8
MELBOURNE
rd. Arundel 18 K20
MELIA
ct. Southport 28 L7
st. Crestmead 261 F8
MELINDA
st. Marsden 261 Q1
st. Southport 29 C18
MELISSA
st. Up Coomera 6 K2
MELITA
st. Currumbin Wtr 70 H8
st. Ormeau 306 C10
MELL
st. Bannockburn 304 H1
MELLIODORA
rd. Waterford W 262 G11
MELLISSAH
cr. Arundel 17 Q20
MELLUM
cct. Pacific Pines 16 P20
MELNIK
dr. Loganlea 262 H4
MELODY
st. Marsden 261 G3
st. Mermaid Wtr 49 M3
MELROSE
pl. Eagleby 264 K14
pl. Southport 28 R11
MELTON
ct. Edens Landing 263 H16
MELVILLE
dr. Pimpama 327 C5
dr. Pimpama 327 D4
MELWOOD
st. Eagleby 264 H17
MEMORIAL
dr. Up Coomera 15 L7
MEMPHIS
dr. Russell I 268 K15
MENDOORAN
ct. Oxenford 16 M1
MENINDEE
av. Coombabah 18 K1
MENORA
rd. Bahrs Scrub 283 D8
MENTON
av. Varsity Lakes 59 D7
MENTONE
av. Bundall 39 D6
MENZIES
cl. Arundel 28 K1
st. Bethania 262 R8
MERANTI
ct. Nerang 36 N9
st. Crestmead 261 L9
MERAUKE
av. Palm Beach 70 M3
MERCANTILE
ct. Molendinar 28 E11
dr. Park Ridge 261 A13
MERCATOR
ct. Carrara 37 P11
MERCEDES
pl. Bundall 39 F7
MERCER
dr. Pimpama 326 R12
MERCURE
pl. Highland Pk 37 D15
MERCURY
dr. Bethania 262 N4
MERCY
cct. Park Ridge 261 G19
MEREDITH
dr. Broadbeach Wtr 39 J16
MEREFORD
rd. Russell I 268 L2
MEREWETHER
ct. Highland Pk 37 H14
MERIDIAN
ct. Tanah Merah 263 G2
wy. Tweed Heads 82 C8
MERIDIEN
av. Varsity Lakes 59 D8
MERINDA
ct. Southport 29 A20
MERINO
dr. Helensvale 17 D4
pl. Terranora 91 H10
st. Park Ridge 261 F17
MERION
ct. Banora Pt 82 E20
ct. Cornubia 264 G1
ct. Robina 48 R19
tce. Hope Island 7 R1
tce. Hope Island 327 R20
MERIVALE
av. Ormeau Hills 305 G18
MERLIN
pl. Ormeau 305 L12
MERLOO
dr. Nerang 36 L7
MERLOT
ct. Tweed Hd S 82 A19
MERMAID
av. Mermaid Bch 49 P3
MERNICK
ct. Bahrs Scrub 283 N9
MERON
ct. Tamborine Mtn 14 A13
st. Russell I 268 M9
st. Southport 29 F15
MEROO
pl. Up Coomera 6 B17
MERRIDOWN
dr. Merrimac 48 A7
MERRILAINE
cr. Merrimac 48 E7
MERRIMAC
bvd.Broadbeach Wtr 39 K20
MERRINA
dr. Ashmore 38 J4
MERROW
st. Mt Warren Pk 284 F9
MERSEY
st. Up Coomera 6 C13
MERSING
ct. Tanah Merah 263 L3
MERTON
dr. Up Coomera 6 M7
MERU
cl. Southport 28 K14
MERVYN THOMAS
dr. Hope Island 8 D12
MESA
st. Yarrabilba 294 A18
MESSEL
pl. Robina, off Watts Dr 59 G1
MESSINES
cr. Miami 50 A16
MESSMATE
ct. Beenleigh 283 L4
METCALF
ct. Ormeau 305 A7
METEOR
ct. Mudgeeraba 48 A19
METRICUP
ct. Mermaid Wtr 49 J15
METRO
cr. Oxenford 17 D13
MEWING
ct. Windaroo 283 R11
MEWS
ct. Oxenford 17 A10
MEWSDALE
row.Tallai 47 M19
MEXICALI
ct. Broadbeach Wtr 39 H15
MEYER
st. Southport 29 D7
MIA
st. Marsden 261 E3
MIAMAX
pl. Logan Res 261 L14
MIAMI
key,Broadbeach Wtr 39 M19
MIAMI SHORE
pde.Miami 50 B18
MIANDETTA
dr. Advancetown 36 F13
MIBBIN
av. Banora Pt 92 M5
MICA
st. Yarrabilba 294 E20
MICHAELS
prm.Coomera 327 G19
MICHEL
dr. Currumbin Wtr 70 M9
MICHELIN
st. Southport 28 Q12
MICHELLE
la. Pimpama 327 D11
MICHELMORE
rd. Carrara 37 Q17
MICHIGAN
dr. Oxenford 16 K1
MICK VEIVERS
wy. Southport 29 B13
MIDDLE
qy. Biggera Wtr 18 L13
st. Labrador 19 C20
MIDDLEHAM
fy. Maudsland 16 F11
MIDDLEMOUNT
st. Holmview 283 E3
MIDDLETON
st. Ashmore 28 P18
MIDGERA
st. Ashmore 38 D4
MIDHURST
ct. Arundel 18 D19
MIDJEE
st. Russell I 268 G10
MIDNIGHT
ct. Runaway Bay 18 Q11
MIDPARK
ct. Helensvale 7 J18
MIDSHIP
ct. Banora Pt 92 K11
MIDSHIPMAN
ct. Surfers Pdse 39 K1
MIDVALE
pl. Helensvale 17 G7
MIDVIEW
ct. Currumbin 70 R9
ct. Currumbin 71 A9
MIDWAY
tce. Pacific Pines 17 B17
MIEKA
cr. Pimpama 326 P13
MIEKE
ct. Burleigh Hd 59 L19
MIKADO
wy. Robina 58 Q2
MIKAELLA
wy. Logan Res 282 B1
MIKE
pl. Mt Warren Pk 284 A5
MIKONOS
ct. Currumbin Wtr 70 K9
MILAN
ct. Surfers Pdse 39 K12
MILBONG
tce. Ashmore 38 J4
MILBROOK
cr. Pimpama 326 Q11
MILBY
st. Yarrabilba 293 R18
MILDARA
ct. Highland Pk 37 M14
MILDRED
st. Southport 28 R18
MILDURA
dr. Helensvale 17 J3
dr. Helensvale 17 J9
MILEHAM
ct. Marsden 261 M5
MILES
ct. Eagleby 264 J10
st. Coolangatta 82 D3
MILING
ct. Robina 49 F19
MILKBUSH
ct. Bonogin 67 H12
MILKINS
wy. Mudgeeraba 57 K3
MILKY
wy. Mudgeeraba 47 R19
MILL
rd. Steiglitz 287 D13
rd. Steiglitz 287 E4
rd. Woongoolba 287 D13
rd. Woongoolba 287 E4
st. Yarrabilba 300 D4
MILLAROO
dr. Helensvale 17 H14
MILLENNIUM
cct. Helensvale 17 H16
MILLER
rd. Logan Vill 294 C3
rd. Logan Vill 294 L5
MILLERS
dr. Currumbin 71 C9
dr. Tugun 71 C9
la. Maudsland 15 Q7
MILLET
pl. Pimpama 326 L16
pl. Up Coomera 326 L16
MILLEWA
ct. Labrador 28 P1
MILLICENT
st. Ormeau 306 A9
MILLIE
ct. Witheren 45 F2
MILLPOND
ct. Up Coomera 326 J18
MILLS
st. Bilinga 71 M17
MILLSEY
rd. Cedar Creek 304 J12
MILLSTREAM
pl. Pimpama 326 L6
rt. Waterford 263 A19
MILLSWOOD
ct. Robina 48 K16
MILLSWYN
ct. Carrara 37 Q10
MILLY
cct. Ormeau 305 M15
MILNE
st. Beenleigh 284 B3
st. Mt Warren Pk 284 B3
MILNE BAY
rd. Witheren 33 M18
MILPARINKA
tce. Ashmore 38 H5
MILTON
av. Paradise Pt 8 P16
MILVERTON
cl. Mudgeeraba 58 N7
MIMI
ct. Mt Warren Pk 284 E9
MIMOSA
rd. Springbrook 66 E14
st. Ormeau 305 Q9
MINA
pl. Southport 29 A20
MINDARIE
st. Ormeau 306 A7
MINDELO
dr. Varsity Lakes 59 B7
MINDEN
cr. Helensvale 17 F3
MINEHAN
rd. Logan Vill 294 F3
MINERS
ct. Mudgeeraba 57 L4
MINERVA
ct. Banora Pt 82 H20
MING
st. Marsden 261 H4
MINGALETTA
dr. Ashmore 38 H1
MINIMBAH
st. Eagleby 264 H17
MINJUNGBAL
dr. Tweed Heads 82 G8
dr. Tweed Hd S 82 J14
MINKA
la. Norwell 305 M4
la. Ormeau 305 M4
MINNESOTA
st. Robina, off Massachusetts Ct. 59 H3
MINNIE
pl. Windaroo 283 P12
st. Southport 29 A15
MINORE
pl. Tweed Heads 82 B6
MINT
wy. Helensvale 17 L18
MINTWOOD
pl. Molendinar 28 G13
MINUGH
ct. Carrara 37 Q15
MINVERA
pl. Waterford 262 R20
MINYON
ct. Pacific Pines 16 Q19
MIRALIE
pl. Ashmore 28 K17
MIRAMBEENA
dr. Pimpama 305 P18
MIRANI
st. Lr Beechmont 46 A7
MIRELLA
ct. Waterford 263 A16
MIRIAM
ct. Parkwood 28 B8
MIRIMA
ct. Waterford 262 R20
MIRIMAR
ct. Currumbin Wtr 70 H9
MIRINAE
cct. Pimpama 326 R9
MIRO
pl. Nerang 37 A8
MIRREEN
dr. Tugun 71 B14
MISKIN
st. Nerang 37 J7
MISSION
dr. Tallai 57 P1
MISSOURI
wy. Oxenford 16 N5
MISTLETOE
cct. Kingscliff 93 B20
ct. Gilston 37 A16
ct. Ormeau 305 C3
MISTRAL
la. Coomera 328 E14
MISTY
ct. Varsity Lakes 59 G4
MITARO
ri. Pacific Pines 17 A14
MITCHAM
pl. Robina 49 B10
MITCHELL
av. Currumbin 70 Q8
av. Molendinar 28 E17
ct. Carrara 38 A12
st. Up Coomera 6 G4
MITCHUM
wy. Crestmead 261 K11
MITRE
pl. Molendinar 28 B14
st. Holmview 263 L16
MITTAGONG
av. Helensvale 17 J4
MOANA PARK
av. Broadbeach Wtr 39 G18
MOBBS
pl. Ormeau 305 C11
MOCHA
wy. Pimpama 326 E9
MOCKINGBIRD
dr. Up Coomera 6 H9
MOFFATT
pl. Edens Landing 263 E13
rd. Waterford W 261 R8
MOIRA
ct. Paradise Pt 8 N17
MOJAVE
dr. Burleigh Wtr 59 L5
MOKERA
av. Palm Beach 60 G13
MOLE
av. Southport 29 A9
MOLLENHAGEN
rd. Stockleigh 293 A8
MOLLOY
pl. Robina 49 F13
MOLLY
ct. Eagleby 264 M11
MOLLYS
pl. Currumbin Wtr 70 R13
MOLOKAI
cr. Pacific Pines 26 R1
MOLONEY
rd. Loganlea 262 L8
rd. Waterford W 262 L8
MOLONGLO
cl. Reedy Creek 58 P16
MOLUCCA
av. Palm Beach 70 Q3
MOLYU
ct. Mt Warren Pk 284 E4
MOMALONG
ct. Buccan 282 K14
MONA
ct. Oxenford 16 P11
dr. Jimboomba 299 A18
rd. Kingscliff 93 A20
MONACO
av. Russell I 268 J6
st. Broadbeach Wtr 39 D15
st. Surfers Pdse 39 L14
MONARCH
av. Up Coomera 6 J13
ct. Bahrs Scrub 283 E5
dr. Canungra 33 A14
dr. Kingscliff 93 B20
pl. Burleigh Wtr 49 M20
MONARO
rd. Mudgeeraba 57 G9
MONASH
av. Russell I 268 J4
rd. Loganlea 262 E2
st. Tugun 71 G13
MONASTERY
la. Tweed Heads 82 J6
MONA VALE
ct. Robina 49 G15
MONDAY
dr. Tallebudgera Vy 68 N6
MONDURAN
st. Marsden 261 L1
st. Marsden 261 L2
MONET
st. Coombabah 18 L9
MONIVAE
cct. Eagleby 264 F10
MONK
st. Eagleby 264 H15
MONMOUTH
st. Eagleby 264 H16
MONOMEETH
av. Bilambil Ht 91 B1
MONROE
ct. Oxenford 17 B12
MONSAL
la. Holmview 283 D2
MONSERRAT
ct. Reedy Creek 58 Q20
MONTAINE
rd. Ormeau 305 R11
MONTANA
cct. Logan Res 282 B2
pl. Coomera 327 D20
rd. Mermaid Bch 49 Q5
MONTE
st. Tamborine Mtn 13 M14
MONTEBELLO
ct. Mermaid Wtr 49 J10
MONTE CARLO
av. Surfers Pdse 39 M15
MONTECLAIR
ct. Mermaid Wtr 49 H10
MONTEGO
ct. Mermaid Wtr 49 G11
MONTEGO HILLS
dr. Kingsholme 325 J2
MONTE-KHOURY
dr. Loganholme 263 R7
MONTEREY
av. Banora Pt 92 E2
ct. Broadbeach Wtr 39 G14
MONTEREY KEYS
dr. Helensvale 7 G14
MONTESSA
st. Cornubia 264 D1
MONTEVIDEO
dr. Clear I Wtr 48 P5
MONTE VISTA
ct. Broadbeach Wtr 39 G16
MONTEZUMA
dr. Burleigh Wtr 59 K6
MONTGOMERY
av. Main Beach 29 M16
MONTREAL
cr. Robina 49 J16
MONTROSE
av. Bethania 263 A10
ct. Benowa 38 P14
MONTSERRAT
ct. Clear I Wtr 49 B3
MONTVILLE
ct. Varsity Lakes 59 B3
MONZA
dr. Oxenford 16 G10
MOODY
ct. Parkwood 28 C8
MOOLA
ct. Broadbeach Wtr 39 F20
MOOLAU
av. Tweed Heads 82 B8
MOOLIGUM
wy. Currumbin Vy 79 Q5
MOOMBA
cr. Piggabeen 80 B10
ct. Bundall 39 E12
MOONAH
av. Southport 28 Q16
ct. Crestmead 261 K8
MOONBEAM
pde.Mudgeeraba 47 R19
MOONBI
la. Coomera 328 B16
MOONDA
ct. Helensvale 17 L7
MOONDANCE
ct. Bonogin 67 Q2
MOONDANI
dr. Gilston 36 Q12
MOONDARRA
st. Pimpama 326 M6
MOONIE
dr. Coomera 327 H15
MOONLIGHT
la. Coomera 327 E16
MOONRAKER
st. Clear I Wtr 48 Q10
MOONSTONE
la. Logan Res 262 A17
st. Pimpama 326 P13

MOORA
st. Ashmore....28 H19
MOORABBIN
pl. Robina....48 R15
MOORABINDA
pl. Bilambil Ht....91 B1
MOORABOOL
st. Park Ridge....261 H14
MOORALLA
st. Tallai....47 N19
MOORE
la. Willow Vale....326 E11
st. Loganlea....262 H7
MOOREA
ct. Pacific Pines....17 A18
MOORES
cr. Varsity Lakes....59 G1
MOORHEN
pl. Burleigh Wtr....59 P4
st. Coomera....327 F17
MOORILLA
pl. Broadbeach Wtr..39 M17
MOORINGS
av. Hope Island....8 E9
MOORINYA
cct. Pimpama....327 E8
MOOYUMBIN
ct. Nerang....37 F4
MORALA
av. Biggera Wtr....19 A15
av. Runaway Bay....19 A3
av. Runaway Bay....19 A8
MORAN
cl. Eagleby....264 L11
dr. Up Coomera....16 C1
MORANE
ct. Pacific Pines....17 E20
MORAY
cr. Benowa....38 R12
ct. Highland Pk....37 F10
MORDIALLOC
pl. Robina....49 A14
MOREA
ct. Varsity Lakes....59 D3
MORELL
st. Tamborine Mtn....14 C10
MORESBY
av. Palm Beach....70 M3
MORETON
dr. Jacobs Well....308 F14
out. Russell I....268 P12
cr. Yarrabilba....300 J8
MORETON BAY
av. Tamborine Mtn....14 F10
MORFANTAINE
tce. Parkwood....28 H5
MORGAN
ct. Up Coomera....16 D2
MORINDA
wy. Labrador....28 P5
MORION
st. Yarrabilba....294 C19
MORISSET
rd. Edens Landing..263 J16
MORLEY
st. Tweed Hd W....82 A9
MORNA
pl. Coomera....327 P15
MORNING SUN
ct. Maudsland....16 H14
MORNING TIDE
la. Coomera....328 D15
MORNINGTON
tce. Robina....49 A14
MOROCCAN
st. Highland Pk....37 D15
MOROTAI
av. Palm Beach....70 M2
MORPHETT
pl. Yatala....284 C20
MORRELL
ct. Ormeau....305 C6
MORRIS
st. Pimpama....327 E11
MORRISON
la. Beenleigh....284 J3
MORROW
st. Crestmead....261 E7
MORSHEAD
st. Tugun....71 G13
MORTENSEN
rd. Nerang....37 F8
MORTIMORE
pl. Up Coomera....6 F6
MORTLEY
la. Varsity Lakes....59 G1

MORTLOCK
rd. Guanaba....24 Q2
MORTON
st. Chinderah....92 P16
st. Waterford....283 B1
MORVEN
ct. Mudgeeraba....57 P1
MORWELL
ct. Helensvale....17 F6
la. Yarrabilba....300 G9
MOSMAN
ct. Robina....49 E16
MOSS
st. Helensvale....17 K17
st. Kingscliff....103 H2
st. Mudgeeraba....58 A3
tce. Pimpama....326 C8
MOSSMAN
pde.Waterford....263 B19
MOTORWAY
cct. Ormeau....305 J6
MOTTEE
ct. Advancetown....46 K3
MOTU
cl. Pacific Pines....17 A20
MOUNT
st. Burleigh Hd....60 E7
st. Nerang....37 K5
st. Up Coomera....6 F5
MOUNTAIN ASH
cct. Robina....58 P5
cr. Stapylton....284 Q7
MOUNTAIN VIEW
av. Burleigh Wtr....49 R19
av. Miami....49 R19
cr. Mt Warren Pk....283 R8
cst. Mt Nathan....25 Q11
MOUNTBATTEN
av. Main Beach....29 M16
MT BILINGA
cct. Bilambil Ht....81 E17
MT ARCHER
rd. Park Ridge....261 E20
rd. Park Ridge....261 H14
MT BALLOW
st. Park Ridge....261 G20
MT BARNEY
st. Park Ridge....261 F20
MT BOWEN
st. Park Ridge....261 G20
st. Park Ridge....281 G1
MT COOROORA
st. Park Ridge....261 G20
MT COTTON
rd. Cornubia....264 P2
MT COUGALL
rd. Tallebudgera Vy...77 L19
MT CROSBY
st. Park Ridge....261 G20
st. Park Ridge....281 G1
MT EDWARDS
st. Park Ridge....261 D20
MT EMERALD
rd. Park Ridge....261 H20
MT GLORIOUS
st. Park Ridge....261 G20
MT GREVILLE
wy. Park Ridge....261 D20
MT HAGEN
dr. Runaway Bay....19 B4
MT HUNTLEY
st. Park Ridge....261 C19
MT MAY
st. Park Ridge....261 G20
MT MEE
st. Park Ridge....261 E20
MT MITCHELL
st. Park Ridge....281 H1
MT MORGAN
pl. Ormeau....305 L4
MT NATHAN
rd. Maudsland....26 B15
rd. Mt Nathan....36 D4
rd. Nerang....36 D4
MT NIMMEL
rd. Austinville....66 M6
rd. Neranwood....66 M1
rd. Springbrook....66 M6
MT OLIVE
ct. Mudgeeraba....58 A12
MT PATTERSON
st. Park Ridge....261 C20
MT PLEASANT
st. Park Ridge....261 E20

MT ROBERTS
st. Park Ridge....261 E20
MT ROYAL
st. Pimpama....326 J3
MT VISTA
pl. Tamborine....2 A20
MT WARREN
bvd.Mt Warren Pk....284 A4
bvd.Mt Warren Pk....284 A7
bvd.Mt Warren Pk....284 F5
bvd.Mt Warren Pk....284 F9
MT WHEELER
st. Park Ridge....261 H20
MOURA
rd. Worongary....37 M17
MOURNE
tce. Banora Pt....92 E10
MOWBRAY
st. Pimpama....326 J4
MOWLA
dr. Ashmore....38 H5
MOXEY
st. Marsden....261 H4
MOYENNE
cr. Varsity Lakes....59 E7
MUALLA
st. Ashmore....38 L2
MUCHOW
ct. Logan Res....261 R20
ct. Logan Res....281 R1
rd. Waterford W....261 R6
rd. Waterford W....262 A6
st. Beenleigh....284 D3
MUDGEE
st. Kingston....262 B1
MUDGEERABA
rd. Mudgeeraba....47 R18
rd. Tallai....47 Q16
rd. Worongary....47 Q16
MUDLO
st. Redland Bay....266 R1
st. Yarrabilba....300 H5
MUGELLO
dr. Oxenford....16 G9
MUGGA
wy. Tweed Heads....82 D5
MUIR
st. Labrador....29 C6
MUIREFIELD
pl. Arundel....28 G3
MUIRFIELD
ct. Cornubia....264 G3
pl. Banora Pt....92 J2
pl. Hope Island....8 E4
pl. Robina....49 A17
MULBERRY
pde.Tugun....71 E14
tce. Pimpama....326 D9
MULGA
pl. Beenleigh....283 M5
MULGRAVE
cr. Varsity Lakes....59 C2
MULKARRA
st. Biggera Wtr....18 Q15
MULL
ct. Merrimac....48 A7
MULLEWA
cr. Helensvale....17 E10
MULLIGAN
wy. Edens Landing..263 F15
MULLINER
tce. Up Coomera....6 G1
MULLINGAR
pl. Carrara....37 N10
MULLINS
st. Ormeau Hills....305 F16
MULTIMEDIA
la. Southport....28 L10
MULWALA
st. Maudsland....26 B5
MULYAN
pl. Ashmore....38 K5
MUMDJIN
ct. Currumbin Vy....79 Q5
MUNDOOLUN
rd. Mundoolun....1 B15
rd. Mundoolun....11 A3
MUNDOOLUN BRIDGE
Mundoolun....11 M6
MUNDOOLUN CONNECTION
rd. Boyland....12 E14
rd. Tamborine....12 A5
rd. Wonglepong....23 A7
MUNDORA
rd. Springbrook....66 N16

MUNDULLA
pl. Helensvale....17 F10
MUNGALA
st. Hope Island....7 Q3
MUNGANA
dr. Up Coomera....6 H3
MUNGERA
st. Biggera Wtr....18 Q14
st. Runaway Bay....18 Q14
MUNGINDIE
ct. Mt Nathan....25 G17
MUNGO
pl. Pimpama....326 N3
pl. Southport....38 R1
MUNIA
ct. Varsity Lakes....59 L3
MUNRO
ct. Tamborine Mtn....33 M5
MUNSTERVALE
st. Tamborine....2 B14
MUNYAROO
la. Up Coomera, off Coomerong Cr....6 A17
MURCHISON
st. Pacific Pines....26 Q2
MURDOCH
ct. Pimpama....326 H13
ct. Varsity Lakes....59 K3
MURESK
ct. Mermaid Wtr....49 J14
MUREV
wy. Carrara....37 Q14
MURIEL
st. Redland Bay....266 R6
st. Redland Bay....267 A7
MURIEL HENCHMAN
dr. Main Beach....29 L4
MURLONG
ct. Palm Beach....60 G12
MURPHY
dr. Loganholme....263 G6
rd. Canungra....33 A16
MURPHYS
la. Oxenford....16 K13
MURRAMI
st. Tanah Merah....263 K1
MURRAY
cct. Up Coomera....6 C9
ct. Russell I....268 P9
pl. Eagleby....264 K11
rd. Logan Vill....294 M8
st. Tugun....71 B11
MURRAYA
wy. Cudgen....102 P2
MURRAYFIELD
ct. Merrimac....48 D9
MURRAY GREY
dr. Tamborine....12 R4
MURRUMBA
ct. Ashmore....38 G1
MURTEN
ct. Hope Island....7 N11
MURTHA
dr. Elanora....70 H7
MUSA
st. Ashmore....38 N1
st. Crestmead....261 D9
MUSCOVEY
av. Paradise Pt....8 R13
MUSGRAVE
av. Labrador....28 M6
av. Labrador....29 A7
av. Southport....28 M6
ct. Banora Pt....91 N1
st. Coolangatta....72 B20
st. Coolangatta....82 E1
st. Yarrabilba....300 H12
MUSICAL
ct. Oxenford....16 R10
MUSK
av. Up Coomera....6 N11
MUSSAU
st. Pacific Pines....17 D19
MUSSON
la. Up Coomera....326 J19
MUSTANG
pl. Up Coomera....6 L8
MUSTIQUE
ct. Burleigh Wtr....60 A9
MUSTON
rd. Carrara....38 A17

MYALICEA
la. Up Coomera....326 H19
MYALL
ct. Oxenford....6 N18
st. Crestmead....261 L7
st. Southport....28 R20
MYCO
ct. Elanora....70 H7
MYE
pl. Stockleigh....293 G7
MYEERIMBA
pde.Tweed Hd W....81 J11
MYERS
st. Yarrabilba....293 R17
MYLOR
st. Nerang....37 F2
MYNA
wy. Burleigh Wtr....59 Q6
MYOLA
ct. Coombabah....18 F1
MYRA
ct. Witheren....45 D4
MYRTLE
av. Norwell....305 Q9
ct. Ormeau....305 Q9
ct. Beenleigh....283 K5
ct. Palm Beach....60 L20
st. Southport....28 R19
st. Kingscliff....93 A20
st. Waterford W....262 A7
MYSTERY
rd. Guanaba....24 M4
MYUNA
ct. Labrador....28 Q1

N

NABARLEK
dr. Worongary....37 M16
NABBERU
st. Maudsland....26 A7
NABILLA
st. Bilambil Ht....81 G14
NAGEL
av. Miami....50 B15
NAGLE
ct. Bilambil Ht....91 A1
NAIRN
ct. Cornubia....264 F2
ct. Highland Pk....37 H15
NAKEN
pl. Russell I....268 H10
NAKINA
st. Southport....28 Q8
NAKITA
ct. Mudgeeraba....58 J4
NAKULA
st. Gaven....27 K11
NALKARI
st. Coombabah....8 L19
NALLA
ct. Palm Beach....60 L17
NALYA
ct. Mermaid Wtr....49 J16
NAMATJIRA
ct. Broadbeach Wtr..38 P19
st. Paradise Pt....8 P13
NAMBA
cct. Yarrabilba....300 H10
NAMBUCCA
cr. Pimpama....326 G13
NAMBUR
st. Runaway Bay....18 Q13
NAMOI
ct. Carrara....38 B19
NANCOL
dr. Tallebudgera Vy...68 L14
NANCY YAUN
ct. Worongary....47 D9
NANDALA
dr. Tanah Merah....263 J1
NANDEWAR
ct. Carrara....38 C19
NANDI
dr. Up Coomera....326 K16
NANDINA
tce. Pacific Pines....17 E18
NANDROYA
dr. Up Coomera....6 E6
NANGANA
st. Tugun....71 E12
NANGAR
st. Pimpama....326 J3
NANKEEN
av. Paradise Pt....8 Q14

NAPA
cct. Holmview....263 E20
NAPIDO
la. Pacific Pines....17 D18
NAPIER
ct. Pacific Pines....16 N14
NAPLES
av. Surfers Pdse....39 K10
dr. Russell I....268 P10
NAPONYAH
rd. Terranora....91 C10
NAPPER
rd. Arundel....27 N3
rd. Arundel....28 F3
rd. Parkwood....27 N3
NARA
cr. Oxenford....16 D9
la. Yarrabilba....300 J7
NARALING
rd. Bahrs Scrub....283 D13
NARANGA
av. Broadbeach Wtr..39 L16
NARANJA
cr. Benowa....38 N12
NARARA
cr. Banora Pt....82 J19
NARBINE
st. Currumbin Wtr....70 R11
NARDOO
st. Robina....58 R2
NAREMBEEN
pl. Elanora....70 J2
NARIANNE
st. Marsden....261 Q1
NARKOOLA
st. Pimpama....326 K5
NAROOMA
pl. Helensvale....17 E7
NARRABEEN
ct. Robina....49 G15
st. Kingscliff....103 G8
NARRABRI
st. Gaven....27 H12
NARRABUNDAH
st. Mudgeeraba....48 A16
NARRACORT
ct. Oxenford....6 Q20
NARRANE
st. Tugun....71 F11
NARRAPORT
cr. Beenleigh....283 R4
NARRIEN
st. Pimpama....326 J5
NARROGIN
pl. Burleigh Wtr....49 K18
NARROW LEAF
ct. Advancetown....46 F1
NARU
st. Chinderah....92 M14
NASH
rd. Worongary....47 N8
st. Pimpama....326 N12
NASSAU
av. Terranora....91 Q12
pl. Jacobs Well....308 F11
NATALIE
ct. Eagleby....264 L12
rd. Buccan....282 C8
NATAN
rd. Mudgeeraba....57 N6
NATASHA
ct. Currumbin Wtr....70 P10
st. Ormeau....305 L7
NATHAN
st. Burleigh Hd....60 G7
NATHAN HOMESTEAD
rd. Mt Nathan....36 A3
NATHANVALE
dr. Mt Nathan....25 N18
dr. Mt Nathan....25 P11
NATHAN VALLEY
rd. Mt Nathan....25 Q19
NATIVE DOG
rd. Redland Bay....266 D2
NATONE
ct. Bethania....263 D13
ct. Edens Landing..263 D13
NATURAL BRIDGE
rd. Natural Br....65 Q20
NATURES
ct. Currumbin Vy....79 N5
NATURE VALLEY
ct. Tallai....46 Q3
NAURU
pl. Pacific Pines....17 D14
NAUTILUS
pde.Russell I....268 H8
pl. Biggera Wtr....18 R15
wy. Kingscliff....103 F14

Map Ref

NAVAJO
rd. Mudgeeraba ... 57 Q1
NAVARS
st. Reedy Creek ... 59 B13
NAVERENO
ct. Mundoolun ... 1 D4
NAVES
dr. Coomera ... 327 F10
NAVIGATION
la. Tweed Heads ... 82 J2
NAVIGATORS
wy. Tweed Heads ... 82 K7
NAVUA
ct. Pacific Pines ... 27 F1
NAYLOR
dr. Tamborine ... 299 J7
NEAGLE
rd. Wolffdene ... 304 D7
NEBO
pl. Helensvale ... 17 G11
NEBRASKA
ct. Oxenford ... 16 N3
NED EASEMENT
Ashmore ... 27 Q20
NEEDHAM
rd. Luscombe ... 304 F10
NEENES
pl. Russell I. ... 268 M2
NEESON
pl. Currumbin Wtr ... 70 R14
NELLA
la. Up Coomera ... 6 E8
NELLS
ct. Coomera ... 6 R11
NELMS
cct. Coomera ... 327 M14
NELSON
av. Hope Island ... 8 H9
ct. Benowa ... 38 N7
rd. Russell I. ... 268 L7
NEMARA
st. Biggera Wtr ... 18 Q14
NEMO
st. Ashmore ... 28 F20
NEPEAN
ct. Varsity Lakes ... 59 B7
NEPTUNE
ct. Surfers Pdse ... 39 L1
NEPTUNES
wy. Paradise Pt ... 9 A10
NERANG
st. Nerang ... 37 H3
st. Southport ... 29 D14
st. Tweed Hd W ... 81 K11
st. Waterford ... 262 M11
NERANG-BROADBEACH
rd. Broadbeach ... 49 H2
rd. Broadbeach Wtr ... 49 A1
rd. Carrara ... 37 L3
rd. Carrara ... 37 G12
rd. Clear I Wtr ... 49 A1
rd. Mermaid Wtr ... 49 H3
rd. Nerang ... 37 K3
NERANG CONNECTION
rd. Nerang ... 37 K2
NERANG-MURWILLUMBAH
rd. Advancetown ... 36 B20
rd. Clagiraba ... 36 B13
rd. Mt Nathan ... 36 B13
rd. Natural Br ... 65 P11
rd. Nerang ... 36 B13
rd. Numinbah Vy ... 65 P9
NERANG RIVER
dr. Nerang ... 37 F4
NERI
cr. Arundel ... 18 C20
NERIDA
dr. Mt Nathan ... 25 K20
la. Coomera ... 328 C16
NERIDAH
st. Loganlea ... 262 M2
NERREMAN
dr. Chambers Ft ... 281 J20
NESBIT
st. Southport ... 29 F17
NEUMANN
dr. Yarrabilba ... 300 G4
NEVADA
av. Park Ridge ... 261 H18
pl. Oxenford ... 16 P3
NEVENIA
st. Labrador ... 19 B18
NEVILLE
av. Southport ... 29 A8
NEVRON
dr. Bahrs Scrub ... 283 N10
NEW
st. Nerang ... 37 J6
NEWBURY
st. Pimpama ... 326 F3
NEWCASTLE
st. Burleigh Hd ... 59 L12
NEWCOMBE
la. Oxenford ... 16 L4
NEW FARM
pl. Banora Pt ... 91 R2
NEWHAVEN
cr. Worongary ... 47 N1
NEWHEATH
dr. Arundel ... 27 K1
NEW HORIZON
av. Bahrs Scrub ... 283 L12
NEWLANDS
ct. Mt Nathan ... 25 R15
NEWLINE
ct. Loganlea ... 262 F6
NEW NORWELL
rd. Norwell ... 306 L4
rd. Woongoolba ... 286 P20
rd. Woongoolba ... 287 A14
rd. Woongoolba ... 306 L4
NEWPORT
dr. Robina ... 49 G16
NEWSHAM
ct. Buccan ... 282 H16
NEWSTEAD
st. Burleigh Wtr ... 60 B3
NEWTON
av. Southport ... 28 R8
NEXUS
cl. Edens Landing ... 263 E15
dr. Pimpama ... 326 J7
NGUNGUN
cl. Loganholme ... 263 N12
NIBBS
ct. Boyland ... 13 B20
NICCY
rd. Coomera ... 327 F19
NICHE GLADE
cct. Maudsland ... 16 G12
NICHOLAS
wy. Reedy Creek ... 58 R11
NICHOLSON
la. Coomera ... 327 H16
NICKEL
st. Pimpama ... 326 N10
st. Pimpama ... 326 P10
NICKLAUS
ct. Merrimac ... 48 L3
NICOLA
wy. Up Coomera ... 6 G6
NICOLE
pl. Crestmead ... 261 F10
st. Bonogin ... 58 F14
NICOLET
dr. Tamborine Mtn ... 13 H11
NICOLIS
ct. Beenleigh ... 283 L2
NICOLSON
ct. Mermaid Wtr ... 49 E8
NIELS
cr. Park Ridge ... 261 D17
NIELSENS
rd. Carrara ... 37 P13
NIEUWENBURG
pl. Tamborine ... 2 M18
NIGHTINGALE
ct. Highland Pk ... 37 F14
NIGHTJAR
dr. Up Coomera ... 326 G19
NIGHTSHADE
cr. Pimpama ... 326 E10
rd. Bonogin ... 67 L9
NIJINSKY
wy. Willow Vale ... 325 G13
NIKAU
cr. Nerang ... 37 A8
NILES
ct. Bahrs Scrub ... 283 B3
NILKARE
ct. Up Coomera ... 6 N12
NIMBUS
ct. Coomera ... 327 E15
NIMMEL
la. Tugun ... 71 E8
NIMRUD
st. Southport ... 28 Q20
NINA
ct. Crestmead ... 261 C12
ct. Ormeau ... 305 Q10
pde.Arundel ... 28 L5
NIND
st. Southport ... 29 E11
NINETEENTH
av. Elanora ... 70 C4
av. Palm Beach ... 60 F18
NINGALOO
dr. Pimpama ... 326 M6
NINIGO
st. Pacific Pines ... 17 D19
NINKY
ct. Waterford ... 263 A17
NINNES
ct. Mudgeeraba ... 58 H4
NINTH
av. Palm Beach ... 60 N19
NIPA
ct. Tamborine Mtn ... 14 C4
NIPPER
pl. Mt Warren Pk ... 284 D4
NIRIMBA
ct. Bilambil Ht ... 91 B1
NIRVANA
ct. Runaway Bay ... 18 P11
NISBET
pl. Merrimac ... 48 B7
NIXON CREEK
rd. Numinbah Vy ... 65 N10
NOARLUNGA
st. Banora Pt ... 92 N6
NOBBY
pde.Miami ... 50 A19
NOCTURNE
la. Coomera ... 328 C16
NOELENE
la. Arundel ... 17 P20
NOELLA
ct. Bundall ... 39 D11
NOFFKE
ct. Logan Res ... 281 L3
ct. Logan Res ... 281 L4
NOLAN
ch. Parkwood ... 27 Q8
ct. Tamborine ... 299 E15
st. Tallai ... 57 M1
NOLINA
ct. Crestmead ... 261 G9
NOLLAMARA
dr. Elanora ... 60 H20
NONGA
ct. Mudgeeraba ... 57 N9
NOOJEE
st. Currumbin Wtr ... 70 N9
NOONARA
dr. Wonglepong ... 23 F14
NOOTKA
ct. Broadbeach Wtr ... 39 A19
NORA
la. Pimpama ... 326 N9
NORAH
st. Crestmead ... 261 M10
NORFOLK
av. Surfers Pdse ... 39 L4
av. Surfers Pdse ... 40 K3
dr. Pacific Pines ... 27 C3
st. Pimpama ... 326 D4
NORMAN
ct. Up Coomera ... 6 J6
st. Southport ... 29 F9
st. Tweed Heads ... 82 D8
NORMANBY
st. Mermaid Wtr ... 49 E8
NORMANDIE
ct. Tamborine Mtn ... 23 N7
NORONG
ct. Tallai ... 47 P18
NORRIS
st. Logan Res ... 262 C20
st. Pacific Pines ... 16 N13
NORSE
cl. Nerang ... 37 D6
NORSEMAN
cr. Worongary ... 37 N17
ct. Surfers Pdse ... 29 J19
NORTH
ct. Currumbin Vy ... 79 C18
qy. Biggera Wtr ... 18 L13
rd. Lr Beechmont ... 46 B2
st. Logan Vill ... 293 N2
st. Nerang ... 27 J19
st. Southport ... 29 D10
st. Tamborine Mtn ... 13 P12
NORTHAMPTON
bvd.Mudgeeraba ... 58 N7
NORTH BANK
st. Helensvale ... 7 B12
NORTHBOW
ct. Tallebudgera ... 69 R11
NORTHCLIFFE
tce. Surfers Pdse ... 39 P9
tce. Surfers Pdse ... 40 P15
NORTHCOTT
wy. Southport ... 28 N7
NORTHERLY
st. Logan Res ... 261 L16
NORTHERN LINK
rd. Coomera ... 6 Q1
rd. Coomera ... 326 Q20
NORTHERN SKIES
tce. Maudsland ... 15 P9
NORTH HILL
dr. Robina ... 48 D17
NORTHLAKES
dr. Elanora ... 69 R6
NORTH POINT
av. Kingscliff ... 103 G8
NORTHPOINT
cl. Robina ... 59 B1
NORTH QUAY
cct. Hope Island ... 7 Q9
NORTH SHORE
av. Varsity Lakes ... 59 D3
NORTH VIEW
st. Hope Island ... 8 E10
NORTHVIEW
pde.Benowa ... 38 E5
st. Mermaid Wtr ... 49 P4
NORTHWARD
st. Up Coomera ... 6 M1
st. Up Coomera ... 326 M20
NORTHWESTERN
ct. Varsity Lakes ... 59 K2
NORTHWOOD
cl. Robina ... 49 G16
NORWELL
rd. Gilberton ... 286 G13
rd. Norwell ... 286 G13
rd. Norwell ... 306 F2
rd. Norwell ... 306 F4
rd. Woongoolba ... 286 G13
NORWELL LAKES
rd. Norwell ... 307 D13
NORWOOD
ct. Yatala ... 284 F18
NOTAR
dr. Ormeau ... 285 F20
NOTELIA
dr. Elanora ... 69 R5
NOTRE DAME
ct. Varsity Lakes ... 59 J4
NOTTINGHAM
pl. Highland Pk ... 37 F12
NOTTINGHILL
pl. Oxenford ... 16 K2
NOTTINGHILL GATE
dr. Arundel ... 17 R14
NOVA
st. Waterford ... 283 A1
NOVAR
ct. Robina ... 48 K16
NOWENDOC
av. Pimpama ... 327 D5
NOWRA
ct. Helensvale ... 17 D3
NOZOMI
st. Burleigh Wtr ... 59 L6
NUBAN
st. Currumbin Wtr ... 70 M12
NUDGEE
st. Banora Pt ... 82 E20
NUGENT
ct. Helensvale ... 17 H6
NUI DAT
rd. Witheren ... 33 M20
NULLARBOR
st. Pimpama ... 326 N6
NUMALLA
ct. Elanora ... 70 E5
NUMBAT
ct. Coombabah ... 18 K2
ct.e,Coombabah ... 18 K2
ct.w,Coombabah ... 18 J3
NUMERALLA
av. Ashmore ... 38 F3
NUMIDIA
st. Currumbin Wtr ... 70 J8
NUNAWADING
ct. Robina ... 49 C10
NUNDAH
av. Miami ... 50 B19
NUSSEY
ct. Mt Warren Pk ... 284 D4
NUTHATCH
st. Burleigh Wtr ... 49 M20
NYAH
st. Beenleigh ... 283 R5
NYANDA
pde.Broadbeach Wtr ... 39 H17
N'YERRUM
la. Currumbin Vy ... 79 N6
NYHOLT
dr. Yatala ... 284 L6
NYMBOIDA
ct. Helensvale ... 7 D17
NYOKA
ct. Elanora ... 69 P7
NYORA
st. Southport ... 29 A17
NYPA
cl. Robina ... 58 Q3
NYRANG
av. Palm Beach ... 60 J11
dr. Pimpama ... 306 E20

O

OAK
av. Miami ... 49 R15
av. Surfers Pdse ... 39 M5
av. Surfers Pdse ... 40 K4
st. Marsden ... 261 Q4
st. Nerang ... 37 E3
st. Pimpama ... 326 N10
OAKDALE
av. Nerang ... 36 Q6
OAK HILL
cr. Parkwood ... 28 G8
dr. Hope Island ... 8 G6
OAKLAND
ct. Burleigh Wtr ... 59 L8
pde.Banora Pt ... 92 C4
OAKLEIGH
cct. Robina ... 49 B10
OAKLYN
pl. Merrimac ... 48 E9
OAKMONT
av. Cornubia ... 264 G2
la. Hope Island ... 8 G7
st. Robina ... 49 A20
OAKOVER
av. Ormeau Hills ... 305 E17
OAKRIDGE
pl. Molendinar ... 28 E14
OAKS
av. Chinderah ... 101 P4
av. Stotts Ck ... 101 P4
OAKVALE
av. Holmview ... 283 G2
cl. Mermaid Wtr ... 49 E6
OAKWOOD
dr. Waterford W ... 261 P8
dr. Waterford W ... 261 Q7
st. Pimpama ... 326 F10
tce. Palm Beach ... 60 J18
OAKY CREEK
rd. Coomera ... 7 H1
OASIS
cr. Elanora ... 70 J6
ct. Marsden ... 261 J3
wy. Kingscliff ... 103 F11
OATLAND
esp.Runaway Bay ... 19 D12
OATLANDS
pl. Banora Pt ... 92 D1
OATLEY
pl. Southport ... 29 A18
OBAN
ct. Eagleby ... 264 F12
la. Southport ... 29 F14
OBERON
wy. Oxenford ... 6 P19
O'BRIEN
ct. Arundel ... 27 R1
OBSERVATION
cr. Hope Island ... 8 E2
OBSERVATORY
dr. Reedy Creek ... 58 L16
dr. Reedy Creek ... 58 R17
OCEAN
av. Kingscliff ... 103 E13
av. Surfers Pdse ... 39 N3
av. Surfers Pdse ... 40 M3
av. Tweed Hd S ... 81 Q17
dr. Chinderah ... 92 R12
dr. Kingscliff ... 92 R12
gr. Currumbin ... 71 A6
pde.Burleigh Hd ... 60 D10
st. Burleigh Hd ... 60 F7
st. Coolangatta ... 82 C2
st. Kingscliff ... 93 B15
st. Mermaid Bch ... 49 R6
st. Runaway Bay ... 18 R13
OCEANBLUE
ri. Up Coomera ... 326 H16
OCEANIC
dr. Mermaid Wtr ... 49 L13
OCEANIS
dr. Oxenford ... 6 P17
OCEAN VIEW
cr. Kingscliff ... 103 E3
pde.Tamborine Mtn ... 24 H14
st. Benowa ... 38 Q6
OCEANVIEW EASEMENT
Mermaid Bch ... 50 B13
OCHNA
st. Crestmead ... 261 K8
OCOLA
ct. Tamborine Mtn ... 13 G12
O'CONNELL
ct. Pimpama ... 326 K14
O'CONNOR
pl. Up Coomera ... 6 C9
st. Tugun ... 71 G9
OCTAL
st. Yatala ... 284 R20
st. Yatala ... 305 A1
ODDIE
rd. Beenleigh ... 263 Q18
O'DOHERTY
av. Southport ... 28 R10
O'DOWD
ct. Nerang ... 37 A5
OFFHAM
ct. Arundel ... 18 C20
OGILVIE
cr. Nerang ... 36 R6
OGLE
pl. Windaroo ... 283 R15
O'GRADY
dr. Paradise Pt ... 8 N13
OHIA
ct. Tamborine Mtn ... 14 B8
OHIO
ct. Oxenford ... 16 Q2
OKINYA
st. Biggera Wtr ... 18 R14
OLAF
lp. Park Ridge ... 261 D16
OLD BAHRS SCRUB
rd. Bahrs Scrub ... 283 B11
OLD BOGANGAR
rd. Kings Forest ... 103 A14
OLD BOGANGAR BRIDGE
Kings Forest ... 103 B17
OLD BURLEIGH
rd. Broadbeach ... 39 P12
rd. Broadbeach ... 39 P17
rd. Surfers Pdse ... 39 P12
OLD COACH
rd. Burleigh Hd ... 59 D14
rd. Molendinar ... 27 M18
rd. Mudgeeraba ... 47 Q20
rd. Reedy Creek ... 59 B11
rd. Tallai ... 47 Q20
rd. Tallebudgera Vy ... 69 J1
rd. Tamborine ... 2 A19
rd. Up Coomera ... 6 F6
rd. Up Coomera ... 326 K20
OLD DAIRY
la. Benowa ... 38 M8
OLD FERRY
rd. Banora Pt ... 92 G12
OLD KENT
rd. Up Coomera ... 6 L5
OLD LOGAN VILLAGE
rd. Waterford ... 262 Q17
OLD MILL
rd. Bannockburn ... 304 H1
OLD PACIFIC
hwy.Coomera ... 6 N1
hwy.Coomera ... 326 H5
hwy.Coomera ... 326 M15
hwy.Oxenford ... 6 Q17
hwy.Pimpama ... 326 H5
hwy.Yatala ... 284 L6
OLD PIGGABEEN
rd. Cobaki L. ... 80 N8
OLD SCHOOL
rd. Springbrook ... 66 G20
OLD TAMBORINE
rd. Oxenford ... 6 G20
OLD TRAFFORD
rd. Bethania ... 263 A8
OLD WHARF
rd. Pimpama ... 306 H17
OLEA
ct. Crestmead ... 261 F8

Map Ref

PARK RIDGE
rd. Park Ridge 261 C16
PARKRIDGE
dr. Molendinar 27 L19
PARKSIDE
av. Arundel 17 M20
av. Hope Island 8 D9
cct. Robina 48 Q15
dr. Crestmead 261 C8
dr. Jacobs Well 308 J14
dr. Tweed Hd S 82 E18
pde.Wongawallan 4 Q14
PARK VIEW
pl. Helensvale 7 R14
PARKVIEW
ct. Southport 29 B12
la. Biggera Wtr 18 L14
st. Bahrs Scrub 283 N15
PARKVISTA
cct. Coomera 327 K16
la. Eagleby 264 M16
PARKWATER
pt. Helensvale 7 L16
tce. Helensvale 7 M15
PARKWAY
cct. Worongary 37 N18
dr. Advancetown 36 A17
PARKWOOD
bvd.Parkwood 28 D8
pl. Terranora 91 K14
PARLIAMENT
st. Bethania 262 R7
PARLOUR
pl. Robina 59 A4
PARMA
ct. Mt Nathan 36 E6
PARNELL
bvd.Robina 58 L3
PARNENO
st. Surfers Pdse 39 J4
PARNHAM
ct. Arundel 18 D19
PARNKI
pde.Palm Beach 60 G13
PARNOO
av. Burleigh Hd 60 E10
st. Surfers Pdse 39 K6
PAROO
ct. Eagleby 264 E11
PAROS
pl. Currumbin Wtr 70 K8
PARR
st. Biggera Wtr 19 B17
PARROT
ct. Ashmore 28 E20
ct. Gilston 36 R15
PARROT VALLEY
rd. Wolffdene 304 E7
PARRY
ct. Windaroo 284 A16
st. Tweed Hd S 82 H12
PARSLEY
rd. Russell I 268 L15
PARTRIDGE
pl. Tugun 71 E15
PARUNA
pl. Ashmore 38 G3
PARVULA
pl. Logan Res 262 C17
PASADENA
ct. Broadbeach Wtr 39 H14
PASCALI
ct. Varsity Lakes 59 F4
PASCOE
rd. Ormeau 304 R4
rd. Ormeau 305 A3
PASS
st. Kingscliff 103 G9
PASTURE
pl. Mt Nathan 25 Q10
PATERSON
pl. Paradise Pt 8 N14
rd. Yatala 284 C18
rd. Yatala 284 F18
PATHFINDER
rd. Coomera 328 C15
PATONGA
st. Ashmore 28 H19
PATRICIA
ct. Nerang 37 C8
PATRICK
ct. Waterford W 262 C4
rd. Nerang 37 L6
PATTERSON
ct. Up Coomera 6 B9
PATULA
ct. Beenleigh 283 M5

Map Ref

PATURA
dr. Ashmore 28 J19
PAUL
av. Coombabah 18 L6
ct. Carrara 37 M8
PAULA
dr. Up Coomera 6 H5
PAULINE
pl. Highland Pk 37 L13
st. Marsden 261 P4
PAULS
la. Varsity Lakes 59 G10
PAUL TOOSE
dr. Hope Island 8 J5
PAVILION
ct. Casuarina 103 D19
PAVILIONS
cl. Hope Island 7 Q10
PEABODY
la. Yarrabilba 293 N20
PEACE
ct. Mt Warren Pk 284 A7
PEACH
dr. Robina 48 M16
PEACHESTER
cl. Ormeau 305 M9
PEACHEY
rd. Luscombe 304 N1
rd. Ormeau 305 A8
rd. Ormeau 305 A9
rd. Yatala 284 H20
rd. Yatala 304 M1
PEACHFACE
st. Loganlea 262 J5
PEACHTREE
ct. Parkwood 28 G7
PEACHWOOD
ct. Robina 58 R7
PEACOCK
av. Beenleigh 264 A14
pl. Burleigh Wtr 59 Q1
PEAFOWL
st. Up Coomera 326 G17
PEAK
av. Main Beach 29 L17
cr. Pimpama 326 J12
la. Yarrabilba 293 P18
PEAL
ct. Carrara 38 B20
PEANBA PARK
rd. Up Coomera 6 C1
rd. Up Coomera 326 J20
rd. Willow Vale 6 C1
rd. Willow Vale 325 R20
PEAR
st. Redland Bay 266 R1
st. Redland Bay 267 A1
PEARCE
ct. Eagleby 264 K14
PEARL
key,Broadbeach Wtr 39 J19
la. Varsity Lakes 59 B4
st. Coomera 327 D19
st. Kingscliff 93 E19
st. Tweed Heads 82 H3
PEARL BAY
av. Russell I 268 L16
PEARL BEACH
dr. Helensvale 8 C17
PEARSE
st. Banora Pt 92 N1
PEARSON
cl. Arundel 17 R19
rd. Yatala 284 Q20
PEARSONS
st. Pimpama 326 E5
PEARWOOD
la. Robina 58 R6
PEASE
ct. Bethania 263 B15
PEATE
ct. Kingscliff 93 B15
PEBBLE
la. Hope Island 7 R1
la. Hope Island 327 Q20
row.Labrador 18 Q20
PEBBLE BEACH
dr. Runaway Bay 18 P8
dr. Windaroo 284 A17
PEBBLE CREEK
rd. Bonogin 58 J16
PECAN
dr. Up Coomera 6 J3
PECKHAM
ct. Pacific Pines 16 P17
PEDDER
pl. Coombabah 18 J1
st. Marsden 261 K4

Map Ref

PEEGAN
pl. Oxenford 16 E9
PEEL
cct. Tweed Hd S 82 B19
st. Holmview 283 D2
st. Up Coomera 6 C13
PEERLESS
av. Mermaid Bch 49 Q3
PEE WEE
pl. Burleigh Wtr 59 Q2
PEGASUS
ct. Currumbin Wtr 70 H13
PEGGS
rd. Burleigh Hd 60 F8
PELEWAN
ct. Tanah Merah 263 J3
PELHAM
st. Logan Res 282 B3
PELICAN
pde.Jacobs Well 307 R7
pl. Mudgeeraba 58 K6
pl. Tweed Hd W 81 M16
PEMBERTON
cl. Mt Nathan 36 B5
PEMBROKE
rd. Bethania 263 B10
st. Maudsland 16 E12
st. Pimpama 326 E4
PENAMBER
ct. Benowa 38 M8
PENDA
ct. Merrimac 48 C9
PENDENNIS
rd. Tamborine 1 E1
PENDLEBURY
ct. Edens Landing 263 G13
PENDRAAT
pde.Hope Island 8 B10
PENDRAGON
ct. Ormeau 305 M11
dr. Coomera 328 G13
PENELOPE
pl. Benowa 38 N8
PENFOLDS
cl. Pimpama 327 B11
ct. Holmview 283 G3
PENGANA
st. Labrador 29 A2
PENGUIN
pde.Burleigh Wtr 60 A1
PENINA
cct. Cornubia 264 H2
PENINSULA
av. Cornubia 264 G4
ct. Mermaid Wtr 49 F10
dr. Bilambil Ht 91 C1
dr. Robina 48 F20
dr. Robina 58 F1
PENINSULAR
dr. Surfers Pdse 39 L9
PENN
st. Russell I 268 M5
PENNANT
ct. Up Coomera 6 K3
PENNESHAW
cr. Ormeau 305 R9
PENNIES
rd. Russell I 268 J10
PENNSYLVANIA
av. Varsity Lakes 59 H4
PENNY
la. Burleigh Hd 59 D13
la. Stapylton 285 C7
pl. Arundel 28 L5
PENOLA
pl. Ashmore 38 G1
PENRHYN
st. Pacific Pines 26 R1
PENRITH
ct. Helensvale 17 D2
PENROCK
pde.Labrador 19 C19
PENSACOLA
ct. Broadbeach Wtr 39 G15
PENTLAND
ct. Helensvale 17 K7
PEONY
wy. Gaven 27 J7
PEPPER
st. Southport 28 R15
PEPPERCORN
ct. Nerang 37 B9
PEPPERINA
ct. Ormeau 305 E5
dr. Stockleigh 293 C6
PEPPERMINT
pl. Banora Pt 92 C4
st. Crestmead 261 L8

Map Ref

PEPPER TREE
dr. Holmview 283 F2
PEPPERTREE
cct. Robina 58 Q5
st. Pimpama 326 Q13
PEPPERWOOD
rd. Bonogin 67 H13
PERAK
ct. Tanah Merah 263 K5
PERCH
pl. Tweed Hd W 81 N15
PERCY
st. Southport 29 E16
PERCY EARL
cr. Pimpama 327 C14
PEREGRINE
cr. Coomera 327 L18
dr. Tweed Hd S 82 F15
st. Reedy Creek 58 P18
PERGER
st. Pimpama 326 M8
PERIWINKLE
cr. Tugun 71 F14
pl. Tugun 71 E14
PERKINS
cl. Reedy Creek 58 P20
PERONNE
av. Russell I 268 N14
PERRY
pl. Biggera Wtr 19 A15
PERSELLS
la. Yarrabilba 300 A1
PERSEVERANCE
wy. Logan Vill 293 P4
PERSIMMON
st. Pimpama 326 E10
PERTH
sq. Highland Pk 37 F12
PESCARA
st. Marsden 261 J3
PETA
pl. Reedy Creek 58 R12
PETER
pde.Mermaid Wtr 49 P13
pde.Miami 49 P13
st. Banora Pt 92 L6
st. Park Ridge 261 J13
wy. Berrinba 261 D2
PETER BLONDELL
dr. Mermaid Wtr 49 L10
PETER MILLS
dr. Gilston 36 Q14
PETERS
st. Pimpama 327 D11
PETER SELLERS
ct. Parkwood 27 R7
PETERSEN
av. Southport 39 E1
PETER SENIOR
ct. Parkwood 28 E9
dr. Hope Island 7 R10
PETER THOMSON
dr. Parkwood 28 F3
PETHERBRIDGE
av. Merrimac 48 C6
PETRA
st. Southport 28 Q20
PETREL
av. Mermaid Bch 49 R10
cr. Worongary 37 J19
pl. Casuarina 103 E14
pl. Jacobs Well 308 A7
PETRIE
st. Coolangatta 72 M19
PETSCH CREEK
rd. Tallebudgera Vy 78 F17
PETTIFER
ct. Up Coomera 6 C19
PETUNIA
ct. Eagleby 264 E16
ct. Miami 49 P18
PETWORTH
ct. Arundel 18 D20
PHAETON
st. Up Coomera 6 J2
st. Up Coomera 326 J20
PHARLAP
av. Mudgeeraba 58 A9
PHEASANT
av. Beenleigh 264 B15
st. Miami 49 R19
PHEENY
la. Casuarina 103 J15
PHIE
st. Loganlea 262 H6
PHILBEN
dr. Ormeau 305 A8

Map Ref

PHILIP
av. Broadbeach 39 P20
st. Currumbin 70 R7
PHILIPPINE
la. Palm Beach 70 N2
pde.Palm Beach 70 N1
PHILLIP
st. Beenleigh 284 B1
st. Chinderah 92 Q13
st. Labrador 29 D5
PHILLIP GRAY
rd. Helensvale 17 G15
PHILLIPS
la. Tweed Heads 82 G6
rd. Russell I 268 K8
PHILP
pde.Tweed Hd S 81 Q12
PHILS
pl. Miami 49 Q14
PHIPPS
pl. Ormeau 305 G8
PHLOX
ct. Waterford W 262 C7
PHOEBE
ri. Bonogin 58 J14
PHOENIX
st. Pacific Pines 17 C15
wy. Crestmead 261 G11
PHOENIX PALMS
dr. Hope Island 7 Q10
PIALLINGO
st. Mudgeeraba 48 B17
PIARI
st. Loganholme 263 M3
PICABEEN
cl. Robina 58 R4
PICCADILLY
pl. Highland Pk 37 F13
PICCOLO
st. Coomera 328 B17
PICKWORTH
ct. Parkwood 28 D9
PICNIC
pl. Canungra 33 B12
PICNIC CREEK
dr. Coomera 327 K19
dr. Coomera 327 L18
PICOLA
pl. Helensvale 17 E5
PICT
ct. Nerang 37 C6
PICTON
ct. Up Coomera 6 A18
PIDGEON
bvd.Crestmead 261 G12
st. Pimpama 327 F10
PIDNA
la. Pimpama 327 D8
PIEBALD
wy. Benobble 33 C8
PIEDMONT
st. Up Coomera 326 H18
PIERRE
la. Eagleby 264 P15
PIERRO
pl. Logan Res 261 L14
PIETA
wy. Coombabah 18 M6
PIGGABEEN
rd. Cobaki L 80 N8
rd. Currumbin Vy 80 E1
rd. Currumbin Wtr 80 E1
rd. Piggabeen 79 G20
rd. Piggabeen 80 G10
rd. Tweed Hd W 81 B11
PIGGOTTS
rd. Guanaba 15 E18
PIKE
la. Willow Vale 326 D9
PILAR
ct. Molendinar 27 Q10
PILBARA
pl. Worongary 37 M15
PILEENA
st. Banora Pt 92 H9
PILGRIM
pl. Southport 28 Q13
PILLIGA
st. Southport 29 A18
PILOT
ct. Mermaid Wtr 49 J10
PIMAGA
pl. Runaway Bay 19 A4
PIMPALA
ct. Tugun 71 B13
st. Loganlea 262 F7

Map Ref

PIMPAMA
st. Waterford 262 N11
PIMPAMA-JACOBS WELL
rd. Jacobs Well 307 K10
rd. Jacobs Well 307 M11
rd. Norwell 306 J15
rd. Norwell 307 A12
rd. Pimpama 306 G17
rd. Pimpama 326 E5
rd. Pimpama 326 G3
PIMPAMA RIVERS
dr. Ormeau 305 M14
PINAROO
cr. Ashmore 28 K19
PINCALLY
cr. Ormeau 305 Q6
PINDAR
av. Ormeau 305 M3
PINDARA
la. Benowa 38 Q10
PINDARI
av. Burleigh Hd 60 E10
PINE
av. Beenleigh 264 C17
av. Surfers Pdse 39 L4
gr. Tamborine Mtn 13 L13
st. Canungra 33 F14
st. Jacobs Well 308 C11
PINEBARK
av. Oxenford 16 M9
PINE CONE
ct. Elanora 70 H6
PINE CREEK
rd. Numinbah Vy 46 B18
rd. Springbrook 46 B18
PINECREST
ct. Oxenford 16 N10
PINEDALE
st. Oxenford 16 M9
PINE FOREST
wy. Kairabah 300 A14
wy. Tamborine 300 A14
PINE GROVE
dr. Crestmead 261 L13
st. Nerang 37 M3
PINEHILL
dr. Oxenford 16 P11
st. Yarrabilba 293 Q17
PINEHURST
dr. Hope Island 8 F5
pl. Robina 48 Q19
PINELANDS
st. Loganlea 262 E4
PINEMOUNT
cr. Oxenford 16 L10
PINENEEDLE
ct. Oxenford 16 M10
PINE RIDGE
rd. Biggera Wtr 18 H15
rd. Coombabah 18 H15
rd. Runaway Bay 18 M11
PINES
la. Elanora 70 L2
PINE TREE
pl. Piggabeen 80 B14
PINETREE
ct. Mudgeeraba 57 A7
PINEVALE
dr. Oxenford 16 N10
PINE VALLEY
dr. Robina 49 E20
PINEVIEW
dr. Eagleby 264 H9
dr. Oxenford 16 M9
rd. Logan Vill 294 E18
PINEWOOD
st. Crestmead 261 K7
st. Up Coomera 16 A1
PINJARRA
pl. Worongary 37 M16
PINKWOOD
dr. Ashmore 38 N2
PINNACLE
ct. Robina 49 E15
dr. Wongawallan 4 N18
pl. Currumbin Wtr 80 H1
wy. Pimpama 326 H12
PINNACLES
st. Yarrabilba 300 H12
PINNAROO
st. Hope Island 7 Q2
PINNINGTON
st. Crestmead 261 F7
PINON
cl. Elanora 70 L6
PINTAIL
cr. Burleigh Wtr 59 Q5

PINTER

ROBYN

Map Ref

RAPHAEL
st. Coombabah 18 K8
RAROTONGA
ri. Pacific Pines 17 A19
RASMUSSEN
av. Marsden 261 M1
RASON
wy. Coombabah 18 K1
R A STEVENS BRIDGE
Nerang 36 P6
RATA
pl. Nerang 37 B8
RATHBONE
ct. Mudgeeraba 57 R4
pl. Labrador 29 D6
RATHKEALE
st. Crestmead 261 F6
RATTAN
ct. Elanora 60 F19
RATU
la. Coomera 327 R15
RAVEL
st. Eagleby 264 N11
RAVEN
pde.Burleigh Wtr 49 L20
RAVENSBOURNE
cct. Waterford 282 Q1
RAVENSTHORPE
st. Ormeau 305 R9
RAVINA
pl. Coomera 327 D20
RAWARD
av. Banora Pt 82 N20
RAWLE
ct. Broadbeach Wtr 49 J2
RAWLINNA
dr. Mermaid Wtr 49 J14
RAWLINS
st. Southport 29 E11
RAWSON
ct. Holmview 283 G2
RAY
st. Runaway Bay 19 B13
RAYES
la. N Tumbulgum 101 F3
RAYLES
la. Terranora 91 L14
RAYMOND
av. Bundall 39 D6
ct. Mt Warren Pk 284 B7
RAYNER
la. Mudgeeraba 57 L6
RAYNUHA
ct. Ormeau 305 L6
RAZORBACK
rd. Tweed Heads 82 F6
RAZORBILL
st. Burleigh Wtr 59 P4
READ
st. Pimpama 326 M9
REAGAN
cl. Pimpama 326 D7
REARDONS
rd. Cudgen 102 L12
REBBECHI
ct. Parkwood 28 B8
REBECCA
cct. Eagleby 264 P16
ct. Broadbeach Wtr 49 L1
dr. Chambers Ft 281 P13
REBHOLZ
dr. Benowa 38 P16
RECREATION
dr. Nerang 37 M6
pl. Jacobs Well 308 F15
st. Tweed Heads 82 G6
RED ASH
ct. Merrimac 48 B9
RED BARON
la. Up Coomera 6 P7
RED BASS
av. Tweed Hd W 81 M15
REDBAY
st. Up Coomera 326 J17
REDBUD
la.n,Robina 48 M15
la.s,Robina 48 M16
RED CEDAR
cct. Kingsholme 325 J1
RED GUM
tce. Coomera 327 J14
REDGUM
pl. Molendinar 28 E14
REDLEAF
ct. Burleigh Wtr 59 K8
REDMAN
rd. Cudgen 102 Q3

Map Ref

REDNAL
ct. Carrara 38 B17
RED OAK
dr. Tallai 46 N3
REDONDO
av. Miami 50 A14
REDSTART
st. Up Coomera 6 H10
REDSTONE
ct. Carrara 38 A18
REDWING
ct. Burleigh Wtr 49 M20
REDWOOD
pl. Molendinar 28 F14
st. Marsden 261 R4
st. Up Coomera 15 Q2
REDZEL
ct. Logan Res 261 M13
REED
pl. Maudsland 26 A11
st. Ashmore 38 C4
st. Coolangatta 82 G3
st. Logan Res 261 R14
REEDMANS
rd. Ormeau 305 L14
rd. Ormeau 305 M16
REEDY CREEK
rd. Burleigh Hd 59 E11
rd. Burleigh Wtr 59 M11
rd. Varsity Lakes 59 E11
REEF
ct. Mermaid Wtr 49 G3
REEMAN
ct. Eagleby 264 G17
REES
ct. Elanora 60 H20
REESE
la. Yarrabilba 293 R20
la. Yarrabilba 299 R1
REEVE
rd. Tamborine Mtn 13 N14
REEVES
st. Nerang 37 B1
REFLECTION
av. Currumbin Wtr 70 K20
REGAL
ct. Highland Pk 37 F13
ct. Ormeau 305 K6
dr. Canungra 33 B13
REGATTA
av. Oxenford 6 M17
av. Oxenford 6 P17
pde.Southport 39 G4
REGELING
ct. Loganlea 262 L6
REGENCY
pl. Mudgeeraba 48 B20
REGENSBERG
cl. Varsity Lakes 59 F4
REGENT
ct. Bahrs Scrub 283 F6
ct. Coomera 327 F18
la. Hope Island 7 R9
la. Southport 29 G13
st. Currumbin 71 B10
REGENTS
cr. Yarrabilba 300 K8
ct. Paradise Pt 9 E10
REGINA
st. Coomera 7 M1
REGNANS
rd. Carbrook 265 Q2
REICHERT
dr. Molendinar 28 A10
REID
ct. Carrara 38 L13
pl. Banora Pt 91 P2
REINDEER
st. Up Coomera 6 M9
REISER
la. Boyland 22 H6
REISERS
rd. Beenleigh 284 F1
RELLAM
rd. Loganlea 262 E3
REMABAY
st. Burleigh Hd 59 M19
REMARO
st. Waterford W 262 G9
REMEMBRANCE
dr. Surfers Pdse 39 M8
dr. Surfers Pdse 40 L12
REMO
st. Surfers Pdse 39 L13
REMOUNT
pl. Carrara 37 P9

Map Ref

RENAE
la. Eagleby 264 M18
RENATE
wy. Benowa 38 P14
RENELLE
st. Marsden 261 N1
RENFORD
ct. Ormeau 305 F8
RENFREW
dr. Highland Pk 37 F15
RENMARK
ct. Helensvale 17 F10
RENMELAIR
ct. Waterford W 262 G9
ct. Waterford W 262 G9
RENO
av. Russell I 268 M8
RENOIR
dr. Coombabah 18 L9
REPEATER STATION
rd. Springbrook 66 M16
RESERVE
rd. Up Coomera 6 D19
rd. Up Coomera 6 G7
st. Burleigh Hd 60 D10
RESERVOIR
st. Beenleigh 284 B1
RESIDENCES
cct. Pimpama 326 H11
RESORT
dr. Robina 49 E11
RESOURCES
ct. Molendinar 28 A17
RESPALL
wy. Arundel 17 Q19
RETHAN
ct. Marsden 261 G3
RETREAT
pl. Robina 48 C17
st. Russell I 268 H7
REUBEN
bvd.Logan Res 282 B2
REYNELLA
rd. Tallebudgera 69 D17
REYNOLDS
av. Labrador 29 C2
rd. Currumbin Vy 78 P15
REYNTON
st. Currumbin Wtr 70 Q10
RHAPSODY
cr. Jacobs Well 308 H18
RHETT
av. Labrador 29 A4
RHIANA
st. Pimpama 326 F5
RHIANNON
dr. Ashmore 27 M20
RHOADES
rd. Witheren 45 G11
RHODES
st. Loganlea 262 H5
RHODIUM
cr. Hope Island 8 B8
RHONE
dr. Holmview 283 E1
RIALTO QUAY
dr. Hope Island 7 P7
RIANA
ct. Helensvale 17 G9
RIBBONWOOD
pl. Terranora 91 E10
RIBERRY
ct. Bonogin 67 J11
dr. Casuarina 103 E15
RICCARTON
pl. Labrador 18 N20
RICE
pl. Varsity Lakes 59 K4
RICHARD
cr. Highland Pk 37 J13
RICHARDS
st. Loganlea 262 E4
RICHARDSON
cr. Up Coomera 6 C9
ct. Edens Landing 263 E17
RICHENDA
st. Ormeau Hills 305 E18
RICHFIELD
cl. Nerang 36 R9
RICHLAND
dr. Bannockburn 304 G1
RICHMOND
av. Bundall 39 E6
cr. Waterford 262 Q20
ct. Hope Island 7 M6
la. Maudsland 16 D11
st. Pimpama 327 A9

Map Ref

RICHTER
ct. Edens Landing 263 F15
RICKARD
cl. Pimpama 327 B11
RIDE
ct. Worongary 37 K17
RIDGE
ct. Oxenford 16 N10
RIDGECROP
st. Up Coomera 6 J5
RIDGELINE
ct. Mt Nathan 25 N17
wy. Highland Pk 37 D13
RIDGEMONT
st. Up Coomera 6 K4
RIDGEMOUNT
st. Bahrs Scrub 283 N16
RIDGEVALE
bvd.Holmview 263 C20
dr. Helensvale 17 H8
rd. Currumbin Wtr 70 L18
RIDGEVIEW
cr. Bonogin 68 L2
la. Yarrabilba 293 P18
RIDGEVISTA
ct. Reedy Creek 58 R12
RIDGEWAY
av. Southport 29 B20
st. Tweed Hd S 81 Q15
RIDGEWOOD
cl. Pacific Pines 27 B3
ct. Burleigh Wtr 59 K7
RIEDEL
rd. Carbrook 266 B9
RIEMORE
cct. Tamborine 1 P17
RIFLEBIRD
st. Coomera 327 M18
RIFLE RANGE
rd. Pimpama 326 D6
rd. Up Coomera 326 K10
RIGEL
ct. Robina 49 D19
RILEY
ct. Windaroo 283 R16
RILL
ct. Nerang 36 P8
RIMATARA
ri. Pacific Pines 16 R15
RIMU
pl. Molendinar 28 F14
pl. Nerang 37 B7
RINA
ct. Varsity Lakes 59 F11
RING
rd. Robina 49 G18
RINGTAIL
st. Clear I Wtr 48 R9
RINGWOOD
ct. Robina 49 B13
RINTO
dr. Eagleby 264 G12
RIORDAN
st. Logan Res 262 C18
RIO VISTA
bvd.Broadbeach Wtr 39 H20
bvd.Mermaid Wtr 49 G4
bvd.Mermaid Wtr 49 J12
RIPARIAN
cct. Logan Res 262 C20
wy. Ormeau 305 P11
RIPOLL
ct. Reedy Creek 59 B13
RIPPLE
ct. Coomera 328 C17
RIPPONLEA
st. Robina 49 B10
RISE
cct. Pacific Pines 16 M20
cr. Pimpama 326 J11
RISEBOROUGH
cr. Crestmead 261 L10
RISING FAST
rd. Mudgeeraba 58 A12
RITA
ct. Mt Warren Pk 284 D10
RITZ
dr. Coomera 327 E18
RIVAGE
pl. Highland Pk 37 E15
RIVAL
la. Coomera 328 D16
RIVENDELL
Tweed Hd S 82 J18
pl. Up Coomera 16 D1
RIVER
cr. Broadbeach Wtr 38 R19
dr. Surfers Pdse 39 L4

Map Ref

rd. Alberton 265 C14
rd. Banora Pt 92 C13
rd. Waterford 262 M11
st. Chinderah 92 N13
st. Eagleby 264 L17
st. Logan Vill 293 N3
tce. Surfers Pdse 39 N10
tce. Surfers Pdse 40 M16
tce. Tweed Heads 82 J6
tce. Up Coomera 6 E18
RIVERBANK
ct. Ashmore 37 R2
RIVERBEND
av. Carrara 38 N19
dr. Canungra 33 C12
RIVER BREEZE
ct. Windaroo 284 A14
RIVERBREEZE
cr. Maudsland 15 Q8
RIVERBROOKE
dr. Up Coomera 6 L13
RIVERCHERRY
wy. Up Coomera 6 D16
RIVER COVE
pl. Helensvale 7 G13
RIVERDALE
ct. Hope Island 7 M7
dr. Hope Island 7 L6
RIVERDOWNS
cr. Helensvale 7 C17
RIVERGLEN
ct. Mt Nathan 25 F17
RIVER GUM
ct. Loganholme 263 H7
RIVERGUM
dr. Nerang 37 B6
RIVER HEIGHTS
bvd.Ashmore, off
Stewart Pde. 38 A2
rd. Up Coomera 6 L12
RIVER HILLS
rd. Eagleby 264 C13
RIVERIA
cct. Bethania 263 A3
RIVERINA
ct. Mudgeeraba 58 D8
RIVERLAND
dr. Loganholme 263 R6
rd. Coomera 7 M2
RIVERLANDS
pl. Banora Pt 82 D20
RIVERLEA WATERS
dr. Nerang 37 A3
RIVERLEIGH
dr. Hope Island 7 H12
pl. Loganholme 263 M12
RIVERLILLY
st. Reedy Creek 59 B17
RIVER LINKS
bvd.e,Helensvale 7 D14
bvd.w,Helensvale 7 B12
RIVER MEADOWS
dr. Up Coomera 6 L13
dr. Up Coomera 6 N11
RIVERMILL
tce. Maudsland 16 A8
RIVERMOUNT
dr. Yatala 284 C18
RIVER OAK
dr. Helensvale 17 A2
pl. Loganholme 263 M11
RIVER PARK
dr. Loganholme 263 H6
RIVERPARK
dr. Nerang 37 A7
RIVER RUN
cct. Ormeau Hills 305 F19
RIVERSDALE
bvd.Banora Pt 82 D20
rd. Oxenford 6 M18
RIVERSIDE
dr. Bungalora 90 Q20
dr. Currumbin Wtr 70 L8
dr. Hope Island 8 H4
dr. Tumbulgum 101 A8
tce. Windaroo 283 R14
RIVERSIDE SANCTUARY
tce. Ormeau 305 P10
RIVER SPRINGS COUNTRY CLUB ACCESS
Nerang 37 G6
RIVERSTONE
av. Logan Res 261 R18
csg.Maudsland 15 N7
csg.Maudsland 16 A8
rd. Helensvale 17 D6

Map Ref

RIVERTREE
av. Helensvale 7 B19
RIVERVALE
st. Ormeau 305 M6
RIVER VALLEY
wy. Wolffdene 304 F7
RIVERVIEW
cr. Hope Island 8 G2
ct. Ormeau 305 J8
pde.Surfers Pdse 39 M5
pde.Surfers Pdse 40 K6
rd. Logan Res 282 D2
rd. Nerang 37 L3
RIVER VISTA
wy. Paradise Pt 9 A10
RIVERVISTA
ct. Eagleby 264 H10
RIVERWALK
av. Robina 58 K1
RIVERWOOD
dr. Ashmore 27 M19
gr. Benowa 38 D4
RIVETT
ct. Mudgeeraba 48 A17
RIVIERA
av. Tweed Hd W 81 M14
ct. Cornubia 264 F4
ct. Windaroo 284 B13
rd. Miami 50 B16
RIVINA
cct. Coomera 327 C18
RIX
dr. Up Coomera 6 J6
RJ HINZE BRIDGE
Witheren 34 G14
ROBA
pl. Ashmore 38 K4
ROB COLE
rd. N Tumbulgum 89 R20
rd. Upper Duroby 89 R20
ROBE
ct. Helensvale 17 D3
ROBERT
dr. Pimpama 326 M8
st. Labrador 29 B5
st. Loganlea 262 E1
st. Mudgeeraba 48 C20
ROBERTA
cr. Bilambil Ht 91 D1
ROBERTS
dr. Maudsland 16 H20
dr. Maudsland 26 H1
ROBERT SOUTH
dr. Crestmead 261 E11
ROBERT STANLEY
dr. Mt Warren Pk 284 G7
ROBIN
av. Paradise Pt 8 P16
cct. Tweed Hd S 81 R16
ct. Ashmore 28 E20
st. Eagleby 264 C13
ROBINA
pky.Clear I Wtr 48 M3
pky.Merrimac 48 M3
pky.Robina 58 K3
ROBINA STATION
rd. Robina 48 J18
ROBINA TOWN CENTRE
dr. Mudgeeraba 48 D18
dr. Robina 48 D18
dr. Robina 48 K20
dr. Robina 48 M18
ROBINIA
ct. Robina 58 P5
ROBIN JOY
cl. Labrador 28 P2
ROBINSON
ct. Berrinba 261 D1
pl. Currumbin Wtr 70 N18
rd. Russell I 268 K15
ROBINSONS
la. Coolangatta 82 E1
rd. Cobaki 80 K11
rd. Piggabeen 80 K11
ROBIUS
ct. Stockleigh 293 G5
ROB ROY
cr. Kingscliff 103 F1
ct. Highland Pk 37 G16
ROBUR
st. Marsden 261 L5
ROBUSTA
ri. Burleigh Hd 69 L1
ROBYN
ct. Logan Vill 293 M5
st. Southport 39 B2

T

WILLOWVALE

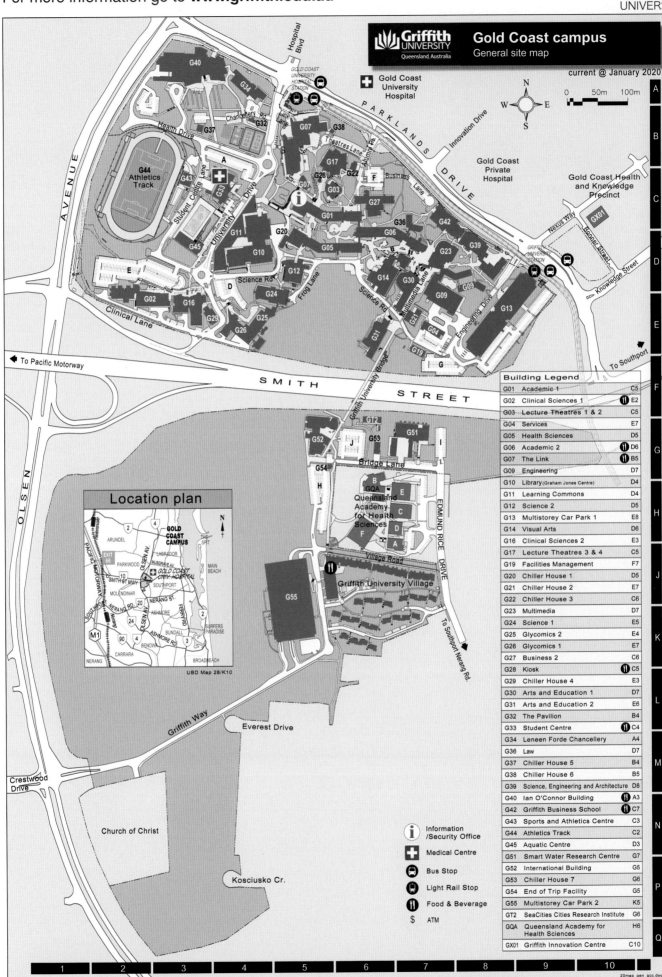

Griffith UNIVERSITY
Queensland, Australia

Gold Coast campus
General site map

current @ January 2020

Building Legend		
G01	Academic 1	C5
G02	Clinical Sciences 1	E2
G03	Lecture Theatres 1 & 2	C5
G04	Services	E7
G05	Health Sciences	D5
G06	Academic 2	D6
G07	The Link	B5
G09	Engineering	D7
G10	Library (Graham Jones Centre)	D4
G11	Learning Commons	D4
G12	Science 2	D5
G13	Multistorey Car Park 1	E8
G14	Visual Arts	D6
G16	Clinical Sciences 2	E3
G17	Lecture Theatres 3 & 4	C5
G19	Facilities Management	F7
G20	Chiller House 1	D5
G21	Chiller House 2	E7
G22	Chiller House 3	C6
G23	Multimedia	D7
G24	Science 1	E5
G25	Glycomics 2	E4
G26	Glycomics 1	E7
G27	Business 2	C6
G28	Kiosk	C5
G29	Chiller House 4	E3
G30	Arts and Education 1	D7
G31	Arts and Education 2	E6
G32	The Pavilion	B4
G33	Student Centre	C4
G34	Leneen Forde Chancellery	A4
G36	Law	D7
G37	Chiller House 5	B4
G38	Chiller House 6	B5
G39	Science, Engineering and Architecture	D8
G40	Ian O'Connor Building	A3
G42	Griffith Business School	C7
G43	Sports and Athletics Centre	C3
G44	Athletics Track	C2
G45	Aquatic Centre	D3
G51	Smart Water Research Centre	G7
G52	International Building	G5
G53	Chiller House 7	G6
G54	End of Trip Facility	G5
G55	Multistorey Car Park 2	K5
GT2	SeaCities Cities Research Institute	G6
GQA	Queensland Academy for Health Sciences	H6
GX01	Griffith Innovation Centre	C10

Location plan

UBD Map 28/K10

(i) Information /Security Office

✚ Medical Centre

🚌 Bus Stop

🚊 Light Rail Stop

🍴 Food & Beverage

$ ATM

20map_gen_goc.dwg

MAP 2
1 KILOMETRE EQUALS 4 GRID SQUARES
JOINS 303
304

A B C D 512E E F G H J K L M 514E N P Q R 515E

1 2 3 4 5 6 7 8 9 10 11 12 13 14 15 16 17 18 19 20

KAIRABAH
4207

PLUNKETT RD

Tamborine Catholic Cemetery

88

95

2410

RD

ALBERT

RIVER

Clutha

Ck

RIVER

ALBERT

WATERFORD

TAMBORINE

PLUNKETT BRIDGE

KIBBLE PL

SONNY

TANDY LA

YORE RD

2659

Creek

WALDRON RD

DURRANT CT

49

31

1

1

1

92

CREAMER RD

15

2

JOINS 3

TAMBORINE
4270

BEENLEIGH

BEAUDESERT

Steele

Tamborine School Pk

Hall

Tennis

2768

RD

92

RFB

Middle Park

Soccer

95

H

Steele

Creek

RACECOURSE PL

LOCHVIEW

ANTRAE

CT

RD

LEACH

TAMBORINE

SIMON SIGANTO BRIDGE

2

MOUNTAIN

36

Steele

MUNSTERVALE

BALL

68

25

10

73

RD

RD

BEENLEIGH

31

J G CAMPBELL LA

88

158

157

NEUENBURG PL

Scenic Rim

CCT

DR

OLD COACH

BULLOCK TEAM WY

BEAUDESERT

95

269

265

RD

92

MT VISTA PL

VERBENA

84

95

15

RD

PALOMINO

218

269

300

RD

RD

HAZEL

48

234

196

669

RD

124

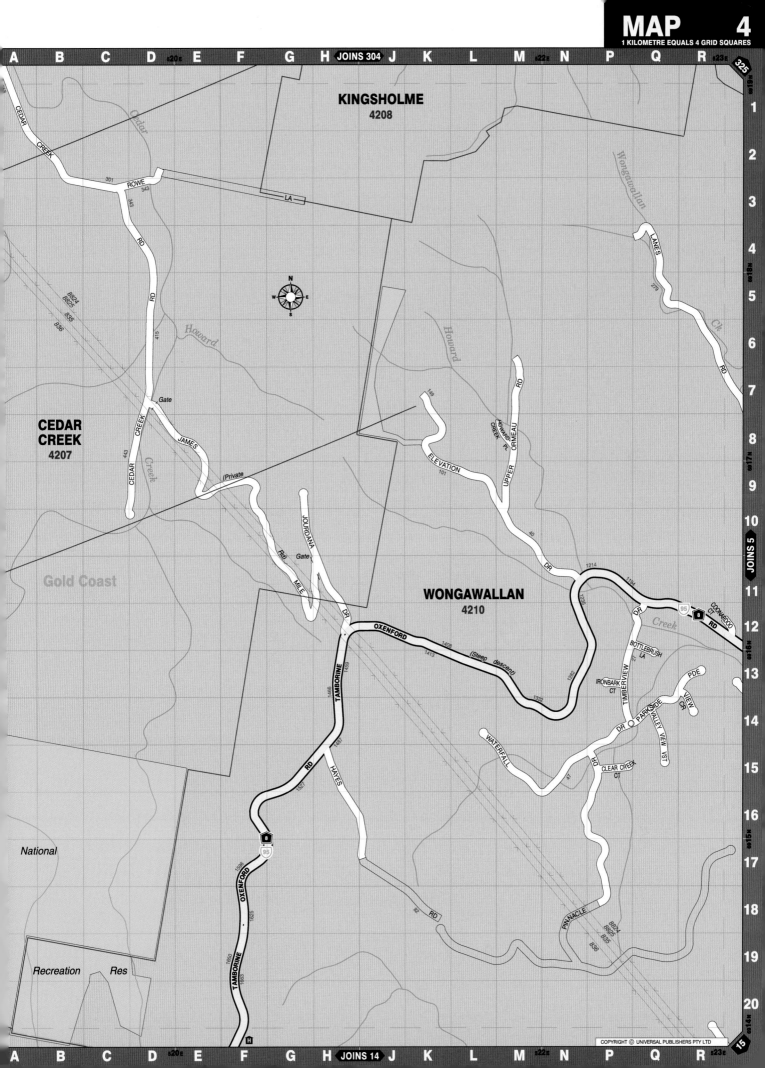

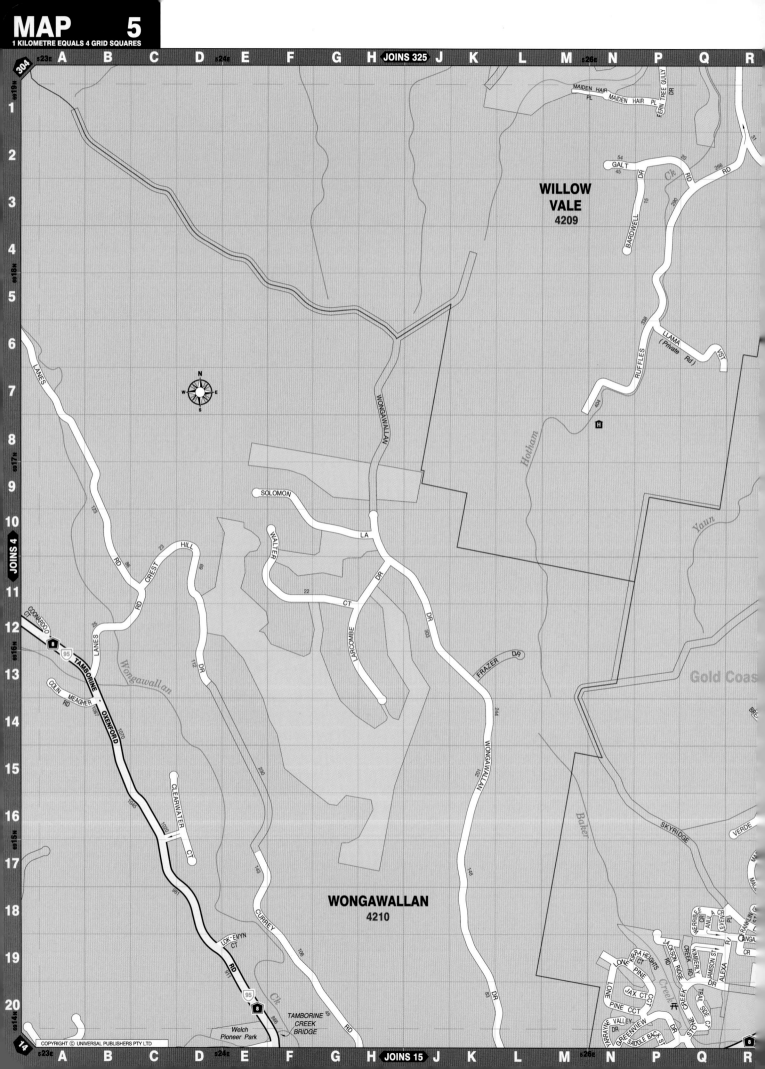

MAP 6

1 KILOMETRE EQUALS 4 GRID SQUARES

JOINS 326

JOINS 16

COOMERA 4209

UPPER COOMERA 4209

OXENFORD 4210

Westfield Coomera

Coomera Anglican College

Assisi Catholic College

Upper Coomera College

Coomera City Centre

Coomera Village

Coomera Primary

Saint Stephens College

Magnolia Homestead Aged Care

Yaun Creek Park

Hargraves Park

Dreamworld

WhiteWater World

Coomera Bridge

Coomera Watersports Club

Ragatta Waters Park

Palm Lake Resort

Seachange Riverside Coomera

Highland Reserve State School

Russell Hinze Pk

Waterhen Lake

Oxenford Reservoir

Oxenford Oval

Pony Club

Gambamora Park

Brygon Creek

Yaun Ck

Coomera River

MAP 7
1 KILOMETRE EQUALS 4 GRID SQUARES

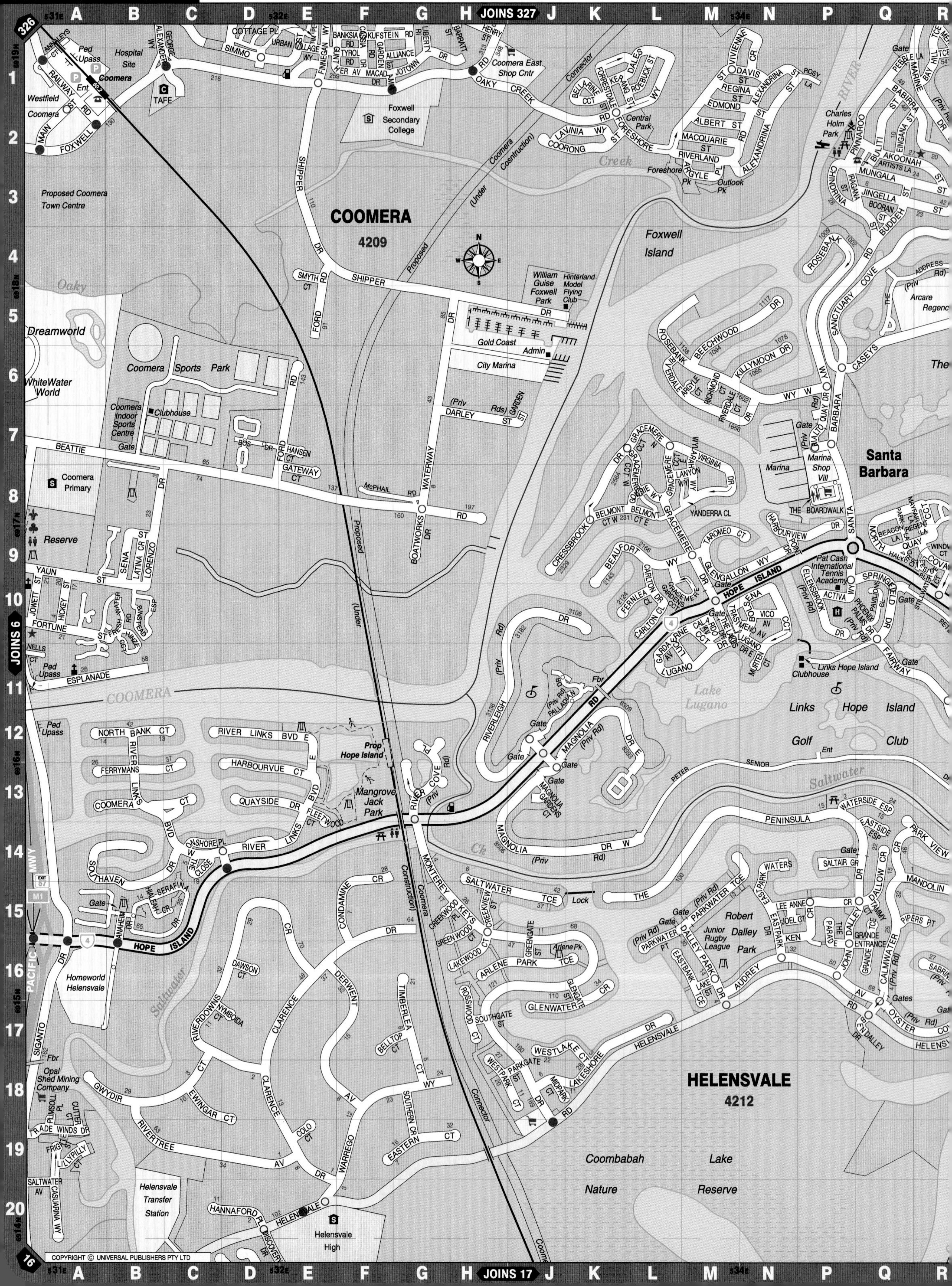

JOINS 327

COOMERA
4209

HELENSVALE
4212

Santa Barbara

Foxwell Island

Dreamworld

WhiteWater World

Westfield Coomera

Hospital Site

TAFE

Coomera Secondary College

Foxwell Secondary College

Proposed Coomera Town Centre

Coomera Sports Park

Coomera Indoor Sports Centre

Clubhouse

Coomera Primary

Reserve

William Guise Foxwell Park

Hinterland Model Flying Club

Gold Coast City Marina

Admin

Coomera East Shop Cntr

Central Park

Charles Holm Park

Marina Shop Vill

THE BOARDWALK

Pat Cash International Tennis Academy

Links Hope Island Clubhouse

Links Hope Island Golf Club

Lake Lugano

Prop Hope Island

Mangrove Jack Park

Homeworld Helensvale

Robert Dalley Park

Junior Rugby League

Opal Shed Mining Company

Helensvale Transfer Station

Helensvale High

Coombabah Lake Nature Reserve

Saltwater

PACIFIC MWY M1

JOINS 6

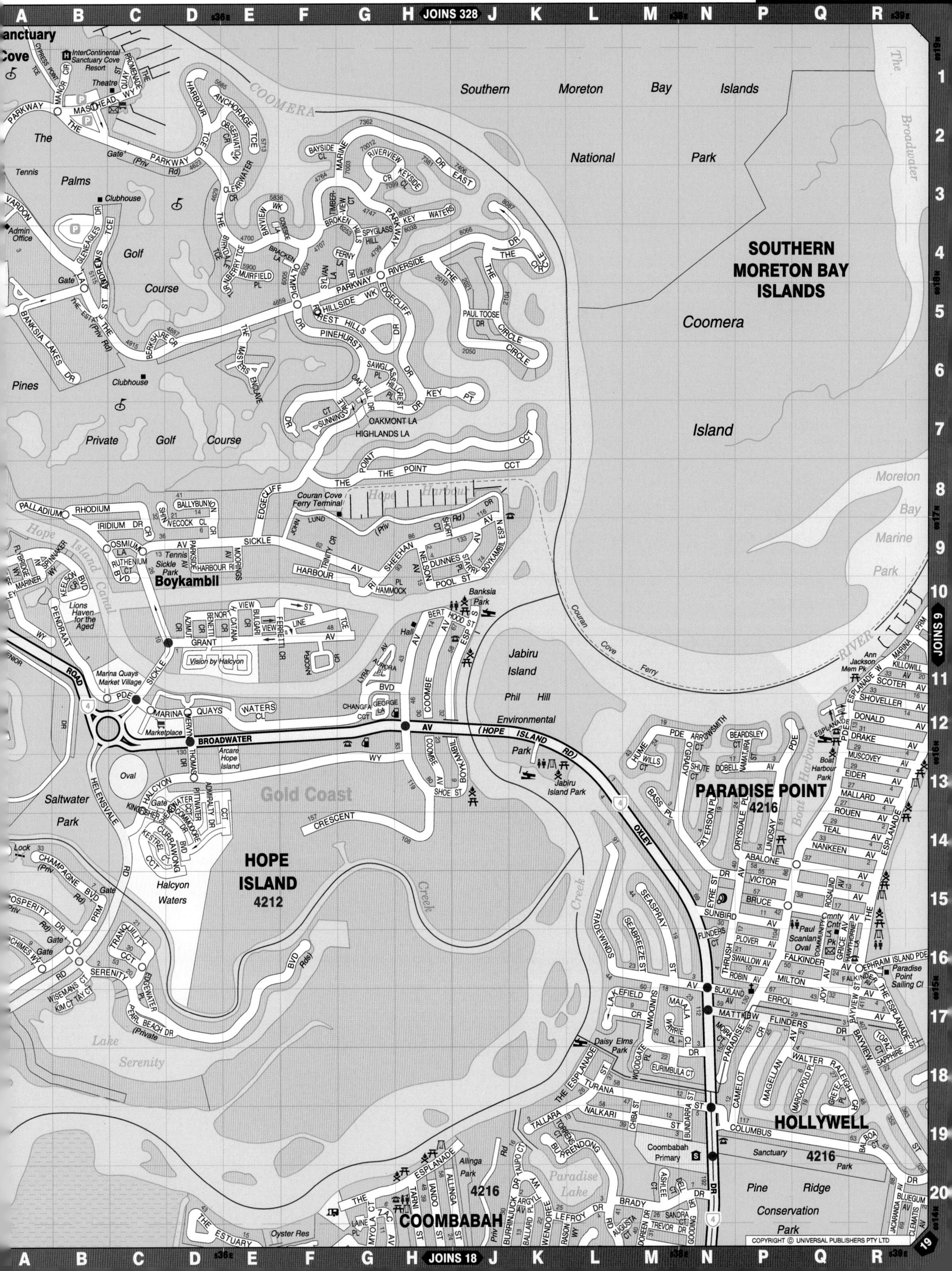

MAP 8
1 KILOMETRE EQUALS 4 GRID SQUARES
JOINS 328
JOINS 18

SOUTHERN
MORETON BAY
ISLANDS

Southern   Moreton   Bay   Islands

National   Park

Coomera

Island

Moreton
Bay
Marine
Park

The Broadwater

Sanctuary Cove

The Palms

Golf Course

Private Golf Course

Pines

Boykambil

Couran Cove Ferry Terminal

Hope Harbour

Hope Island Canal

Lions Haven for the Aged

Marina Quays Market Village

Vision by Halcyon

Marina Quays Marketplace

Arcare Hope Island

Jabiru Island

Phil Hill Environmental Park

Jabiru Island Park

Banksia Park

Hall

Gold Coast

Saltwater Park

HOPE ISLAND
4212

Halcyon Waters

Oval

Lake Serenity

Lake

PARADISE POINT
4216

Paul Scanlan Oval

Paradise Point Sailing Club

Ephraim Island Pde

Boat Harbour Park

HOLLYWELL
4216

Sanctuary Park

Pine Ridge Conservation Park

Paradise Lake

Coombabah Primary

COOMBABAH
4216

Allinga Park

Daisy Elms Park

Oyster Res

The Esplanade

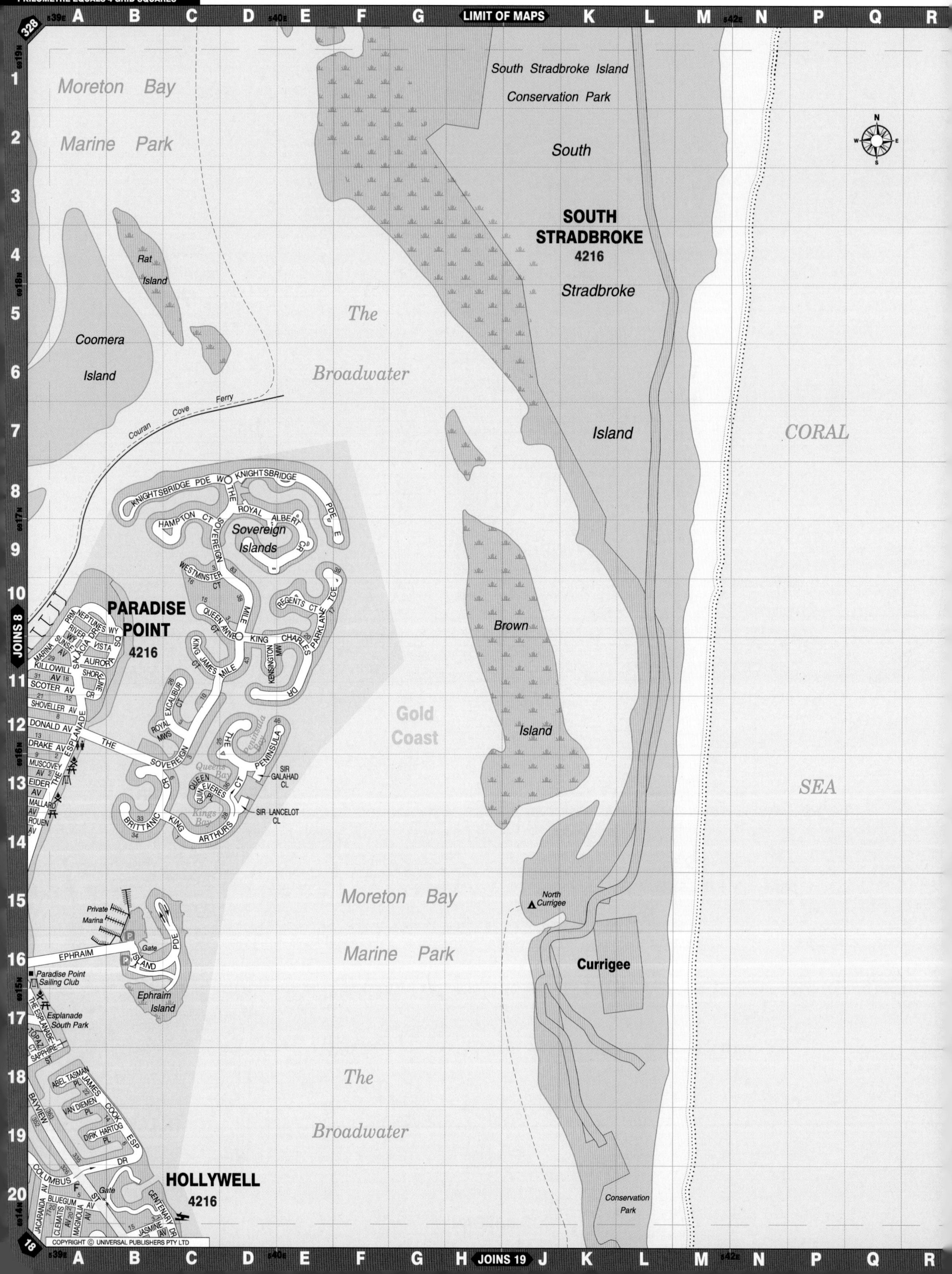

MAP 9
1 KILOMETRE EQUALS 4 GRID SQUARES

328

LIMIT OF MAPS

A B C D E F G H K L M N P Q R

Moreton Bay

Marine Park

South Stradbroke Island
Conservation Park

South

SOUTH STRADBROKE
4216

Stradbroke

Rat Island

The

Island

Broadwater

CORAL

Coomera Island

Couran Cove Ferry

KNIGHTSBRIDGE PDE W
KNIGHTSBRIDGE
THE
HAMPTON CT
ROYAL ALBERT
PDE E
Sovereign Islands

WESTMINSTER CT
REGENTS CT
PARKLANE TCE

PARADISE POINT
4216

QUEEN ANNE
KING
CHARLES
MILE
KING JAMES CT
KENSINGTON MW
Brown

NEPTUNES WY
AURORA
KILLOWILL AV
SCOTER AV
Island

SHOVELLER AV
ROYAL MWS
EXCALIBUR CT
THE PENINSULA
Gold Coast

DONALD AV
THE ESPLANADE
THE SOVEREIGN CR
Queens Bay
SIR GALAHAD CL

DRAKE AV
MUSCOVEY AV
QUEEN GUINEVERES
SIR LANCELOT CL

EIDER AV
Kings Bay
KING ARTHURS
SEA

MALLARD AV
ROUEN AV
BRITTANIC

Moreton Bay

North Currigee

Private Marina

Marine Park

EPHRAIM
Gate
PDE
ISLAND

Currigee

Paradise Point
Sailing Club

THE ESPLANADE

Esplanade South Park

Ephraim Island

TOPAZI CT
SAPPHIRE ST

The

ABEL TASMAN PL
JAMES ST
VAN DIEMEN PL

Broadwater

BAYVIEW
COOK ESP
DIRK HARTOG PL

COLUMBUS DR
F
Gate
HOLLYWELL
4216

JACARANDA AV
BLUEGUM AV
CLEMATIS
MAGNOLIA AV
CENTENARY DR
JASMINE

Conservation Park

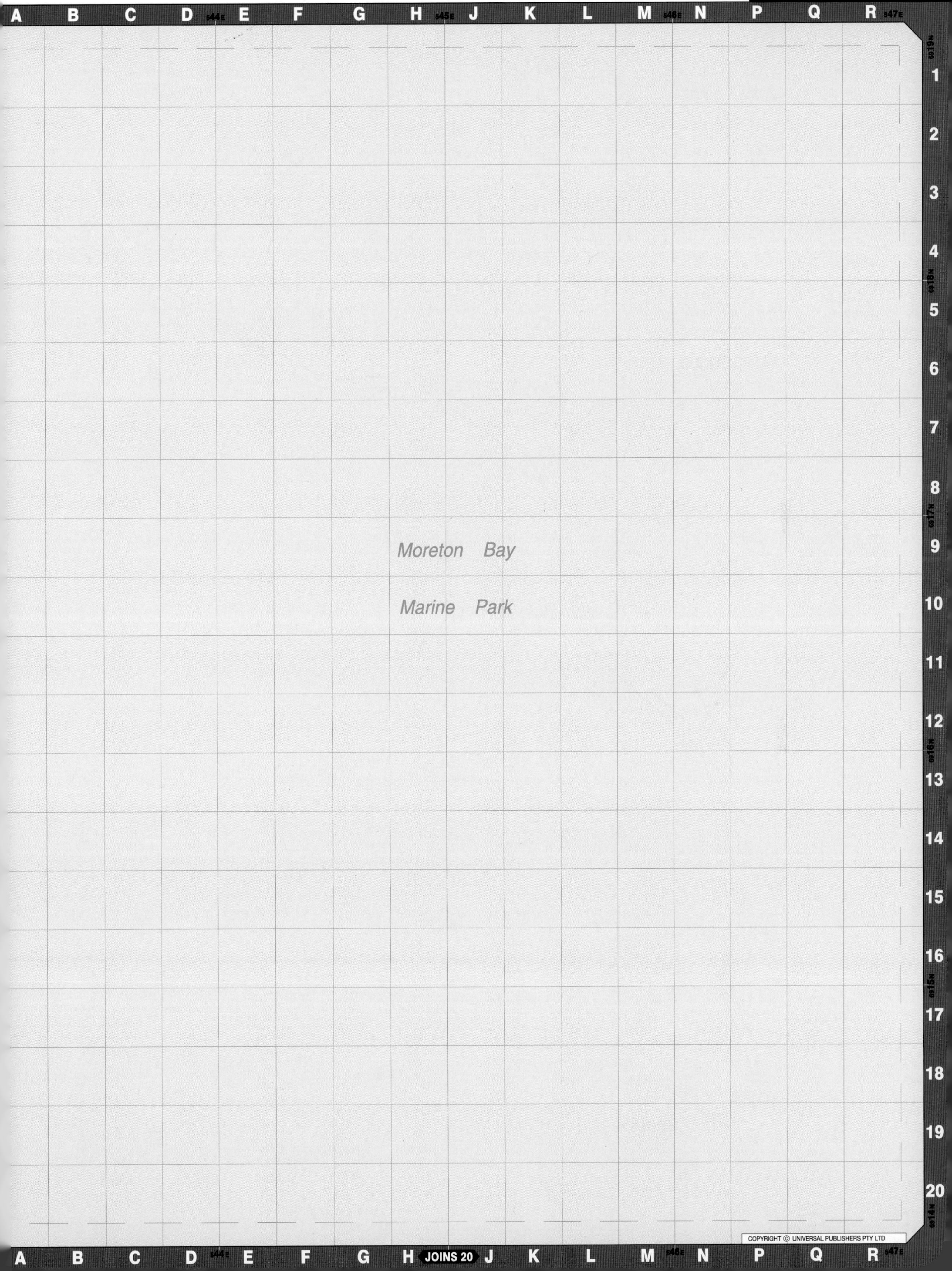

MAP 10
1 KILOMETRE EQUALS 4 GRID SQUARES

A B C D s44e E F G H s45e J K L M s46e N P Q R s47e

1 2 3 4 5 6 7 8 9 10 11 12 13 14 15 16 17 18 19 20

s19n s18n s17n s16n s15n s14n

Moreton Bay

Marine Park

MAP 11
1 KILOMETRE EQUALS 4 GRID SQUARES

A B C D s08ᴇ E F G H **JOINS 1** J K L M s10ᴇ N P Q R

s07ᴇ

MUNDOOLUN
4285

Logan

LIMIT OF MAPS

St Johns
Cemetery

ALBERT RIVER

BEAUDESERT
MUNDOOLUN
BRIDGE

Albert River
Wines

RIVER

Canungra

Fred
Bucholz
Park

WALNUT RD

BEENLEIGH

VINEYARD

WY

90

LARCH

MUNDOOLUN

RD

16 90

RD

FOUR MILE

TREMAYNE RD

BEATTIE RD

Ck

Flagstone
Creek
Park

BEENLEIGH

RD

ALBERT

3074

FLAGSTONE CREEK

RFB

BEAUDESERT

Flagstone

Scenic Rim

LA

BIRNAM
4285

90

16

A B C s08ᴇ D E F G H **JOINS 21** J K L M s10ᴇ N P Q R

MAP **12**
1 KILOMETRE EQUALS 4 GRID SQUARES

A B C D s12E E F G H **JOINS 2** J K L M s14E N P Q R s15E **3**

s14H

1

TAMBORINE
4270

2

HAZEL RD 124

RD 218

92

RD

RD

LA

PALOMINO

STRINGYBARK RD 66

LEACH

3

PARKES CT 34
186

144 DEVON 37
CHANINA 28 CT 5

DR 71

4

VONDA YOUNGMAN 232
DONALD CT 2
49

CURIO CT 18
MURRAY 88 DR

s13H

5

MINDOOLUN

RD 89
CHESTNUT 10 37 RD

IRONBARK RD 2

GREY 20 DR 61

RD 127

6

CONNECTION 869

N
W E
S

7

810

s12H

8

9

10

JOINS 13

11

ROAD 796

BOYLAND
4275

12

s11H

13

90
0

MUNDOOLUN

14

15

CONNECTION 815

16

s10H

17

Ck

18

19

RD 470
BIDDADDABA

ROAD

20

90
0

s09H

A B C D s12E E F G H **JOINS 22** J K L M s14E N P Q R s15E **23**

MAP 13
1 KILOMETRE EQUALS 4 GRID SQUARES

JOINS 3

TAMBORINE
4270

Forest

Reserve

Tamborine Mountain
Caravan & Camping

Thunderbird Park
Tourist Complex

The Sentinel

Transfer
Station

Tamborine Rainforest
Skywalk

TAMBORINE
MOUNTAIN
4272

Falls

Cameron
Falls

Tamborine National Park

Tamborine Mtn
(Hendersons Knob)
551m

John Dickson
Conservation
Park

Mt Tamborine
Convention Centre
(Camp Panorama)

KESWICK RD

BEACON

CIBOLA

CHALMETTE

FREEMONT

SIERRA

DR OCOLA CT

COLVILLE

WINEMA

WITCHES CH

CHALLIS DR

LASSEN DR

SEQUOIA

NICOLET DR

SHILOH DR

BOISE CT

KOOTENAI

PUATT PL

North
Tamborine

BEACON

Scenic Rim

Tamborine
Mountain
College

North
Tamborine
Sports
Centre

SES

Cmnty
Cntr

GEISSMANN ST

NORTH TOOMAN

RACQ
BANK

Cncl
Off

YUULONG

RD

Capo Di Monte
FIGTREE
PINE
GR
CASUAR
(Priv Rds)

CAPO LA

MONTE ST

GRIFFITH ST

Doughty
Pk

KIDD ST

REEVE RD

MAIN ST

RD

Tamborine
National Park

GEISSMANN

TAYLOR LA

TAYLOR

PresCare
Roslyn
Lodge

Youngman
Family
Park

CURTIS

Tamborine

Manitzky
Park

MANITZKY

Witches
Falls
Winery

RD

MOUNTAIN

Cem

Mason
Wines

ROSLYN CT

Jeh Wit

Tamborine
Mountain
High

BOYLAND
4275

National

Witches
Falls

Park

Witches
Falls
Park

WESTERN

TAMBORINE RD

HARTLEY

HOLT

Holt
Pk

The Cedar Creek Estate
Vineyard & Winery
Glow Worm
Caves

Rotary
Lookout

MAIN RD

WEST

LONG RD

Netball

Tamborine

JOINS 23

MAP 14
1 KILOMETRE EQUALS 4 GRID SQUARES

JOINS 4

WONGAWALLAN
4210

Eagle Heights
4271

Tamborine National Park

Tamborine National Park

Botanic Gardens

Tamborine National Park

Tamborine Heights Pk

Tamborine National RD Park

Info Bay

Justins

Harold Jenyns

OXENFORD RD

TAMBORINE

MACDONNELL

WONGAWALLAN

Eagle Heights RD

Witches Chase Cheese Company

Tamborine Mtn Heritage Cntr

Tamborine Mountain Pmy

Lions Park

CURTIS

Tamborine National Park

GUANABA
4210

Tamborine National Park

Gold Coast

Jenyns Falls

Stony Ck

Running Ck

Tamborine Ck

WELCHES RD

Guanaba Ck

GUANABA CREEK

Hollindale Family Park

Hollindale Ck

WHITTINGS RD

JOINS 15

JOINS 24

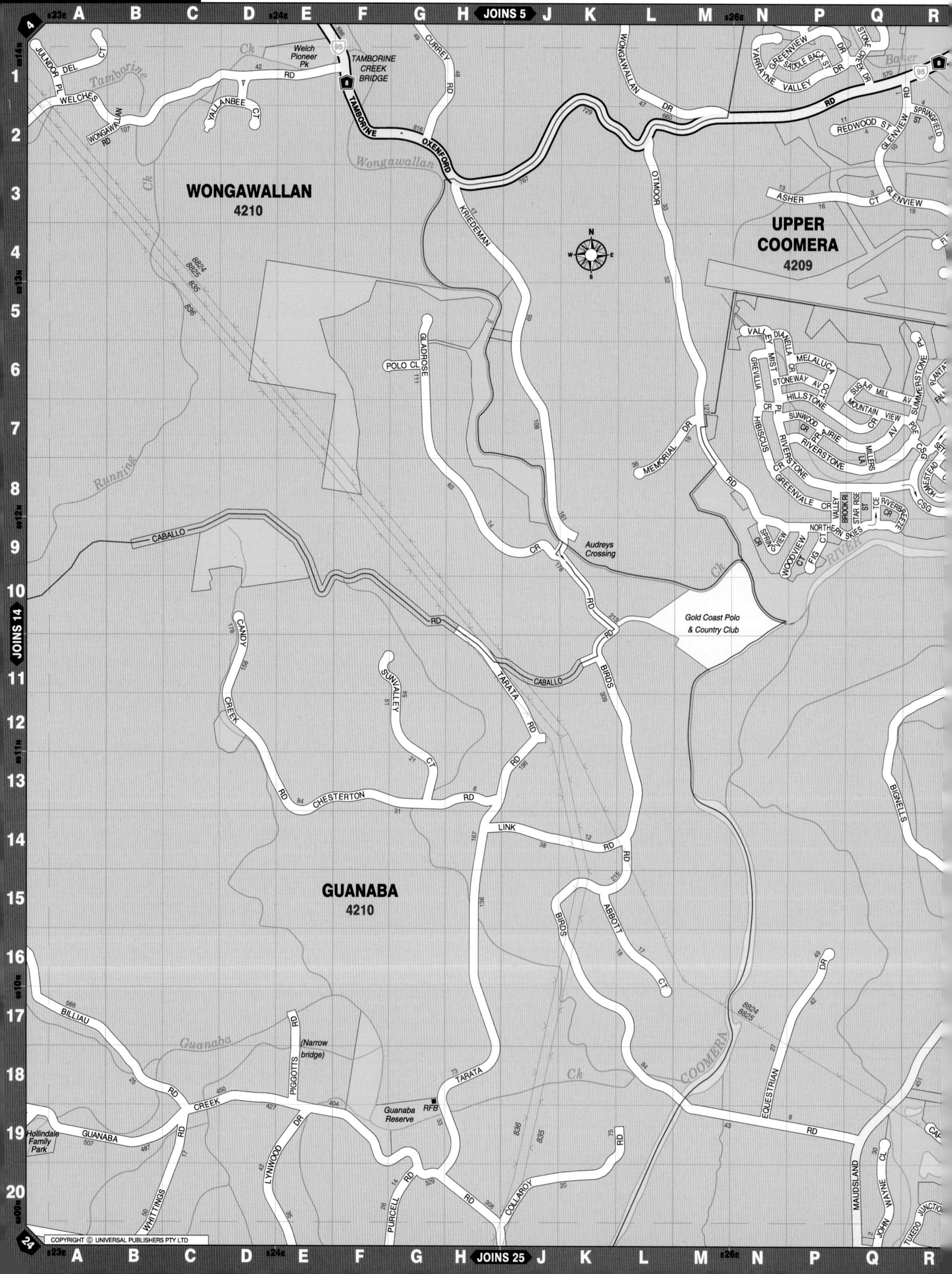

MAP 15
1 KILOMETRE EQUALS 4 GRID SQUARES

JOINS 5

WONGAWALLAN
4210

UPPER COOMERA
4209

GUANABA
4210

Tamborine Ck

Welch Pioneer Pk

TAMBORINE CREEK BRIDGE

Wongawallan Ck

Running Ck

Audreys Crossing

Gold Coast Polo & Country Club

Guanaba Reserve

RFB

Hollindale Family Park

(Narrow bridge)

Guanaba Ck

Coomera Ck

JOINS 14

JOINS 25

MAP 16
1 KILOMETRE EQUALS 4 GRID SQUARES

JOINS 6 (top)

JOINS 26 (bottom)

JOINS 17 (right side)

Gold Coast

OXENFORD 4210

MAUDSLAND 4210

PACIFIC PINES 4211

Studio Village

Warner Bros Movie World Film Studios

Paradise Country

Australian Outback Spectacular

Wet 'N' Wild Water World

Gold Coast Holiday Park

Gambamora Park

Oxenford Primary

Oxenford Quarries

John Muntz Causeway

JOHN MUNTZ CAUSEWAY

TAMBORINE

Cades County Substation

Gaven Primary

Saltwater Park Skate Park

Park Lake Pmy

AFL Oval

Waterstar Pk

Jubilee Pmy

Superfish

COOMERA

Saltwater

COPYRIGHT © UNIVERSAL PUBLISHERS PTY LTD

MAP 17
1 KILOMETRE EQUALS 4 GRID SQUARES

JOINS 7

HELENSVALE
4212

Helensvale
Golf Club

OXENFORD
4210

Studio Village

PACIFIC PINES
4211

GAVEN
4211

Warner Bros Movie World

Australian Outback Spectacular

Wet 'n' Wild Water World

BIG4 Gold Coast Holiday Park

Helensvale High

Helensvale Primary

Discovery Park

Pacific Pines Primary

Pacific Pines High

Westfield Helensvale

Arcare Helensvale

Helensvale Plaza

Coombabah Lake

Ivan Gibbs Wetlands Reserve

Lakeside Country Club

Careel Reserve

Banksia Park

Reservoir Park

Railway Reserve

William Duckett White Park

JOINS 27

JOINS 16

MAP 18
1 KILOMETRE EQUALS 4 GRID SQUARES

JOINS 8

HOLLYWELL
4216

COOMBABAH
4216

Pine Ridge

Conservation

RUNAWAY BAY
4216

Park

Avalon Residential Resort

Emerald Gardens

Grassy Pk

Gateway Lifestyle Coombabah

Coombabah

Lakelands

Conservation

Area

Lake Runaway

Paradise Lake Care Cntr

Lake

Runaway Bay Sporting Complex Western Tennis Grounds

Sports Super Centre

Indoor Sports Complex

Netball

SES

Coombabah Waste Water Treatment Plant

Laboratory

Admin

Nursery

Animal Welfare

Coombabah Reserve

PEBBLE BEACH

THE BOWSPRIT

THE YARDARM

SMUGGERS

Bupa Runaway Bay

Coombabah Lake Conservation Park

Sunny Ridge Gardens

Gold Coast

Coombabah

Lakelands

Conservation

Area

Settlers Village

Coombabah High

Mason Field Southport

RUNWAY

DOUG BRUHN (Private Road) WY

Pine Ridge

Harbour Quays

COMPASS

NORTH QY

MIDDLE QY

SOUTH COMPASS

PARK VIEW LA

Grand Canal

Harbour Town

ARUNDEL
4214

A B Paterson College

O'Brien & Proud Families Park

BIGGERA WATERS
4216

HWY

Junior Motorcycle Club

Business Centre

Harbour Town

Cinema

Harbourside Residential Resort Over 50's

Treasure Island

LABRADOR
4215

Roy Neal Reserve

Ngulli Bui Park

Morrie Glasman Oval Golden Wheel

Rotary Park

Woodlands Lodge

AFC

Cooke Murphy Oval

Industrial Area

COPYRIGHT © UNIVERSAL PUBLISHERS PTY LTD

JOINS 28

JOINS 19

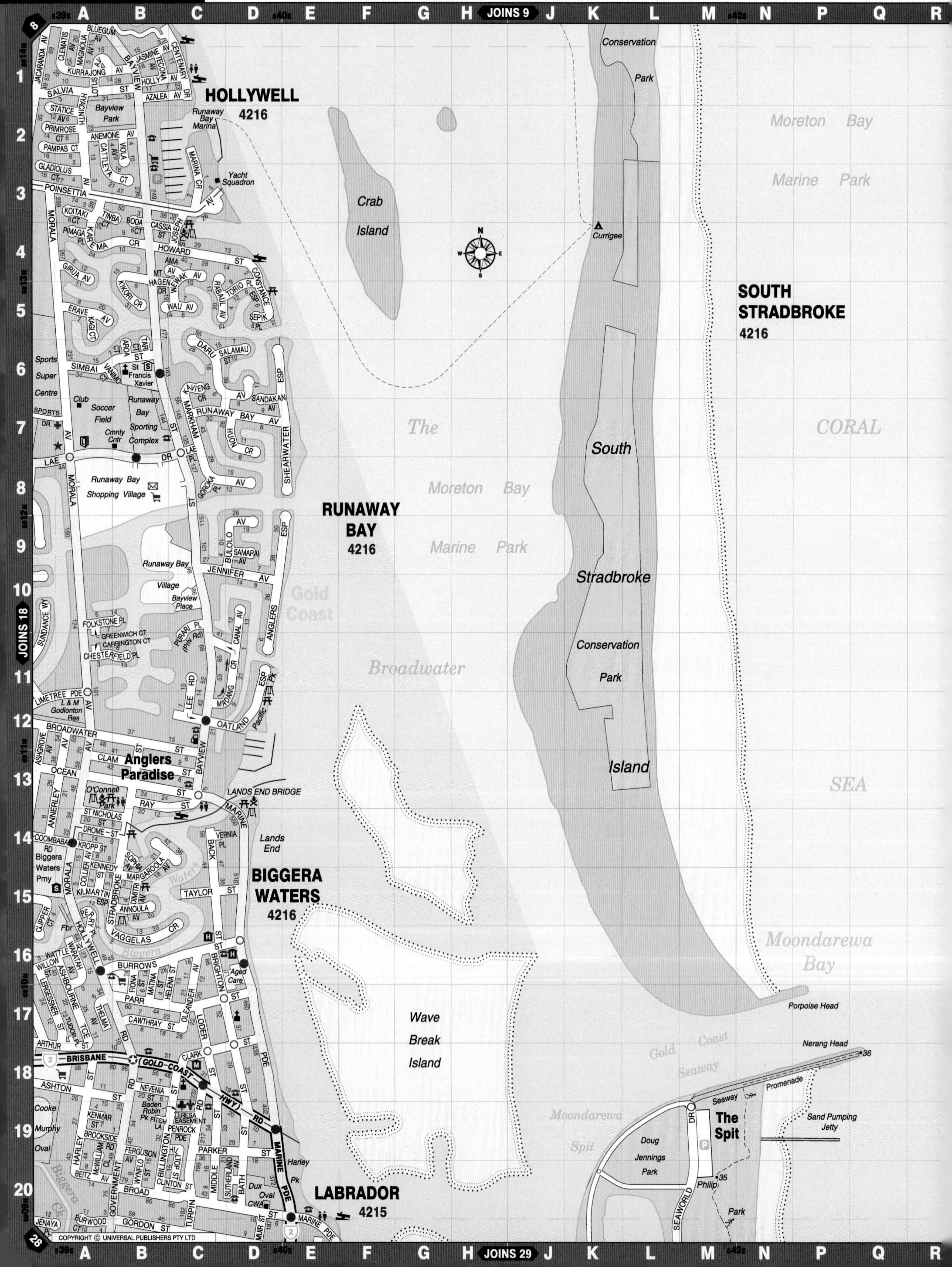

MAP 19
1 KILOMETRE EQUALS 4 GRID SQUARES

JOINS 9

HOLLYWELL
4216

RUNAWAY BAY
4216

SOUTH STRADBROKE
4216

Conservation Park

Moreton Bay

Marine Park

Crab Island

Currigee

South Stradbroke

Conservation Park

Island

The

Moreton Bay

Marine Park

Broadwater

CORAL

SEA

Gold Coast

Anglers Paradise

BIGGERA WATERS
4216

Lands End

LANDS END BRIDGE

Wave Break Island

Moondarewa Bay

Porpoise Head

Nerang Head

Gold Coast Seaway

Moondarewa Spit

Seaway Promenade

Sand Pumping Jetty

Doug Jennings Park

The Spit

Seaworld

Philip Park

LABRADOR
4215

Runaway Bay Marina

Yacht Squadron

Bayview Park

St Francis Xavier

Runaway Bay Sporting Complex

Soccer Field

Club

Cmnty Cntr

Runaway Bay Shopping Village

Runaway Bay Village

Bayview Place

Sports Super Centre

SPORTS

Godlonton Res

O'Connell Park

St Nicholas

Aged Care

Biggera Waters Pmy

Brisbane

GOLD COAST HWY

JOINS 18

JOINS 29

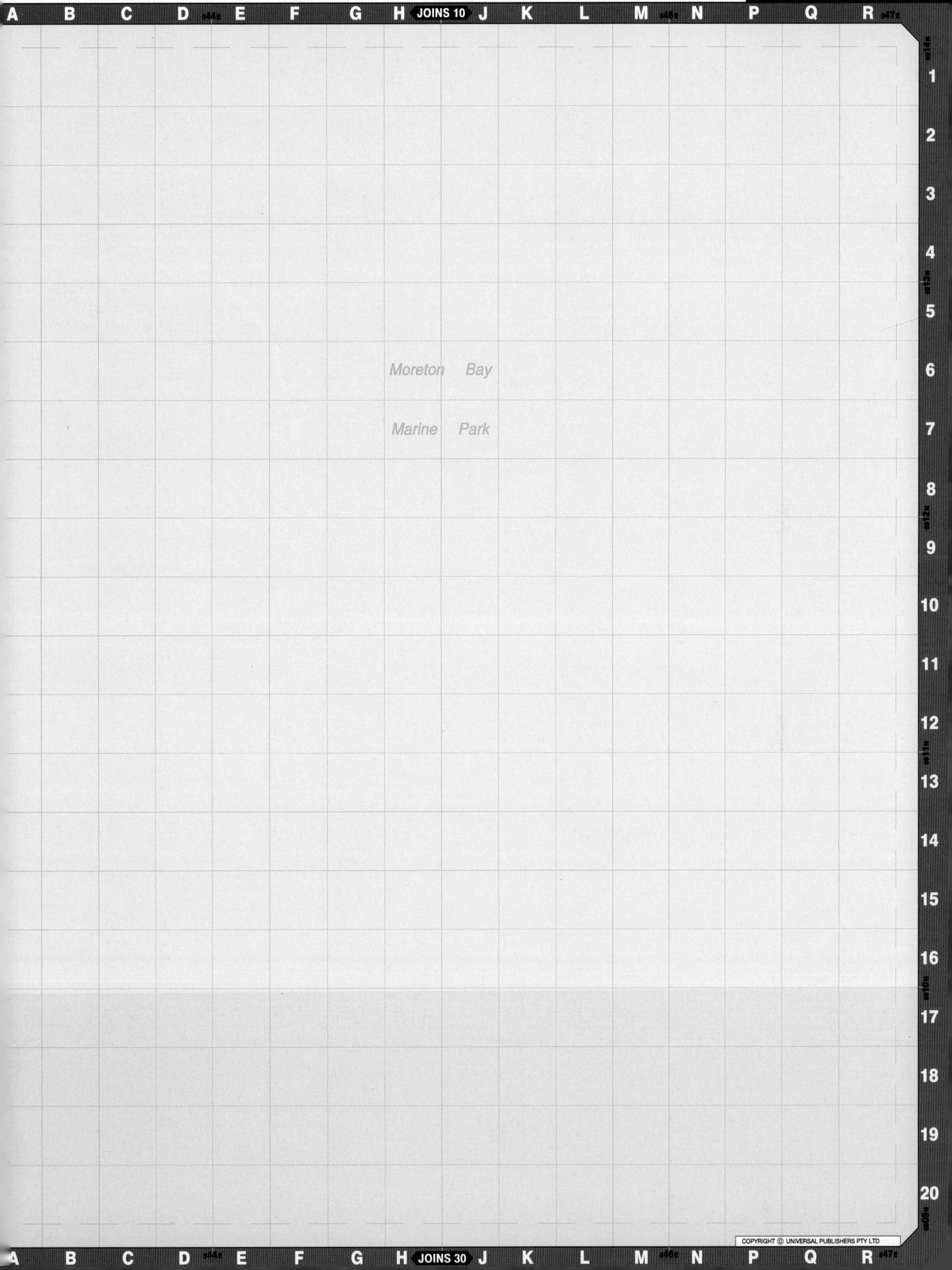

MAP 20
1 KILOMETRE EQUALS 4 GRID SQUARES

A B C D E F G H **JOINS 10** J K L M N P Q R

Moreton   Bay

Marine   Park

JOINS 10

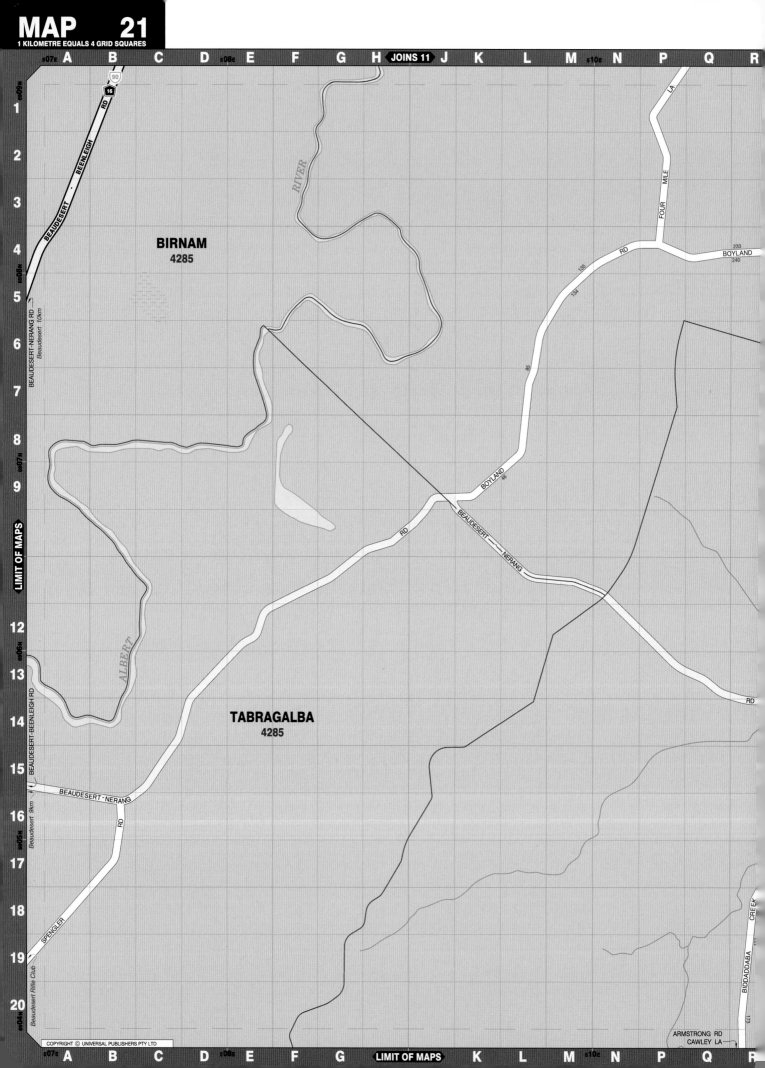

MAP 22
1 KILOMETRE EQUALS 4 GRID SQUARES

BOYLAND
4275

WONGLEPONG
4275

BIDDADDABA
4275

BENOBBLE
4275

Scenic Rim

CAVELL
BRIDGE

JOINS 12

JOINS 23

MUNDOOLUN CONNECTION ROAD

BEAUDESERT - NERANG

BIDDADDABA RD

CLARK RD

GRAHAMS DIP RD

REISER LA

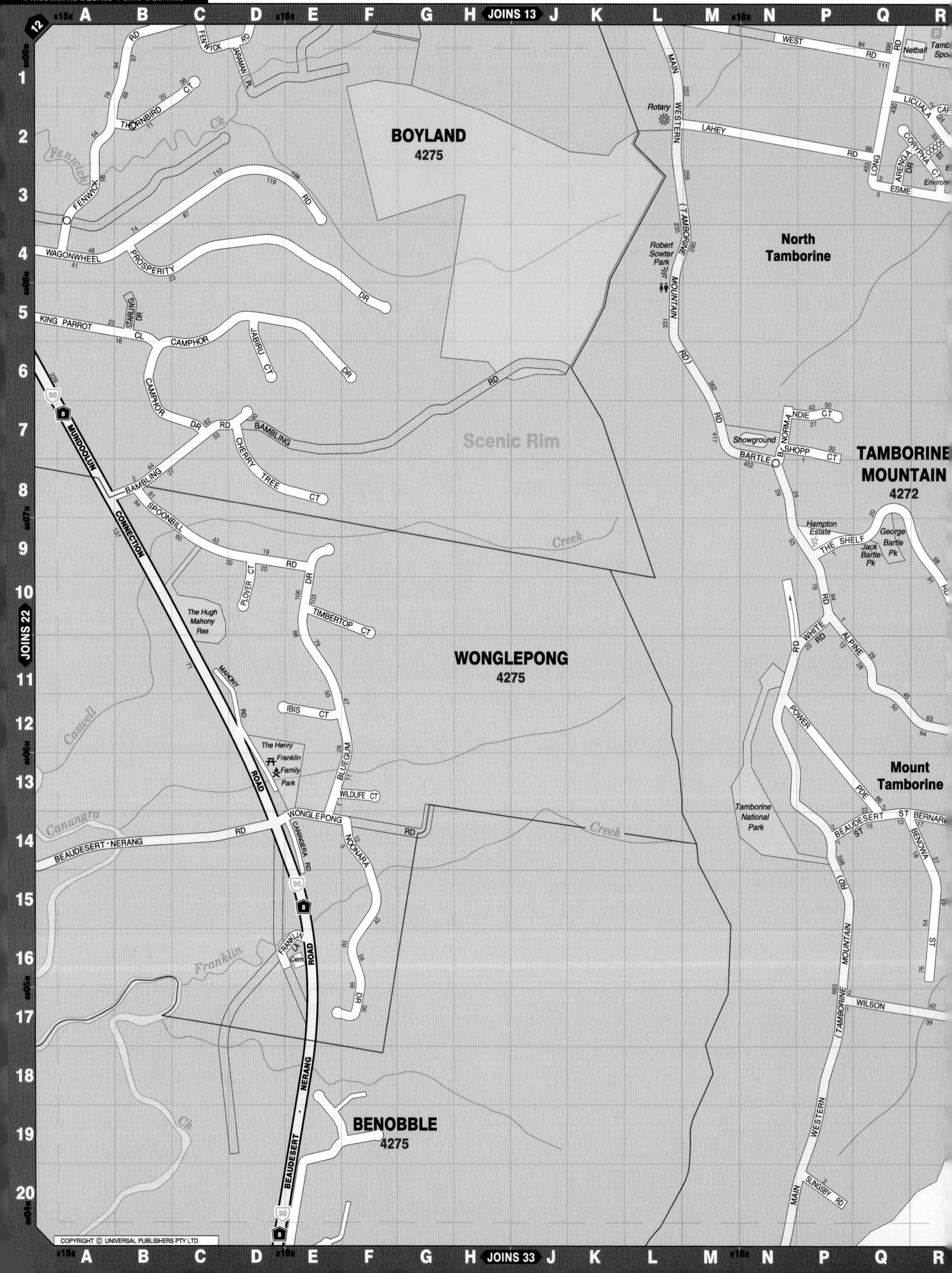

MAP 23
1 KILOMETRE EQUALS 4 GRID SQUARES

12

A B C D E F G H **JOINS 13** J K L M N P Q R

BOYLAND
4275

North Tamborine

Scenic Rim

TAMBORINE MOUNTAIN
4272

WONGLEPONG
4275

Mount Tamborine

BENOBBLE
4275

Rotary

Robert Sowter Park

Showground

Hampton Estate

THE SHELF

George Bartle Pk
Jack Bartle Pk

Tamborine National Park

The Hugh Mahony Res

The Henry Franklin Family Park

Cem

MUNDOOLUN CONNECTION ROAD

BEAUDESERT - NERANG ROAD

NERANG ROAD

BEAUDESERT ROAD

CANUNGERA RD

Fenwick Ck
Caswell Ck
Canungra Ck
Franklin Ck

Creek

THORNBIRD RD
JARMAN PL
FENWICK
WAGONWHEEL
PROSPERITY
KING PARROT
CAMPHOR DR
CAMPHOR RD
JABIRU CT
BAMBLING
CHERRY TREE CT
SPOONBILL
PLOVER CT
TIMBERTOP CT
IBIS CT
BLUEGUM
WILDLIFE CT
WONGLEPONG RD
NOONARA
MAHONY RD
FRANKLIN LA

MAIN WESTERN
LAHEY
TAMBORINE MOUNTAIN RD
WEST RD
Netball
LICUALA
CORYPHA CT
ARENGA DR
ESME
LONG RD
NORMA
BARTLE
SHOPP
NDIE CT
WHITE RD
ALPINE
POWER
BEAUDESERT RD
BERNARD ST
BENOWA ST
PDE
TAMBORINE MOUNTAIN RD
WILSON
MAIN WESTERN
SLINGSBY RD

90
8

COPYRIGHT © UNIVERSAL PUBLISHERS PTY LTD

JOINS 22

MAP 24
1 KILOMETRE EQUALS 4 GRID SQUARES

A B C D s20e E F G H **JOINS 14** J K L M s22e N P Q R s23e

15

Creek

GUANABA
4210

WHITTINGS RD

UZI WY

MORTLOCK RD

SHERLOCK CT

Millet Pk

CAREY PDE

CADE AV

JUSTIN DR

AV

Gorge

Guanaba

MYSTERY

GUANABA RD

ROMANA CT

RD

LEONA CT

Gold Coast

Rope, Little Red Lower Falls

HENRI

BALI

JAVA CT

SUMATRA CT

ROBERT

MADURA

BORNEO

KAISER

SUMBA CT

FLORES CT

LOMBOK CT

CELEBES CT

CLAGIRABA
4211

BOOGARD PL

JOINS 25

TAMBORINE CT

AMBOINE CT

TIMOR CT

Guanaba

GUANABA RD

Wilsons Lookout

NERANG

KING PARROT CT

St Bernard Falls

TCE

ALPINE

St Bernard Pmy

BEN NEVIS ST

SIGANTO

Guanaba Park

GOLF COURSE ST

RD

Tamborine Mountain Golf Club

Clubhouse

JENYNS

PACIFIC

LOOKOUT PDE

OCEAN VIEW PDE

DR

STAGHORN

ELKHORN RD

LANDMAN

RD CT

WILDFLOWER CT

MACROZAMIA

DR

SCHOOL RD

ROSSER ST

Rosser Pk

BIANO RD

MANNKA CT

RD

WOO VERA

LAMINGTON PDE

GORGE

PROSPECT ST

BATEKE

YOUNG ST

Land Warfare Centre

WITHEREN
4275

A B C D s20e E F G H **JOINS 34** J K L M s22e N P Q R s23e

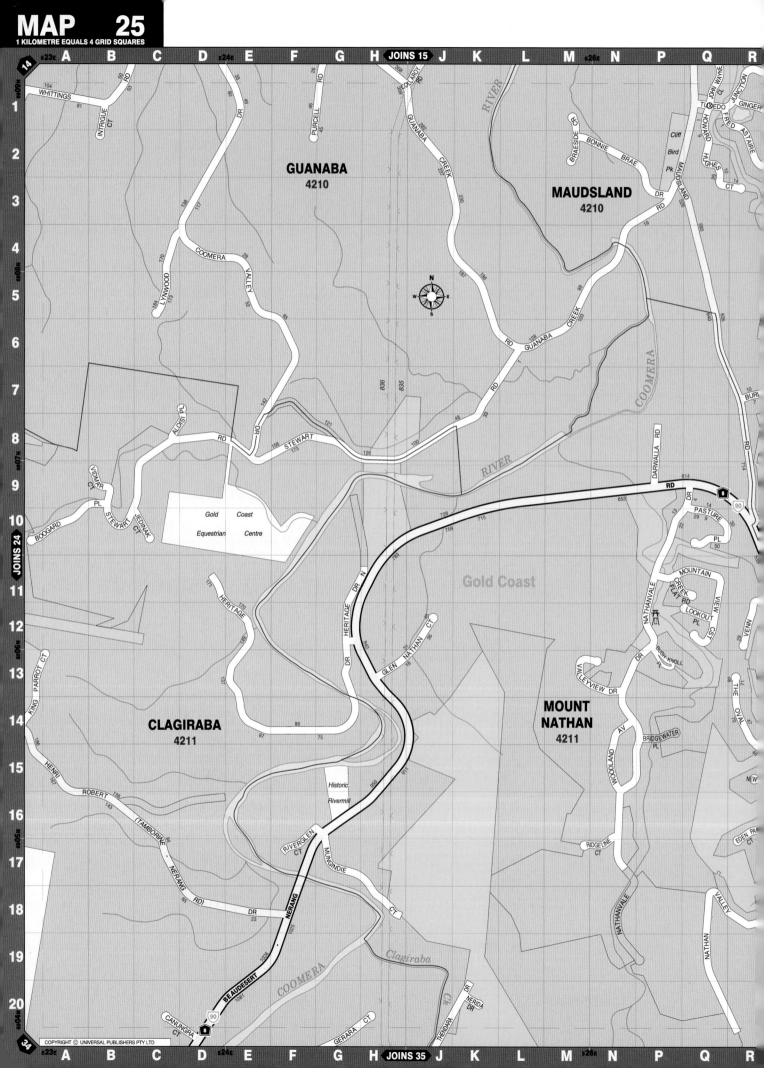

MAP 26
1 KILOMETRE EQUALS 4 GRID SQUARES

JOINS 16

JOINS 36

JOINS 27

PACIFIC PINES
4211

Nerang

NERANG
4211

Forest   Reserve

Restricted   Vehicle   Access

Saltwater Ck

Coombabah

MAP 27
1 KILOMETRE EQUALS 4 GRID SQUARES

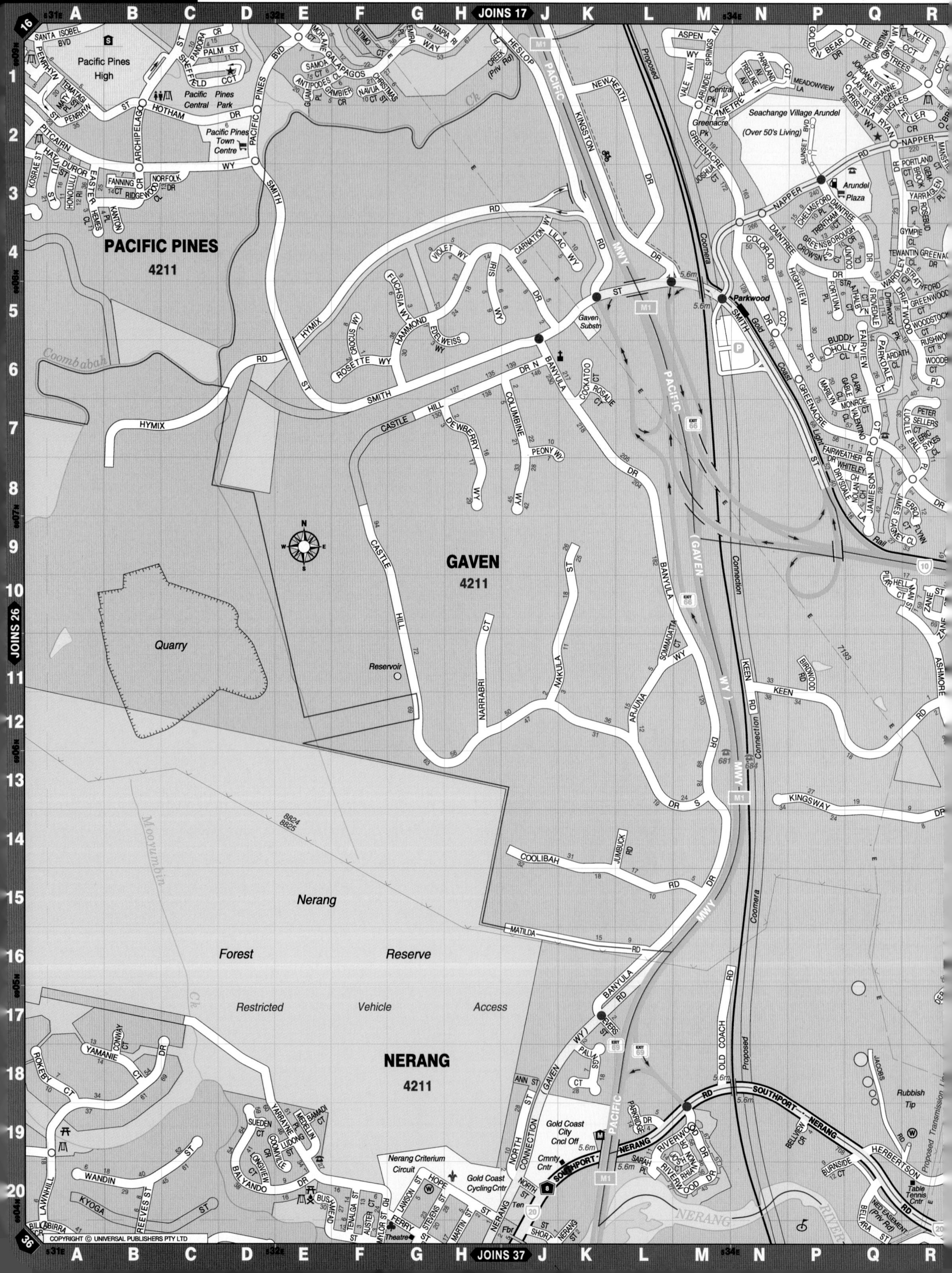

JOINS 17

PACIFIC PINES
4211

GAVEN
4211

NERANG
4211

Nerang

Forest   Reserve

Restricted   Vehicle   Access

Quarry

Reservoir

Pacific Pines High

Pacific Pines Town Centre

Seachange Village Arundel
(Over 50's Living)

Arundel Plaza

Parkwood

Gaven Substn

Nerang Criterium Circuit

Gold Coast Cycling Cntr

Gold Coast City Cncl Off

Rubbish Tip

Table Tennis Cntr

JOINS 26
JOINS 16
JOINS 36

MAP 28
1 KILOMETRE EQUALS 4 GRID SQUARES

JOINS 18

ARUNDEL 4214

LABRADOR 4215

PARKWOOD 4214

Parkwood International Golf Course

Gold Coast

MOLENDINAR 4214

SOUTHPORT 4215

ASHMORE 4214

Griffith University Gold Coast Campus

FOR MORE DETAIL SEE PAGE 71

Gold Coast Uni Hospital
GC Uni Hospital
Gold Coast Private Hospital
2018 Commonwealth Games
Athletes Village

Griffith University Gold Coast Campus (CHANCELLERY)

Qld Academies Health Sciences Campus

Griffith University Village

Gold Coast Pistol Range

Guardian Angels Catholic Pmy

Aquinas College

De Paul Villa

De Paul Manor Estate

Trinity Lutheran College Middle & Senior Schools

Trinity Lutheran College Pmy Sch

Bicentennial Park

Substation

Musgrave Park

Musgrave Hill Pmy

Southport Special Sch

Soccer Club

Keith Hunt Park

Hockey Club

Wally Fankhauser Sports Res

Southport Sharks

Southport Lawn Cemetery

Arthur Angove Park

Ashmore City

Ashmore Plaza

PCYC

Tenpin Bowl

Athletic Track

Ashmore Palms Holiday Village

Aveo The Domain Country Club

Aveo Ashmore

Hill View House

Ashmore Apex Park

Arundel Primary

Abbott Park

Clubhouse

Cmnty Cntr

JOINS 29

SMITH STREET

MOTORWAY

GOLD COAST

LABRADOR-CARRARA RD

NERANG ST

SOUTHPORT RD

ASHMORE RD

JOINS 38

COPYRIGHT © UNIVERSAL PUBLISHERS PTY LTD

19

MAP 29
1 KILOMETRE EQUALS 4 GRID SQUARES

JOINS 19

LABRADOR
4215

Heydon Heights

Musgrave Hill

Gold Coast

The Spit

SEAWORLD

Philip

Volunteer Marine Rescue

Sea World Resort

Sea World

Park

Port of Gold Coast Oceanside Cruise Ship Terminal Site

CORAL

Broadwater

Tuesley Park

Tuesleys Jetty

Broadwater Parklands

Grande Pacific

Anzac Park

Pier

Southport High

Southport Transit Cntr

Central Qld Uni
TAFE QLD Southport Campus

Washington Waters Park

Swimming Enclosure

Marina Mirage

Sheraton Mirage F'br

Mariners Cove

Water Police

Hollindale

Australian Navy Cadets

SOUTHPORT
4215

Ned Twohill Equestrian Centre
Pony Club

Cemetery

Southport Leagues Club

Southport Primary

Owen Park

Junior Rugby Sporting Hall of Fame

Gymnastics

St Hilda's

Business Centre

Court Hse

Southport

Australia Fair

Cinema

Liberty Swing

Southport Mall

Surgery Cntr

Nerang Street

Southport Substation

Southport South

Southport Hosp

Theatre Park

Queens

Andrews Family Centenary Park

RIVER

Marina

Southport Yacht Club

MAIN BEACH
4217

Main Beach

Southport SLSC

Surf Shed

Ret Vill

Spiritus Abri Home for the Aged

Rugby

James Overell Park

GOLD COAST BRIDGE

NERANG

Main Beach

SURFERS PARADISE
Paradise Waters
4217

The Southport School

Keebra Park High

Golden Age Ret Vill

The Southport School Preparatory School

Oval

Marana Gardens

Southport Park Shopping Centre

The Southport School

Macintosh Island

Narrow Neck

JOINS 39

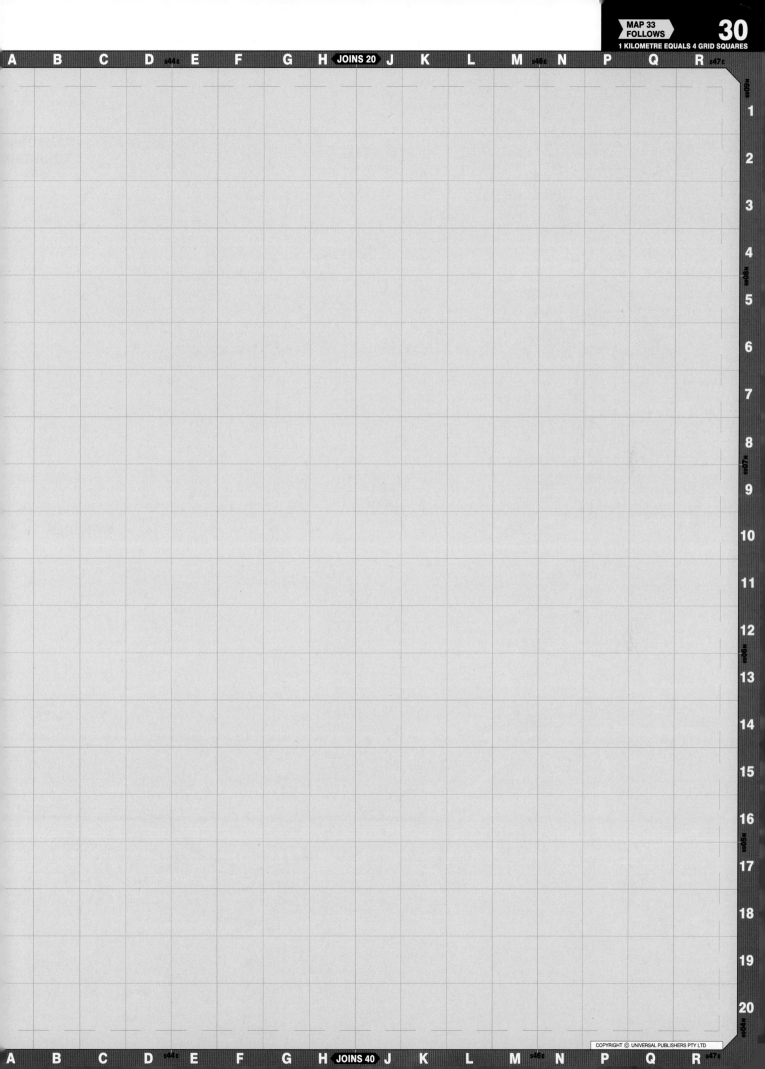

MAP 33
FOLLOWS
30
1 KILOMETRE EQUALS 4 GRID SQUARES

BENOBBLE
4275

TAMBORINE
MOUNTAIN
4272

Canungra

Daniels

NERANG

MALGUM

SHELLY CT

FENWYKE RD

KARRAKAS WY

BIRINBURRA

DANIELS

WENHAM CT

CCT

BEAUDESERT

RI

Creek

Scenic Rim

MAIN WESTERN RD

lane

RD

One

McCARTHY LA

Laheys

ADELAIDE CT

Lookout

MUNRO CT

Park

LAHEYS

DR

PIEBALD

DR

KNIGHT

WY

RI

BIMBUL CT

SEYMOUR

WOJEI

RI

Upper
Hairpin
Bend

WITHEREN
4275

Boike

Rd

ROXBOROUGH

BEASLEY

WY

ST

FINCH

Creek

PICNIC

HOWARD

RIVERBEND

WARUP CT

Riverbend
Drive
Park

FINCH RD

MANOR

CANUNGRA ST

DR

PL

BEAUDESERT

NERANG

LIMIT OF MAPS

REGAL DR

CT

MONARCH

SOVEREIGN CT

CHRISTIE

COBURG

Pmy

Lions Park

DJ Smith Pk

Moriarty
Community
Sporting
Complex

Canungra
Sports &
Recreation
Ground

ST

FINCH

KIDSTON

LAWTON

APPEL

FRANKLIN

TAMBORINE

ANZAC LA

STRACHAN

KIDSTON

KING

RD

ST

RSL

DUNCAN

PINE ST

JEROME ST

ST

TAMBORINE

ROAD

RFS

MOUNTAIN

CANUNGRA
4275

MURPHY
(Private)

LAWSON CT

LOHMANN

PARK

MAURITA CT

RD

GEIGER RD

NATIONAL

LAMINGTON

DOUBLE CROSSING RD

DARLINGTON

RANGE

Laheys
Tramway
Tunnel

CEMETERY RD

Works
Depot

Cem

NERANG

BEAUDESERT

BEECHMONT

BOIKE
(Private Rd)

Gate (Private Rd)

WAU

MILNE BAY RD

BORNEO

Gate (Private Rd)

DA NANG

NUI DAT

Gate
(Private Rd)

TARAKAN
(Private Rd)

FRANKLIN

KAPYONG WY

MAHONY

LAHEY CT

SKELLY PL

MASSEY PL

Gate

Private

BACK CREEK

FORMEYS

ALLOAH WY

RD

Kokoda
Barracks

O'Reillys Vineyards Canungra Valley

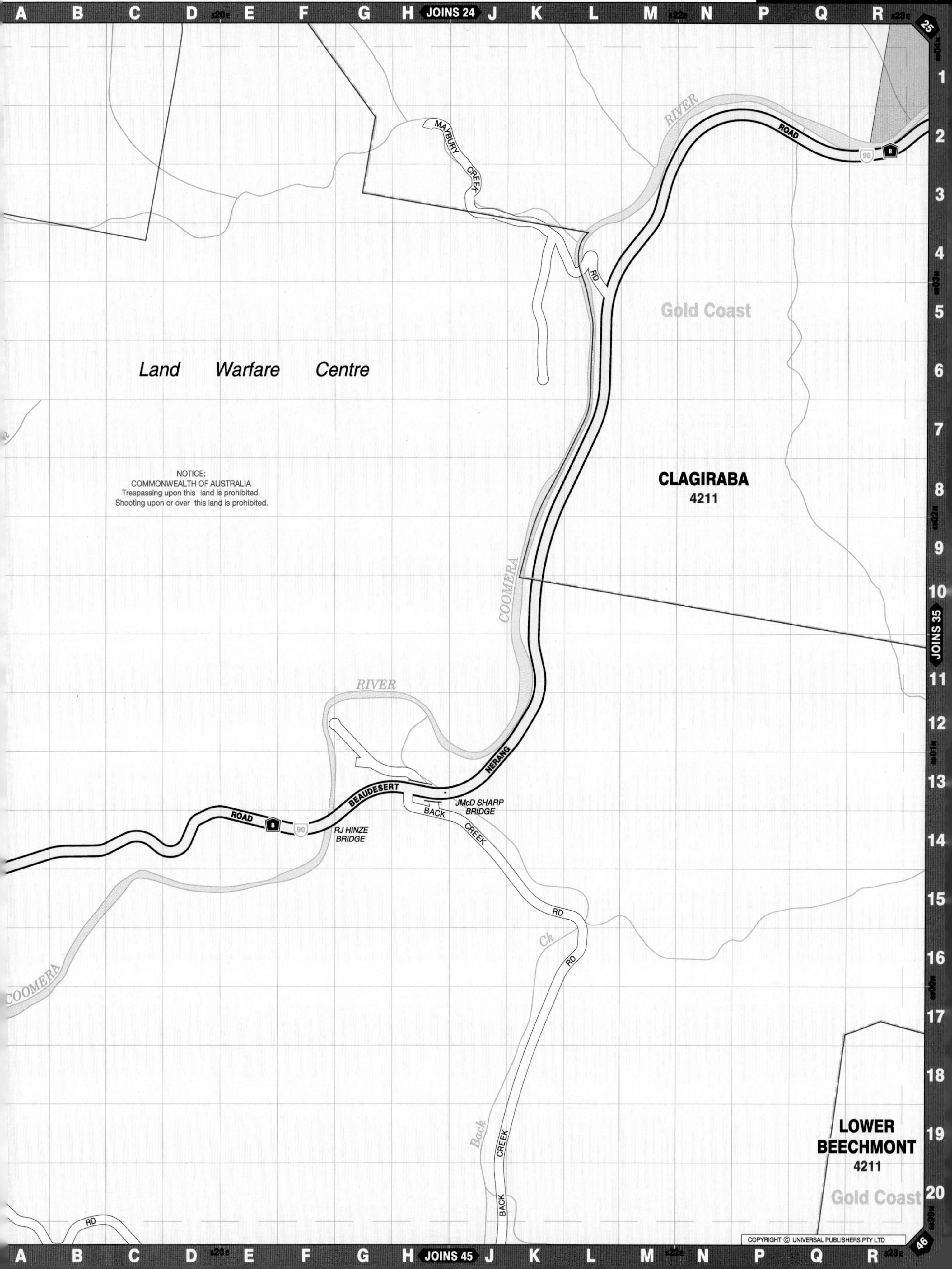

MAP 34
1 KILOMETRE EQUALS 4 GRID SQUARES

A B C D s20E E F G H JOINS 24 J K L M s22E N P Q R s23E 25

JOINS 24

MAYBURY CREEK

RIVER

ROAD

90 8

Gold Coast

RD

Land Warfare Centre

CLAGIRABA
4211

NOTICE:
COMMONWEALTH OF AUSTRALIA
Trespassing upon this land is prohibited.
Shooting upon or over this land is prohibited.

COOMERA

RIVER

NERANG

JOINS 35

BEAUDESERT

ROAD 8 90

RJ HINZE
BRIDGE

BACK

JMcD SHARP
BRIDGE

CREEK

RD

RD

Ck

COOMERA

Back

CREEK

BACK

LOWER
BEECHMONT
4211

Gold Coast

MAP 35
1 KILOMETRE EQUALS 4 GRID SQUARES

JOINS 25

A B C D E F G H J K L M N P Q R

COOMERA

RIVER

CANUNGRA CT

CLAGIRABA

(Causeway)

GERARA

FG WALKER BRIDGE

BEAUDESERT · NERANG

WITHEREN

CCT

GLEN

RD

Clagiraba

THENDARA

Little Clagiraba Reserve

RFB

(Causeway)

Mount Nathan Winery

MOUNT NATHAN
4211

Mt Nathan 286m

Land

Warfare

Centre

CLAGIRABA
4211

Ck

CLAGIRABA

DIAMANTINA CT

BARCOO

Ck

BELLISS RD

N
W E
S

Scenic Rim

Clagiraba

Little

Clagiraba

Gold Coast

HELLFIRE PASS

FREEMANS

CADAGI RD

Ck

Restricted Vehicle Access

BEECHMONT RD

BEECHMONT

Oaky

LA

Clagiraba

ADVANCETOW
4211

LOWER BEECHMONT
4211

BOTTLETREE

BEECHMONT

Scenic Res.

HOOP PINE CT

Ck

JOINS 34

JOINS 46

A B C D E F G H J K L M N P Q R

MAP 36

1 KILOMETRE EQUALS 4 GRID SQUARES

JOINS 26

JOINS 46

NERANG 4211

GILSTON 4211

Nerang Forest Reserve

Restricted Vehicle Access

State Forest

Silkwood Steiner

Reservoir

Nerang Pony Club

R A Stevens Bridge

Kamholtz Family Park

Hurst Family Park

Terry & Carol Moore Park

Riverpark

Homesteads Aged Care

The Grand Golf Club

Clubhouse

Private

Advancetown

Faust Family Park

Latimers Crossing

Gilston Hall

JOINS 37

MAP 38
1 KILOMETRE EQUALS 4 GRID SQUARES

SOUTHPORT

ASHMORE
4214

BENOWA
4217

Gold Coast

CARRARA
4211

Cypress Gardens

JOINS 39

MAP 39
1 KILOMETRE EQUALS 4 GRID SQUARES

JOINS 29

MAIN BEACH 4217

Paradise Waters

Cronin Island

Chevron Island

SOUTHPORT 4215

Southport Golf Club

Gold Coast

SURFERS PARADISE 4217

FOR MORE DETAIL SEE MAP 40

BENOWA 4217

Home of the Arts

Isle of Capri

BUNDALL 4217

Gold Coast Turf Club

Gold Coast Event Centre

Southport Racecourse

Girung Island

Sorrento

Rio Vista

Florida Gardens

BROADBEACH 4218

Rialto
Park

Surfers Paradise Rugby Union Club

BROADBEACH WATERS 4218

Moana Park

Cypress Gardens

Miami Keys

The Star Casino

Broadbeach Island

NERANG

NERANG-BROADBEACH RD

JOINS 49

JOINS 38

MAP 45 FOLLOWS

40

1 KILOMETRE EQUALS 8 GRID SQUARES

A B C D s44E E F G H JOINS 30 J K L s42E M N P Q s42SE R

1 2 3 4 5 6 7 8 9 10 11 12 13 14 15 16 17 18 19 20

CORAL SEA

CORAL

SEA

SURFERS PARADISE
4217

PARADISE PL
HIGMAN ST
SURFERS
Surfers Paradise Marriott Resort & Spa
Alpha Sovereign Hotel
ACACIA AV
BIRT AV
Paradise Resort Gold Coast
BLONDELL AV
OCEAN AV
Surfers Paradise North
ESPLANADE
NORFOLK AV
PANDANUS AV
(Priv Rd)
OAK
PINE AV
STAGHORN AV
QT
FERNY
PALM AV
Ocean Development Site
Bungy
Sling Shot
Vomitron
Adrenalin Park
Mini Golf
CYPRESS AV
Cypress Av
RIVERVIEW PDE
VIEW AV
Light
Wax Mus
Mantra on View Hotel
Piazza on the Boulevard
ELKHORN
Gold Coast
Chevron Renaissance Centre
AV
Vibe Hotel
Monte Carlo
ORCHID AV
Appel Pk
The Mark Centre
Circle on Cavill
Tenpin Bowl
Peppers Soul Surfers Paradise
Cavill Av
The Cavill Hotel
FERNY
CAVILL
Minus 5 Ice Lounge
AV
RSL
Paradise Centre
Hotel Grand Chancellor Surfers Paradise
BEACH RD
BLVD
Tenpin Bowl
SLSC
Transit Cntr
HANLAN ST
Islander Resort Hotel
ALISON
Underground
APPEL
SURFERS
TRICKETT ST
REMEMBRANCE
Pk
Mantra Legends Hotel
Laws & Hamilton Park
Eileen Peters Park
LAYCOCK ST
PARADISE ISLAND
Jack Philip McKinney Pk
CLIFFORD ST
voco
Surfers Paradise Q1
Gold Coast
NORTHCLIFFE
HAMILTON AV
Syn
PARADISE
MARKWELL AV
TCE
John Fraser Memorial Park
ENDERLEY AV
Light
GARFIELD
RIVER
VISTA ST
VIA
ROMA
Northcliffe
CAPRI BRIDGE
THORNTON
BMD Northcliffe SLSC
Sydney Hamilton KCSJ Family Park
AUBREY
DR
D'arcy Arms Motel
GOLD COAST HWY
FREDERICK ST
MARGHARITA PL
BRINDISI AV
AMALFI
FERN ST
TCE
Gold Coast
Beach
Surfers Paradise

JOINS 33

JOINS 34

CANUNGRA
4275

WITHEREN
4275

Scenic Rim

Land   Warfare   Centre

NOTICE:
COMMONWEALTH OF AUSTRALIA
Trespassing upon this land is prohibited
Shooting upon or over this land is prohibited.

FERNY GLEN
4275

COOMERA

FLYING FOX
4275

BEECHMONT
4211

Numinbah

Forest

Reserve

Restricted
Vehicle
Access

Rosins
Lookout

Conservation

Park

Rosins Lookout

ILLINBAH
4275

TUCKER   RIVER

LIMIT OF MAPS

No Through Rd

James Sharp
Mem Pk

(Low level
narrow
bridge)

BEECHMONT

Beechmont Pmy

JOINS 65

MAP 46
1 KILOMETRE EQUALS 2 GRID SQUARES

JOINS 35

JOINS 36

JOINS 37

JOINS 47

JOINS 57

JOINS 66

JOINS 67

LOWER BEECHMONT
4211

GILSTON
4211

TALLAI
4213

ADVANCETOWN
4211

MUDGEERABA
4213

Boomerang Farm Golf Course

NUMINBAH VALLEY
4211

NERANWOOD
4213

Advancetown Lake

Gold Coast

Cedar Lake Country Resort

Hinze Dam

Waterside Park

Spillway

(Narrow bridge)

Gate

Frank Chaston Sporting Field

Guinea Family Memorial Park

Numinbah Environmental Education Centre

Numinbah   Forest   Reserve

Restricted   Vehicle   Access

Gates closed between 6pm - 6am daily

Gate

RFB

Scenic Res

MURWILLUMBAH

NERANG

NERANG RIVER

RIVER

HOOP PINE CT

NARROW LEAF RD

TANGARA RD

ADVANCETOWN RD

GILSTON RD

PRENDER CT

DUNCAN RD

RED OAK DR

THE PANORAMA

PANORAMA RD

WORONGARY RD

ZIMMERMAN CT

ADVANCETOWN / MUDGEERABA RD

RANGE RD

LITTLE NERANG RD

LITTLE NERANG RD

GOLD COAST - SPRINGBROOK RD

MURWILLUMBAH

PINE CREEK

NORTH

OUTLOOK LA

BRUSHBOX RD

LOOP RD

FERNTREE LA

TARLINGTON LA

MIRANI

LOWER BEECHMONT SCHOOL RD

FREEMANS RD

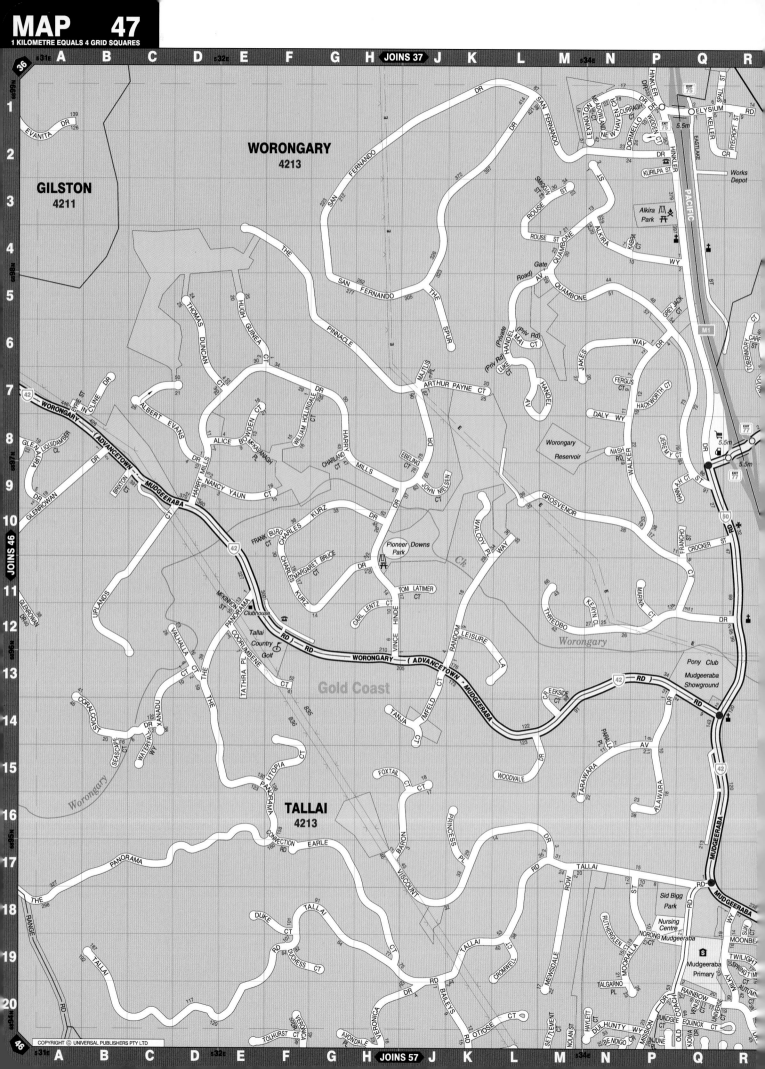

MAP 47
1 KILOMETRE EQUALS 4 GRID SQUARES

WORONGARY
4213

GILSTON
4211

TALLAI
4213

Gold Coast

Worongary

Worongary

Worongary Reservoir

Pioneer Downs Park

Alkira Park

Works Depot

Pony Club Mudgeeraba Showground

Sid Bigg Park

Nursing Centre Mudgeeraba

Mudgeeraba Primary

Tallai Country Golf

Clubhouse

JOINS 46

COPYRIGHT © UNIVERSAL PUBLISHERS PTY LTD

MAP 49

1 KILOMETRE EQUALS 4 GRID SQUARES

JOINS 39

Surfers Paradise

BROADBEACH WATERS
4218

Miami Keys

The Star Casino Broadbeach Island

Broadbeach South

Pacific Fair

CLEAR ISLAND WATERS
4226

MERMAID WATERS
4218

Mermaid Island

Lake Intrepid

Rumrunner Lake

Lake Hugh

ROBINA
4226

Robina Common

Emerald Lagoon

Lake Wonderland

Robina Waters

West Lake

Miami Primary

Pizzey Park Sporting Complex

Burleigh Heads Rugby League Club

Gold Coast Burleigh Golf Club

Clubhouse

Palmer Gold Coast Golf Course

Bond University
4229
University Centre

McKenzie Aged Care

Central Park

Lake Orr

BURLEIGH WATERS
4220

BARCELONA WY	3
LILLE ST	5
PORTO BVD	6
TOURS WY	1
VALENCIA BVD	2
VENICE ST	4
VERONA CCT	7

JOINS 59

JOINS 48

MAP 57
FOLLOWS
50
1 KILOMETRE EQUALS 4 GRID SQUARES

A B C D s44E E F G H **JOINS 40** J K L M s46E N P Q R s47E

s99N

1

2

3

BROADBEACH
4218

4

5

6

MERMAID
BEACH
4218

CORAL

7

8

s97N

9

10

11

Nobby
Beach

12

SLSC

13

SEA

s96N

14

Miami
High

North
Nobby

15

MIAMI
4220

16

s95N

17

18

South Nobby

19

BURLEIGH
HEADS
4220

20

s99N

A B C D s44E E F G H **JOINS 60** J K L M s46E N P Q R s47E

COPYRIGHT © UNIVERSAL PUBLISHERS PTY LTD

JOINS 47

TALLAI
4213

MUDGEERABA
4213

AUSTINVILLE
4213

FRANKLIN

Reservoir

Reservoir

Creek

Mudgeeraba

Mudgeeraba

Laver Family Park

Mudgeeraba Creek Primary

War Museum

Waterworks Reserve

Boomerang Farm Golf Course

(Causeway)

Nature

Nature Trail

Trail

RFB

JOINS 46

TALLAI RD
TOLHURST CT
VERONICA CT
AVONDALE PL
GRANDVIEW TCE
COASTVIEW CR
VERONICA DR
CHRIS AV
BERRIGANS RD
KAGOOLA DR
BERRIGANS AV
ELAINE AV
JULIE
MARK WY
WY
PINETREE CT
GILWARD DR
LITTLE NERANG ST
TYALGUM DR
ARKANA ST
HORSESHOE DR
JOHN ROGERS RD
JOHNS RD
BOOMERANG RD
SPRINGBROOK
BELMONT PARK DR
GOLD COAST
SWANSON PL
AUSTINVILLE RD
LILLIAN LA
BROMFIELD DR
MONARO
MANUKA RD
RD
RAYNER LA
BERRIGANS WY
ALLEENA CT
VALLANDRA
WILKINS
KERALA CT
STOCKMAN CT
STOCKMAN CT
STRIKE WY
ALTOS CT
BURKE
BAILEY'S RD
OTIOSE CT
UNDERHILL PL
NOLAN LA
SUGARGLIDER
OPHIR CT
SETTLEMENT CT
HOLTERMAN CT
COLONIAL CT
PROSPECTOR RD
LALOR CT
MARCUS
SWAGMAN
HARRISON
HAYLETT
DULHUNTY WY
BALLARAT CT
BENDIGO CR
BIRDSVILLE RD
MISSION DR
CAPE
MORVEN
AUGATHELLA
SARATH
ZIEDAN
SOMA
DOUMA
ANTONSON
KERSHAN ST
RATHBONE ST
SCHNEIDO ST
DOWSON
McLACHLAN
BUNDGEE CT
EQUINOX CT
OLD COACH RD
INJUNE
CHINCHILLA CR
KIOWA CT
NAVAJO
CHEROKEE
ACOMA TCE
COBAI
CHIPPEWA
SERENE
ATOMI CT
NATAN RD
CURRONG CR
BIBBA CT
TARRANT
CARRAMA
BERTANA DR
AKAMA CT
NONGA CT
BAGAN
WALLABY DR
WALLA CT
WALLABY
ORANGE CT
ADIOS CT
KULAN CT
GIDYA RD
AMULLA CT
UMPARA
SHETLAND PL
STRAWBERRY
RAFFLES CT
BARAKA
LEYSHON
SEHMISH
GLENMORE
SAUNDERS
STRAWBERRY

MAP 58
1 KILOMETRE EQUALS 4 GRID SQUARES

JOINS 48

ROBINA 4226

The Glades Golf Club

Robina Town Centre 4230

Robina — Woods

Golf Course

REEDY CREEK 4227

BONOGIN 4213

Gold Coast

Hinterland Regional Park

Somerset College

Clover Hill Pmy Sch

Australian Industry Trade College

Kings Christian College

Hillcrest Christian College

Firth Park

Warra Park

Gemvale Park

Lancaster Park

Substation

Reservoirs

PACIFIC

GOLD COAST - SPRINGBROOK RD

M1

JOINS 68

MAP 59
1 KILOMETRE EQUALS 4 GRID SQUARES

JOINS 49

ROBINA
4226

VARSITY LAKES
4227

BURLEIGH WATERS
4220

REEDY CREEK
4227

TALLEBUDGERA VALLEY
4228

TALLEBUDGERA
4228

West Burleigh

Palmer Gold Coast Golf Course

Marymount Catholic College

Gold Coast Christian College

Hillcrest Christian College

Reedy Creek Commercial Wastes Only Landfill

Reedy Creek Waste & Resource Recovery Centre

Gold Coast Junior Motorcycle Club

Miami Lake

Lake Heron

Lake Orr

Swan Lake

Silvabank Lake

Burleigh Sports Club Cmnty Cntr

Caningeraba Primary

St Andrews Lutheran College

St Andrews Lutheran Aged Care

MAP 65 FOLLOWS — 60 — 1 KILOMETRE EQUALS 4 GRID SQUARES

Gold Coast

JOINS 50

BURLEIGH HEADS 4220

PALM BEACH 4221

ELANORA 4221

Burleigh Head

Burleigh Head National Park

Big Burleigh

Burleigh Lake

Koala Park

David Fleay Wildlife Park

Tallebudgera Creek Conservation Park

Tallebudgera Creek Environmental Park

Tallebudgera Ck Cons Park

Tallebudgera Recreation Camp Leisure Cntr

Tallebudgera Creek Tourist Park

Burleigh Ridge Park

Marjorie St Henry Park

Stockland Burleigh Heads

Ozcare Ozanam Villa Burleigh

Maher Hall

All Star Sports Club

Croquet Lawn

Hockey Fields

Palm Beach Soccer Club

Awonga Lake

Waidup Lake

Rio Martin

Rio Barracuda

Rio Dolphin

Rio Swordfish

Rio Barramundi

Palm Beach Pmy

Elanora Water Quality Control Centre

Burleigh Heads Primary

Burleigh Heads Stn

Prop Second Av Burleigh Stn

Prop Burleigh Heads Stn

Proposed Light Rail Due for completion 2024

John Laws Pk

Justins Pk

Club SLSC

SLSC

CORAL

SEA

Pacific

Beach

Martin Shell Pk

Jeh Wit

Gate

PROPOSED PACIFIC RAILWAY

M1

EXIT 92

GOLD COAST HWY

Burleigh Connection Rd

JOINS 70

COPYRIGHT © UNIVERSAL PUBLISHERS PTY LTD

JOINS 45

BEECHMONT
4211

ILLINBAH
4275

Scenic Rim

Numinbah

Correctional

Centre

NUMINBAH VALLEY
4211

Yalbaroo

Lamington

National

O'REILLY
4211

Park

BINNA BURRA
4211

Binna Burra Lodge

Kiosk

Caves

Lamington

Kooloobano
Lookout

National

Park

NATURAL BRIDGE
4211

Yangahla
Lookout

Koolanbilba
Lookout

Ballunjui Falls

NERANG

MURWILLUMBAH

Numinbah
Valley Pmy

Priems
Crossing

(Narrow
bridge)

Nixon
Creek
Rd

Staffords Rd
(Causeway)

Ent

Dussek
Rd

Hall
RFB

Beechmont
Pmy
Graceleigh
Pk
Tennis
Pk
RFB

Summerville Rd

Durbar Rd

Tabletop Rd

Mackenzie Rd

South West Rd

Binna Burra

Timbarra Dr

Boongala

Gwingana Ct

Oonah Dr

Bibaringa Ct

Illinbah

Coomera

Coomera River

Great Walk

Ships Circuit

Stem

Circuit

Caves Cct

Bochow
Pk

Lyons
Crossing

Nerang River

Chesters Rd

Maple Ct

Willow Ct

Prunius Ct

Acacia Ct

Lilac Tree Ct

Munnies Ct

Pocket

DAVES CREEK RD
NATURAL BRIDGE RD
BAKERS RD
SOLITUDE LA
HAYTERS RD
Camp Bornhoffen 2km
Murwillumbah 32 km

LIMIT OF MAPS

MAP 66
1 KILOMETRE EQUALS 2 GRID SQUARES

NERANWOOD 4213

AUSTINVILLE 4213

SPRINGBROOK 4213

Numinbah

Forest

Reserve

Restricted Vehicle Access

Springbrook National Park

Numinbah Forest Reserve

Restricted Vehicle Access

Neranwood Youth Camp

Water Supply Reserve

Scenic Res

Great Walk

Little Nerang Dam

Woonoongoora Walkers Camp

Wunburra

Apple Tree Park

Gold Coast

Springbrook National Park

Forest Reserve

Restricted Vehicle Access

Great Walk

Forest Reserve

Waterfall Creek Rd

Forest Reserve Restricted Vehicle Access Reserve

Purling Brook Falls

Springbrook Research Observatory

Springbrook Pmy

Hall

RFB

CARRICK'S

The Settlement Campground Transfer Station

Springbrook Glow Worms

Springbrook National Park

Hardys

(East Branch) Little Nerang

Warrie Cct

Gooroolba Falls

Twin Falls

INSET

JOINS MAP AT H20

Wedge Bluff Lookout

Repeater Station

Canyon Lookout

Springbrook National Park

Goomoolahra Picnic Area

Goomoolahra Falls

Tallanbana Picnic Area

Rainbow Falls

Twin Falls

Warrie

Best Ever Lookout

Gold Coast

SPRINGBROOK 4213

MAP 67

1 KILOMETRE EQUALS 4 GRID SQUARES

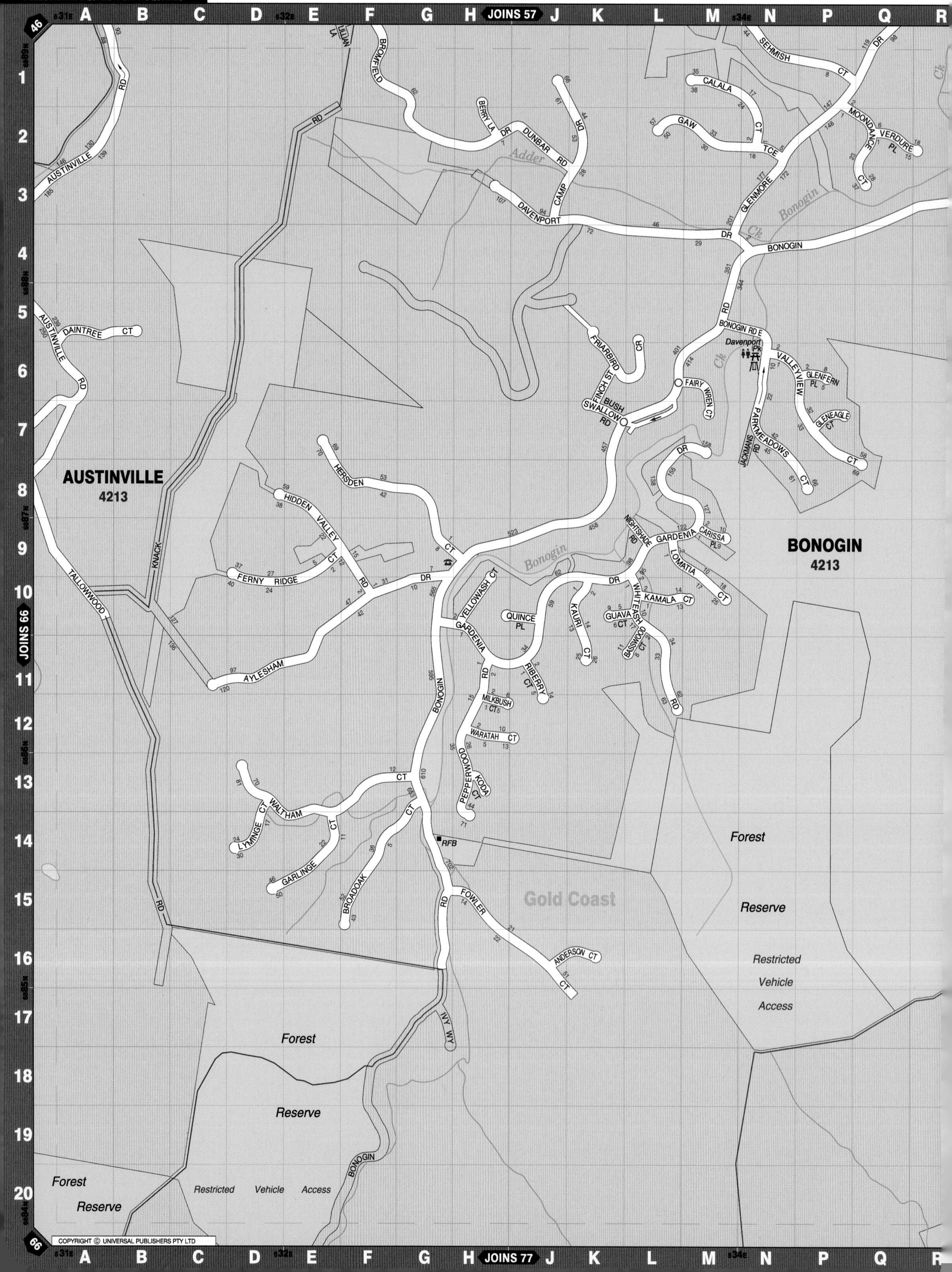

JOINS 57

AUSTINVILLE
4213

BONOGIN
4213

Adder

Bonogin Ck

Davenport Pk

Forest

Reserve

Restricted

Vehicle

Access

Gold Coast

Bonogin

Forest

Reserve

JOINS 66

Forest

Reserve

Restricted   Vehicle   Access

COPYRIGHT © UNIVERSAL PUBLISHERS PTY LTD

JOINS 77

Street labels: AUSTINVILLE RD, DAINTREE CT, TALLOWWOOD RD, KNACK RD, BROMFIELD RD, BERRY LA, DUNBAR RD, DAVENPORT DR, CAMP DR, FRIARBIRD, FINCH ST, BUSH SWALLOW RD, FAIRY WREN CT, HERSDEN, HIDDEN VALLEY CT, FERNY RIDGE, AYLESHAM, BONOGIN RD, GARDENIA, YELLOWASH CT, QUINCE PL, KAURI CT, MILKBUSH CT, WARATAH CT, RIBERRY CT, PEPPERWOOD, KODA, WALTHAM CT, LYMINGE CT, GARLINGE CT, BROADOAK, FOWLER, ANDERSON CT, WY WY, BONOGIN, GLENMORE DR, SEHMISH CT, CALALA CT, GAW TCE, MOONDANCE, VERDURE PL, BONOGIN RD E, VALLEYVIEW, GLENFERN PL, GLENEAGLE CT, PARKMEADOWS, NIGHTSHADE RD, GARDENIA, CARISSA PL, LOMATIA, KAMALA CT, WHITEASH, GUAVA CT, BASSWOOD, RFB

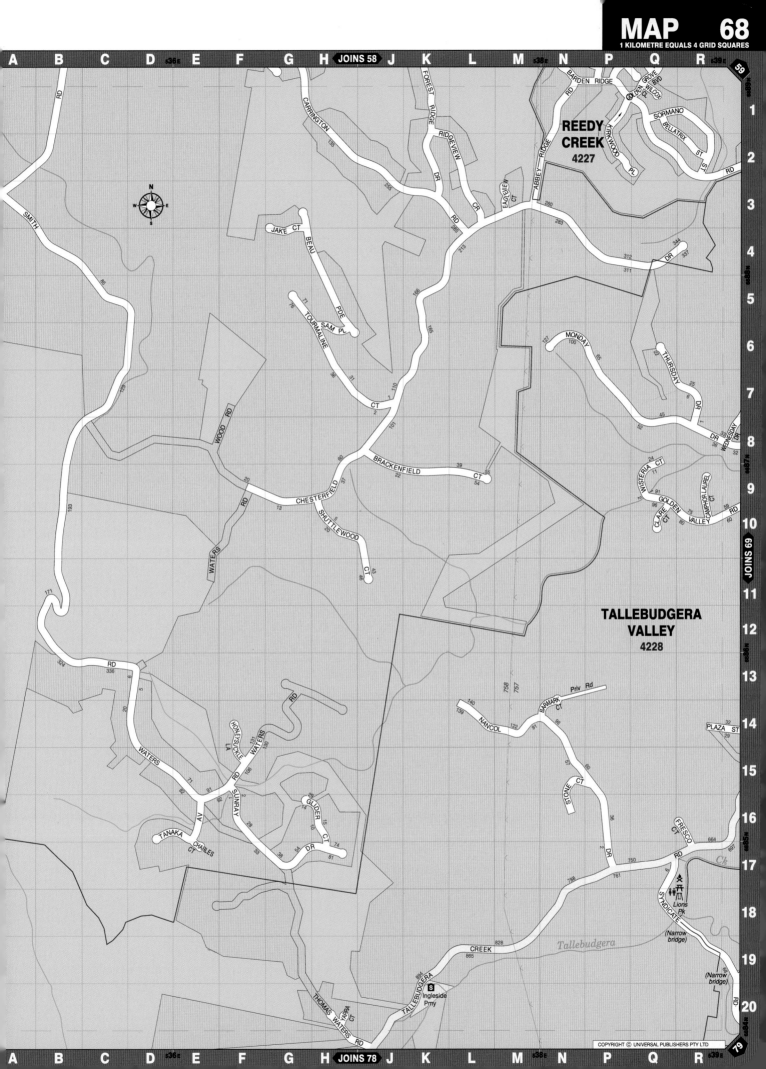

MAP 69
1 KILOMETRE EQUALS 4 GRID SQUARES

A B C D E F G H JOINS 59 J K L M N P Q R

REEDY CREEK
4227

TALLEBUDGERA
VALLEY
4228

TALLEBUDGERA
4228

St Andrews
Lutheran College

Burleigh Heads
Golf Range

Cem

TALLEBUDGERA

Coplick Family
Sports Park

Soccer

Baseball
Clubhouse

Pony
Club

Tallebudgera
(Coplicks)
Golf Course

Clubhouse
Ent

Tallebudgera
Creek

Tallebudgera Prmy

Archery
Club

Golden Valley

Staatz
Ct

Hidden
Cov

Gray
St

Meadow
Park
Golf Course

Ent

Reservoir

Cmnty
Hall

Robinson
Park

Plaza St

Gate
(Priv Rd)
Jeremy

Trees

Dungoge

Tally
Springs

Talleyhaven

Conservation Park

Reservoir

Narrow
bridge

Narrow
bridge

Syndicate

Tallebudgera Creek

Tallebudgera

Street names visible: SCHRANO ST, BARDEN RIDGE RD, MONDAY, TUESDAY DR, WEDNESDAY DR, GOLDEN VALLEY RD, TALLEBUDGERA CREEK RD, BENAROON CT, COORABIN CT, KARRAGATA, CURRINGA CT, COORABIN CT, YANDALA PL, GOOLABAH DR, GOOLABAH CT, JEDDA, BODALLA PL, ARANGA WY, CARAPOOK CR, RONELLE CT, REYNELLA, YALLA CT, DERMOT PL, GOOLABAH, GOLINE CT, KOOMBAHLA GR, TREES, TREES RD, KOORINGAL CT, TOBIN, DWYER CT, STOCKYARD CT, VALLEY WY, GREEN LA, JASMARIN DR, DUDGEON DR, MARY BALE DR, JERSEY CT, FRIESIAN CT, BRAHMAN CT, KEERONG CT, DALWOOD, ISABELLA CT, TERRAMA CT, JAMBEROO CT, ROSEBANK CT, NORTHBOW, VALLEY DR, TIPUANA DR, TUSSOCK, CASUARINA, NYORA CT, BAEKEA DR, PULTENEA DR, TALLY VALLEY, GUINEAS, COPLICKS LA, TALLEBUDGERA CONNECTION RD, YARRAMAN PL, CREEK DR, SAMUEL, ANDREWS RD, LITA CT, JOYCE CT, FENTON DR, CLYDE RD, ORCHNA ST, TIPU, ROBUSTA ST, GLAUCA ST, PULLIA RD, COWELL, BENGAL DR, OLD COACH RD, LARCH, ELM ST, DAFFODIL RD, LILLEE, JOANNE CT, STACKPOLE CT

JOINS 68

JOINS 79

MAP 70
1 KILOMETRE EQUALS 4 GRID SQUARES

JOINS 60

CORAL SEA

PALM BEACH
4221

Palm Beach Parklands

Palm Beach Currumbin High

Winders Park

CURRUMBIN
4223

ELANORA
4221

Schusters Park

Elanora Water Quality Control Centre

Elanora High

Elanora Pmy

The Pines Shopping Centre

Bay of Palms Resort

Isle of Palms Resort

Pine Lake

Community Centre

Merv Craig Sporting Complex

CURRUMBIN WATERS
4223

Currumbin Community Special School

St Augustines Cath Pmy

RSL Care Galleon Gardens Retirement Community

Palm Beach Currumbin Rugby Union Club

Sports Fields

Gold Coast

Tweed

Currumbin District Horse Club

Wendts Bridge

COBAKI LAKES
2486

CURRUMBIN VALLEY
4223

Pococks Bridge

Currumbin Creek

QUEENSLAND
NEW SOUTH WALES

JOINS 80

JOINS 71

81

MAP 71
1 KILOMETRE EQUALS 4 GRID SQUARES

CURRUMBIN 4223

TUGUN 4224

BILINGA 4225

COBAKI LAKES 2486

Tweed

Gold Coast

Gold Coast Airport

CORAL

SEA

John Flynn - Gold Coast Private Hospital

GCCC Desalination Plant

QUEENSLAND

NEW SOUTH WALES

JOINS 70

MAP 77
FOLLOWS

72

1 KILOMETRE EQUALS 4 GRID SQUARES

A B C D s52E E F G Pt H s53E J K L M s54E N P Q R s55E

1
2
3
4
5
6
7
8
9
10
11
12
13
14
15
16
17
18
19
20

s89N
s88N
s87N
s86N
s85N
s84N

Snapper
Rocks

Rainbow
Bay

Capt Cook
Mem

Point
Danger

Volunteer Marine
Rescue

**TWEED
HEADS**
2485

COOLANGATTA
4225

North
Kirra
Beach

Kirra
Pt

Kirra
Beach

Coolangatta
Beach

Greenmount
Beach

Duranbah
Beach

MUSGRAVE
WINSTON
COYNE ST
HWY
SOUTH ST
CREEK
ST

MARINE

GARRICK
ST

Queen
Elizabeth
Park SLSC

MARINE

PDE

SLSC

Pat
Fagan
Pk

MARINE

EDEN
PDE

BOUNDARY
ST

WARD ST

CORAL ST

PETRIE
AV

SLSC RD
SNAPPER ROCKS

TWEED
ST

HILL

CORAL
ST

BOUNDARY

JOINS 82

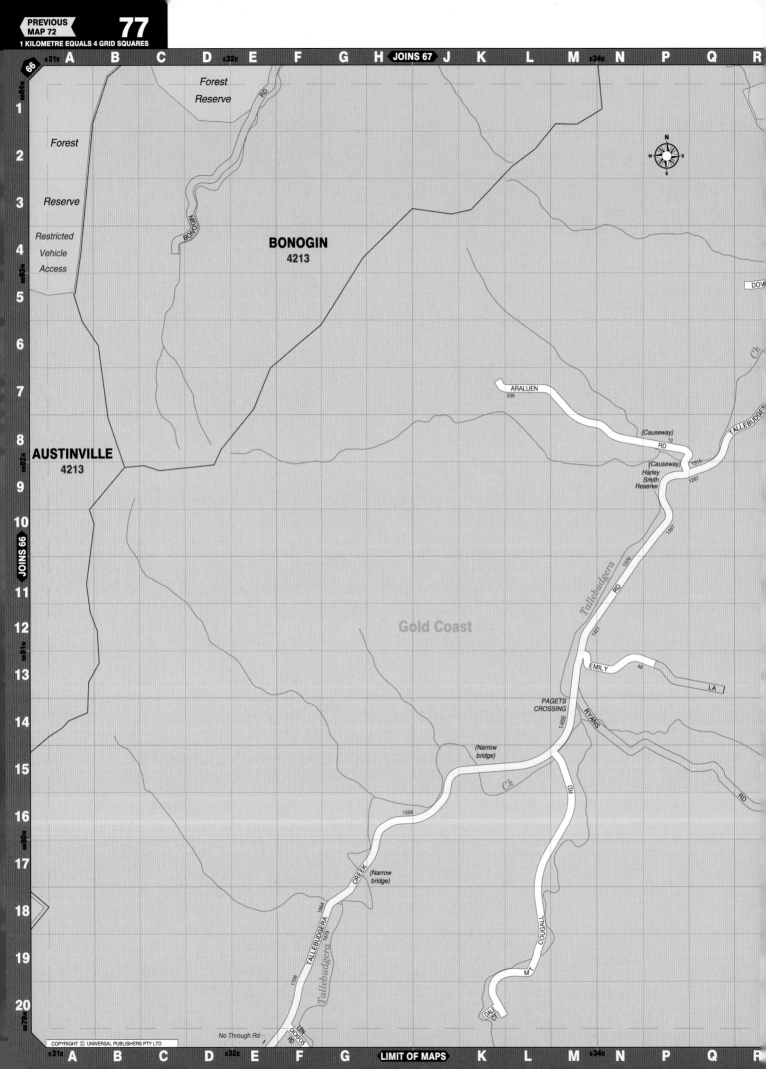

A B C D E F G H JOINS 67 J K L M N P Q R

Forest
Reserve

Forest

Reserve

Restricted
Vehicle
Access

BONOGIN
4213

AUSTINVILLE
4213

JOINS 66

Gold Coast

ARALUEN
338

(Causeway)
RD 12

(Causeway)
Harley
Smith
Reserve

TALLEBUDGERA

Tallebudgera RD

EMILY 48

LA

PAGETS
CROSSING

RYANS

(Narrow
bridge)

Ck

1598

RD

COUGALL

CREEK

(Narrow
bridge)

TALLEBUDGERA

Tallebudgera

LEN
DICKSON
RD

DALE
CT

No Through Rd

A B C D E F G LIMIT OF MAPS K L M N P Q R

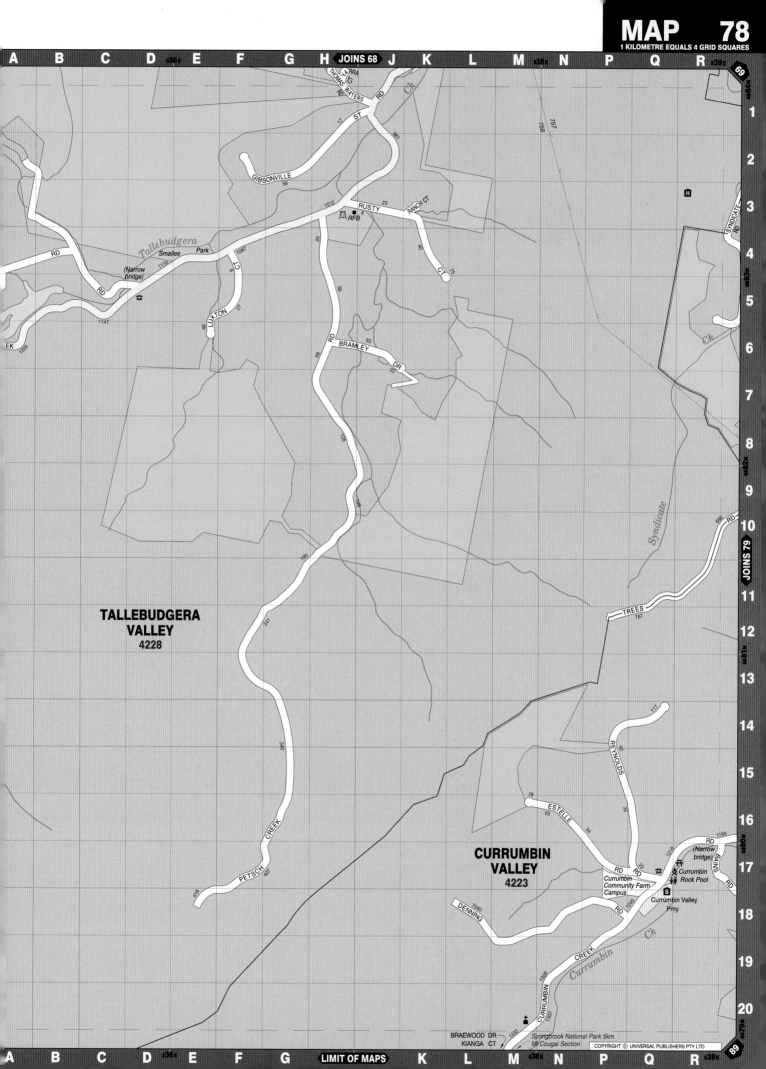

MAP 78
1 KILOMETRE EQUALS 4 GRID SQUARES

JOINS 68

TALLEBUDGERA
VALLEY
4228

CURRUMBIN
VALLEY
4223

Tallebudgera

Smailes
Park

(Narrow
bridge)

GIBSONVILLE

RUSTY
RFB
RANCH CT

LUXTON CT

BRAMLEY
RD
DR

PETSCH
CREEK

Syndicate

SYNDICATE
RD

JOINS 79

TREES

REYNOLDS

ESTELLE

RD
RD
BAINS RD

Currumbin
Rock Pool

Currumbin
Community Farm
Campus

Currumbin Valley
Prmy

DENNING
RD

CURRUMBIN

Currumbin Ck

BRAEWOOD DR
KIANGA CT

Springbrook National Park 5km
Mt Cougal Section

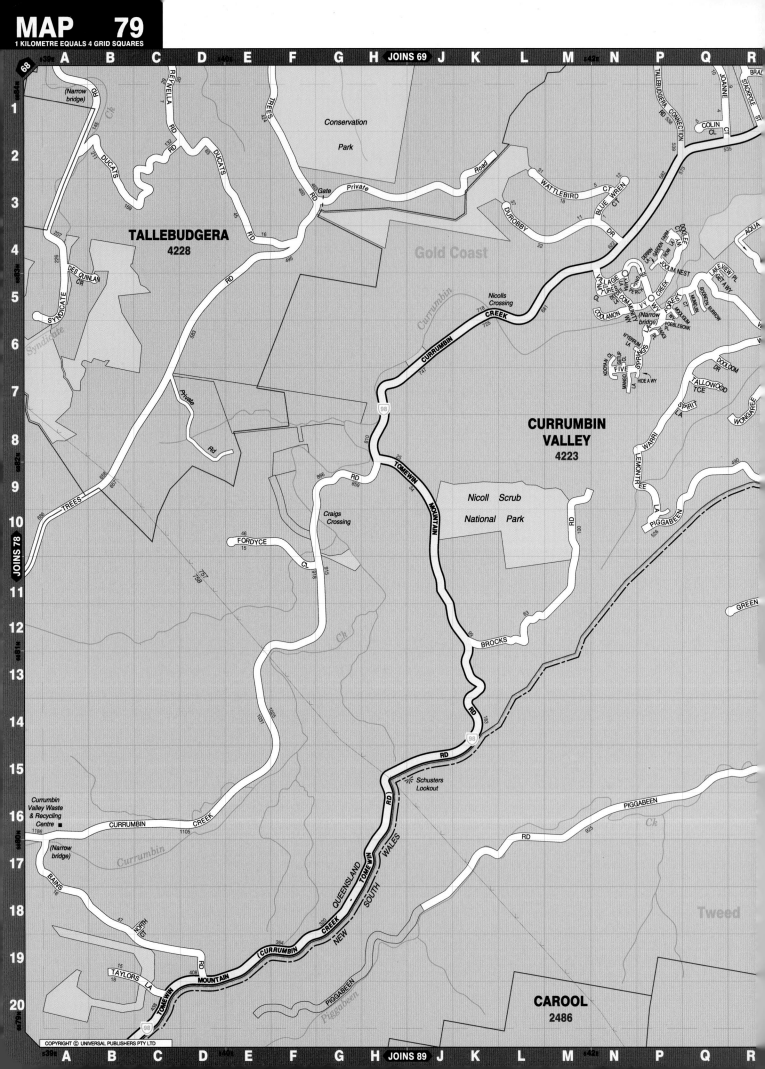

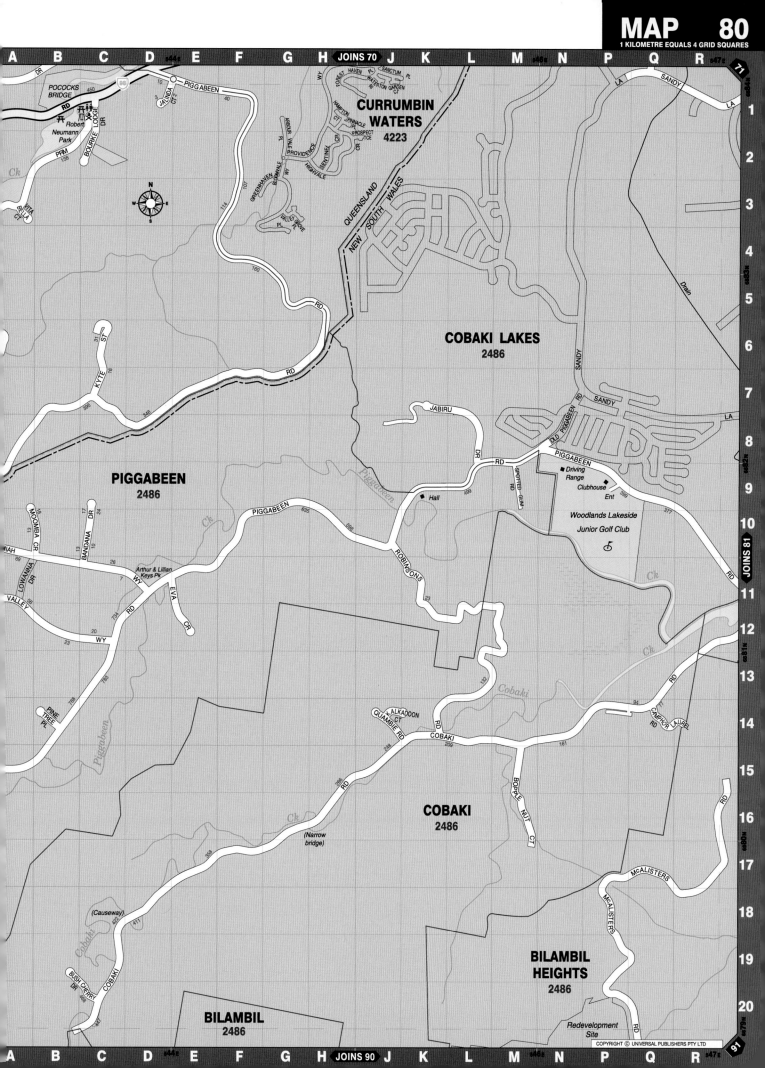

MAP 80
1 KILOMETRE EQUALS 4 GRID SQUARES

CURRUMBIN
WATERS
4223

COBAKI LAKES
2486

PIGGABEEN
2486

Woodlands Lakeside
Junior Golf Club

COBAKI
2486

BILAMBIL
HEIGHTS
2486

BILAMBIL
2486

Redevelopment
Site

POCOCKS
BRIDGE

Robert
Neumann
Park

Arthur & Lillian
Keys Pk

(Narrow
bridge)

(Causeway)

JOINS 70

JOINS 81

JOINS 90

COPYRIGHT © UNIVERSAL PUBLISHERS PTY LTD

MAP 81
1 KILOMETRE EQUALS 4 GRID SQUARES

JOINS 71

BILINGA
4225
QLD
NSW

Terminal 1 Qantas
Short Term
Long Term

Gold Coast

Airport

Southern Cross Uni

M1

PROPOSED

RUNWAY

MAIN

BPS

RAILWAY

4.6m

Tunnel

MWY

4.6m

COBAKI LAKES
2486

Cobaki

Broadwater

PKY

Drain

SANDY LA

Creek

Cobaki

TWEED HEADS WEST
2485

SUSSYER AV

Sewage Treatment Works

HAKEA DR

BANKSIA

GRAY ST

MARIAN ST

TRINGA ST

TATTLER

LIMOSA

PLOVER

Cobaki Broadwater Village Homes

CIRCULAR DR

FIRST AV
SECOND AV
THIRD AV
FOURTH AV
FIFTH AV
SIXTH AV

LAKE-SIDE DR

Tweed

N
W E
S

ANCONIA AV

The Boyd Family Park

Lions Pioneer Pk

KENNEDY

Tweed Maritime & Heritage Museum

Inspection Point

William Campbell Pk

Caddys Island

Terranora

PIGGABEEN RD

COBAKI

JOINS 80

SKYLINE DR

STOTT CL

BENSON ST

CAFFREY

Jeh Wit 135

BAILEY

BURGESS

Ent

CARRAMAR RD

SILKWOOD TCE

LAUREL PL

TULGI

PIGGABEEN

MYEERIMBA

LALUNA

NERANG

NERANG PDE

ANCONIA

MWY

RD

13

102

6

The Boyd Family Park

Piggabeen Sports Complex

Terranora Valley Assisted Living Apartments & Opal Tweed Heads

CUPANA CT

INLET DR

LAKES DR W

KLUDA DR

GULL PL

Clarrie Englert

GOLLAN

LAKES DR

JACARANDA

KOALA PL

RIVIERA

SUNSET

Tweed Broadwater Village

PHILP PL
STEPHEN PL
KIRKWOOD
Ent

229 PL

ACA

Daveys Island

PANORAMA

ALBATROSS

TERN

CCT

BIRDS BAY DR

CURLEW WY

Seagulls Club

JACARANDA ST

POINSETTIA ST

RED BASS AV

PELICAN PL

PERCH BVD

SUNSET PL

SUNSET

Birds Bay

BILAMBIL HEIGHTS
2486

WARRINGA DR

KARINGAL AV

NABILLA ST

MALU TCE

BOLWARRA PL

WALMSLEYS RD

BILINGA CCT

SCENIC DR

MT BILINGA

McALISTERS RD

RD

Bingam Bay

Womgin Island

Big Island

Resvr

LAKEVIEW PDE

OCEAN AV

MARIE ST

HILLCREST ST

GLENYS ST

SEAVIEW

BURGUNDY CT

THE GRANGE

THE HERMITAGE

CHAMPAGNE

VINTAGE

BODEN

PORT

MEDOC PL

CHARD

MUSGRAVE

BOTANICAL CCT

Terranora

Broadwater

Dog Bay

PENINSULA DR

DIANE TCE

YVONNE

COBAKI CR

BANORA TCE

LAKEVIEW TCE

TERRANORA

CORAL

SIMPSON DR

PULKARA CT

BUENAVISTA DR

SCENIC

PENINSULA

ESP

MAP 82
1 KILOMETRE EQUALS 4 GRID SQUARES

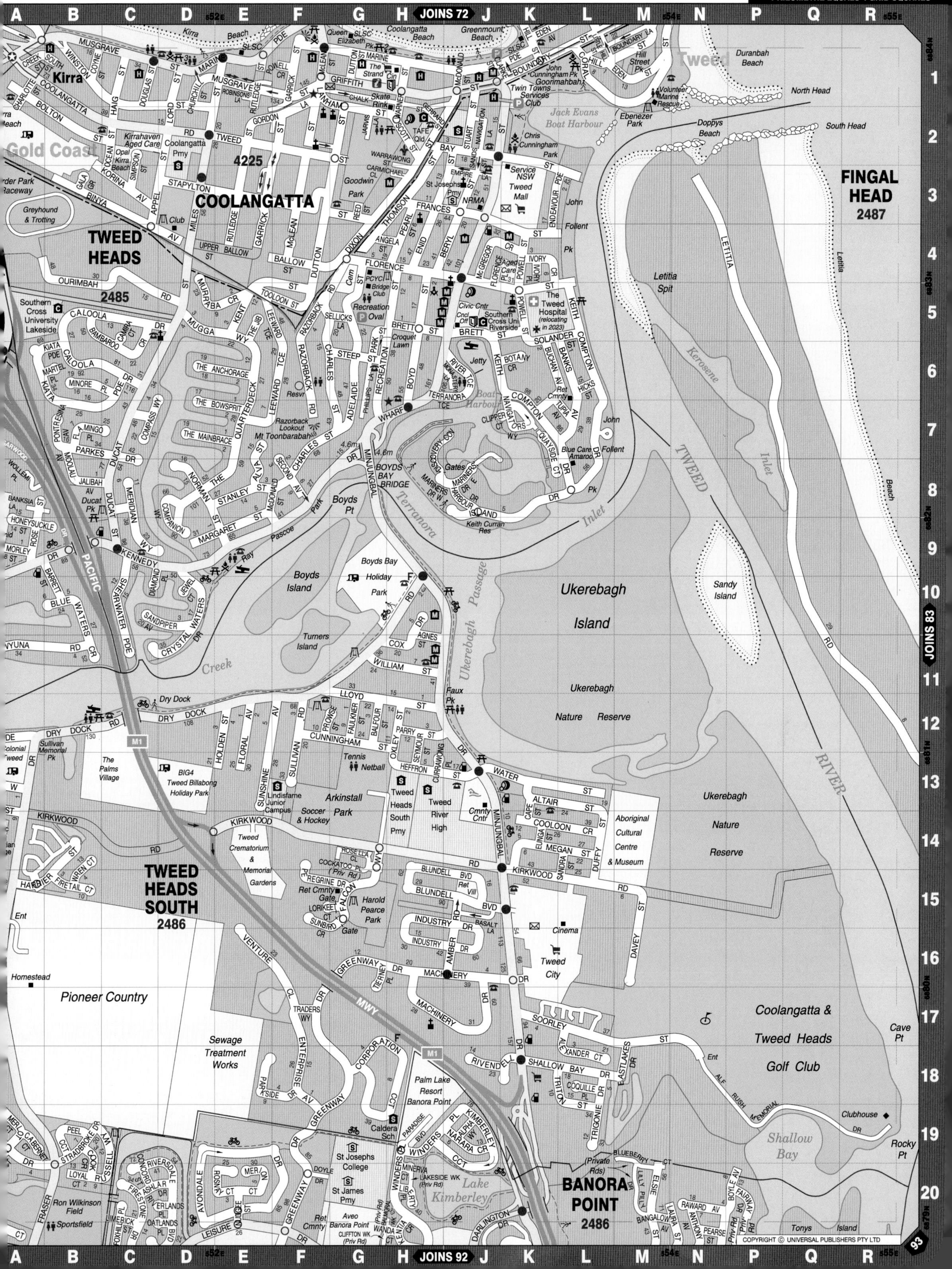

JOINS 72

Kirra

Kirra

Gold Coast

TWEED HEADS 2485

COOLANGATTA 4225

Southern Cross University Lakeside

Greyhound & Trotting

Boyds Pt

Boyds Island

Turners Island

TWEED HEADS SOUTH 2486

Pioneer Country

Sewage Treatment Works

Palm Lake Resort Banora Point

BANORA POINT 2486

Lake Kimberley

St Josephs College

Ukerebagh Island

Ukerebagh Nature Reserve

Ukerebagh Nature Reserve

Aboriginal Cultural Centre & Museum

Tweed City

Cinema

Coolangatta & Tweed Heads Golf Club

Clubhouse

Shallow Bay

Rocky Pt

Cave Pt

Tonys Island

FINGAL HEAD 2487

Tweed

Duranbah Beach

North Head

South Head

Doppys Beach

Letitia Spit

Sandy Island

Kerosene Inlet

TWEED RIVER

Jack Evans Boat Harbour

Ebenezer Park

Boyds Bay Holiday Park

BIG4 Tweed Billabong Holiday Park

The Palms Village

Arkinstall Park

Harold Pearce Park

Sullivan Memorial Pk

Tweed Crematorium & Memorial Gardens

COPYRIGHT © UNIVERSAL PUBLISHERS PTY LTD

JOINS 83

MAP **83**
1 KILOMETRE EQUALS 4 GRID SQUARES

A B C D E F G H J K L M N P Q R

72

CORAL

SEA

JOINS 82

Fingal Head

Tweed

LETITIA

DUKE ST

RD

Tweed Holiday Parks

Fingal Head Rovers SLSC

Fingal Head Pmy

PRINCE

QUEEN

MARINE

PDE

Beach

Fingal Head

Family Park

Giants Causeway

Cook Island

HEALY

MAIN

KING ST

RD

ST

PDE

38

FINGAL HEAD
2487

TWEED

CHITTICKS LA

ELIZABETH ST

BAMBERRY ST

LIGHTHOUSE

Beach

Cave Pt

Boat Harbour

RD

DUNE ST

SHORT ST

LAGOON

Dreamtime

RIVER

Clubhouse

Rocky Pt

Wommin Lagoon

38

FINGAL

92

A B C D E F G H JOINS 93 J K L M N P Q R

MAP 89
FOLLOWS

84

1 KILOMETRE EQUALS 4 GRID SQUARES

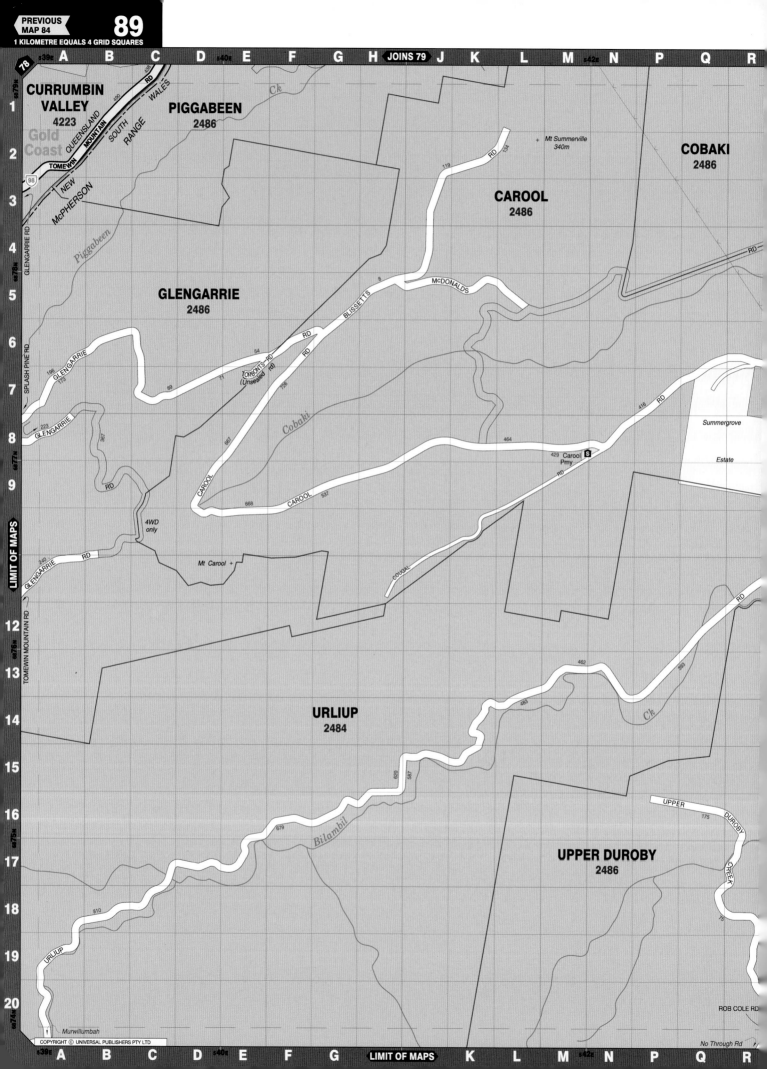

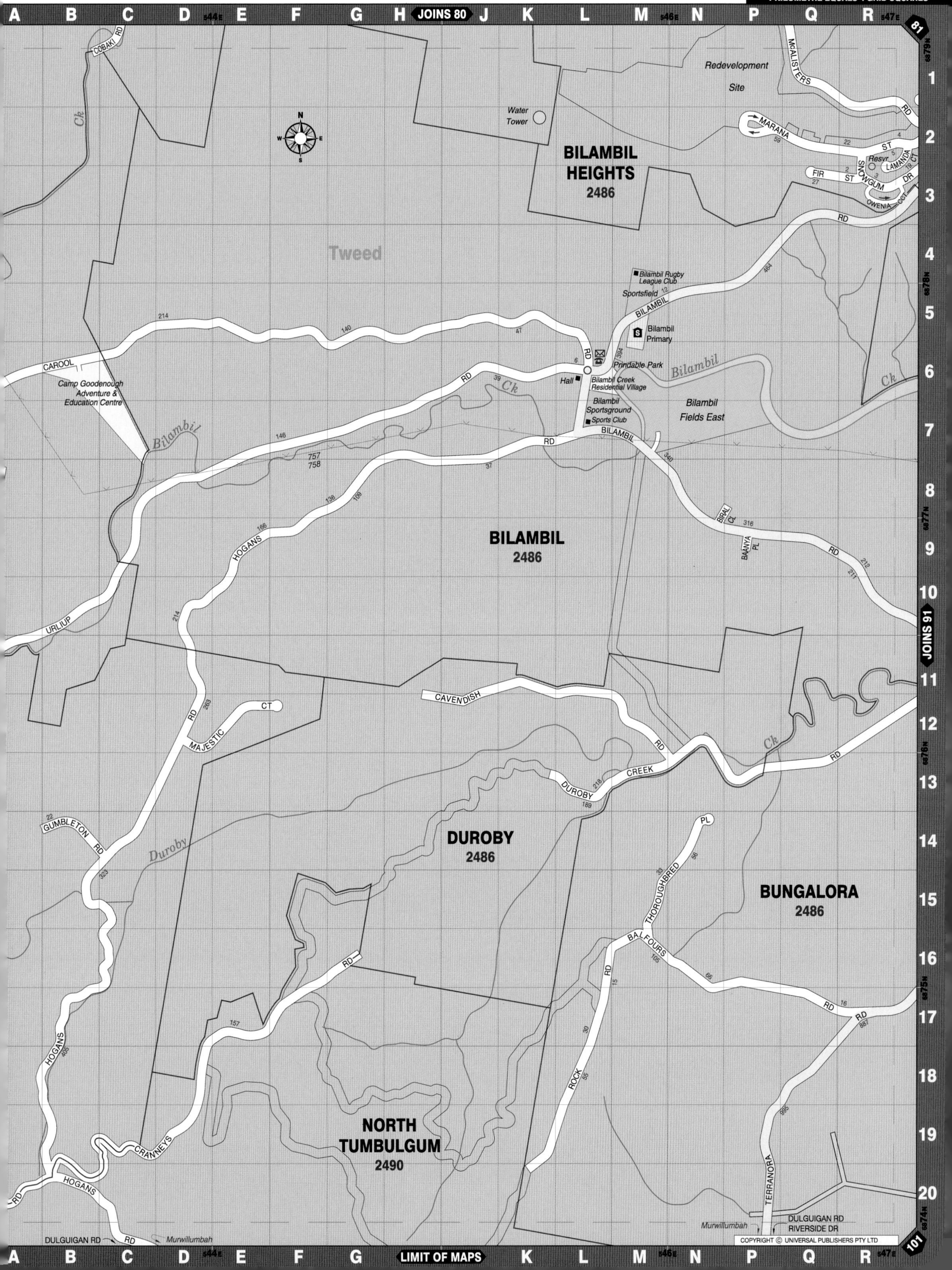

MAP 90
1 KILOMETRE EQUALS 4 GRID SQUARES

JOINS 80

JOINS 81

COBAKI RD

Water
Tower

**BILAMBIL
HEIGHTS
2486**

Redevelopment
Site

MARANA
59

Resvr

FIR
27

SNOWGUM ST
ST

LAMANDA

OWENIA
RD

MCALISTERS RD

Tweed

CAROOL

Camp Goodenough
Adventure &
Education Centre

Bilambil

Bilambil Rugby
League Club
Sportsfield

BILAMBIL
RD

Bilambil
Primary

Prindable Park

Bilambil Creek
Residential Village

Bilambil
Sportsground
Sports Club

Bilambil
Fields East

Bilambil Ck

Hall

Ck

RD

RD

BILAMBIL

RD

BILAMBIL
RD

BANYA
PL

**BILAMBIL
2486**

HOGANS

URLIUP

RD

MAJESTIC

CT

CAVENDISH

RD

DUROBY

CREEK

Ck

RD

RD

GUMBLETON RD

Duroby

**DUROBY
2486**

PL

THOROUGHBRED

BALFOURS

**BUNGALORA
2486**

RD

RD

HOGANS

RD

CRANNEYS

ROCK

**NORTH
TUMBULGUM
2490**

RD

RD

TERRANORA

DULGUIGAN RD

RIVERSIDE DR

Murwillumbah

DULGUIGAN RD

RD

Murwillumbah

HOGANS

JOINS 101

MAP 91
1 KILOMETRE EQUALS 4 GRID SQUARES

JOINS 81

BILAMBIL HEIGHTS 2486

BILAMBIL 2486

TERRANORA 2486

BUNGALORA 2486

NORTH TUMBULGUM 2490

Terranora Broadwater

Charles Bay

Trutes Bay

Tommys Island

Tweed

Tweed Broadwater

Creek

Bilambil Creek

Beltana

Duroby Creek

Lindisfarne Grammar Middle & Senior Campus

Terranora Pmy

Terranora Substation

Bungalora Outlook

Resvr

JOINS 80

JOINS 90

JOINS 101

MAP 92
1 KILOMETRE EQUALS 4 GRID SQUARES

JOINS 82

JOINS 102

JOINS 93

BANORA POINT 2486

FINGAL HEAD 2487

CHINDERAH 2487

Tonys Island

Tims Island

Banora Pt

Palm Lake Resort

Barneys Pt

BARNEYS POINT BRIDGE

Lillies Island

Chinderah Bay

Club Banora Golf Course

Club Banora Sports Complex

Banora Green Soccer

Chinderah Island

Dodds Island

Boyds

Chinderah Channel

TWEED RIVER

Chinderah Village

Ingenia Holidays Kingscliff

The Homestead

Tweed Super Sports

Tweed River Hacienda

Tweed Shores & Chinderah Lakes

Turnock Pk

Corowa Pk

Royal Pacific

Cemetery

Chinderah Golf Course & Driving Range

Tweed Shire Sustainable Living Centre

Noble Lakeside Australia

Chambers Lookout

Banora Point High

Banora Point Primary

Centaur Primary

Twin Towns Juniors

Dave Burns Field

RSL Care Darlington Ret Cmnty

RSL Care Winders Ret Cmnty

Aveo Banora Point

Funeral Cntr

Wilson Pk

SES HQ

COPYRIGHT © UNIVERSAL PUBLISHERS PTY LTD

103

MAP 93
1 KILOMETRE EQUALS 4 GRID SQUARES

JOINS 83

CORAL

SEA

TWEED RIVER

FINGAL HEAD
2487

Dreamtime

Wommin Lake

Beach

Tweed

JOINS 92

PACIFIC MWY

Wommin Bay Hostel

McKISSOCK DR

Ingenia Holidays Kingscliff

Club

Walter Peate Rec Res

MURPHYS RD

BRADSHAW PL

AVOCA ST

OCEAN DR

WOMMIN BAY RD

Merv Edwards Field

Reg Dalton Oval

Tweed Holiday Parks

KINGSCLIFF ST

MARINE PDE

SAND

SHELL ST

EDDY

WORAM PL

YAXA

TERRACE

SURF ST

OCEAN ST

KINDE

PEATE CT

OZONE ST

Kingscliff

KINGSCLIFF ST

CHINDERAH
2487

PACIFIC

ZEPHYR ST

Jack Bayliss Park

ISI PL

ELROND

BEACH

SANDBANK WY

SHOAL PL

CHANNEL PL

SHORE

LORIEN

Ret Vill

DRIF LA

SPOONBILL

PEARL

Aged Care

Noble Lakeside Australia

CORMORAN

QUAIL

BLUE JAY

OSPREY PL

LES NOBLE PDE

MARY ST

DANIELLE

DANIEL

MYRTLE

MONA RD

BELLBIRD DR

DOVE

KEITH ST

KINGSCLIFF
2487

KINGFISHER

MONARCH

LOO

TURNOCK

Kingscliff Shop Vill

St Anthonys Cath Pmly

Tweed Holiday Parks

Central Park

Hall

MARINE PDE

SLSC

Kingscliff Lions Park

HUNGERFORD

Faulks Park

SEGVIEW

Beach

Cudgen Headland

JOINS 103

MAP 101
FOLLOWS

94

1 KILOMETRE EQUALS 4 GRID SQUARES

A B C D s48E E F G H JOINS 91 J K L M s50E N P Q R

BUNGALORA
2486

TERRANORA
2486

NORTH TUMBULGUM
2490

RAYES

JOYDON LA

TWEED

RIVER

RIVER

DULGUIGAN RD
TERRANORA RD

McAULEYS

TWEED

Stotts   Island

Nature   Reserve

OAKS

TWEED VALLEY

RIVERSIDE DR
Murwillumbah

TWEED

Hogans
Park

VALLEY

WY

Bruce
Chick
Park

CUDGEN

40
17

Ck

LEDDAYS CREEK

Mcleods

59

62

114

RD

TUMBULGUM
2490

RD

STOTTS CREEK
2487

LIMIT OF MAPS

Leddys

LEDDAYS CREEK

CREEK

RD

PACIFIC

DURANBAH

122 105

Duranbah

S

Pmy

DURANBAH

■ Dog
Pound

*Stotts Creek
Resource
Hecovery
Centre*

Ck

TWEED VALLEY WY

BARTLETTS

SAUNDERS

HAWKENS

PACIFIC

MWY

BRINSM
R

EVIRON
2484

HAWKENS
LA

M1

HAWKENS LA
EVIRON RD

HAWKENS
LA

EVIRON
RD

CLOTHIERS
CREEK RD

LIMIT OF MAPS

A B C D s48E E F G H J K L M s50E N P Q R

MAP 102
1 KILOMETRE EQUALS 4 GRID SQUARES

A B C D s52E E F G H **JOINS 92** J K L M s54E N P Q R s55E 93

CHINDERAH
2487

Melaleuca
Station
Memorial
Gardens

Tweed Shire
Sustainable
Living Centre

ALTONA RD

Pacific Views
Estate

Cudgen
Prny
Oval

Cudgen War
Memorial

DENMAN DR
MURRAYA WY
COLLIER ST
THE VILLAGE LA
CRESCENT
CLARKE
REDMAN RD
JOHN ROBB WY
GUILFOYLE PL
STERLING CT
JOHN ROBB
BOWEN
SUGAR MILL RD
PRICHARD
TWEED COAST
MONA RD

Substation

Tweed

CUDGEN RD

PLANTATION RD

CUDGEN
2487

McCOLLUMS RD

CUDGEN RD

MELALEUCA

REARDONS RD

TWEED COAST RD

JOINS 103

RFB

Tropical Fruit World

RD

OLD BOGANGAR RD

SECRET LA

DEPOT

KINGS FOREST
2487

DURANBAH
2487

LODERS RD
ANDERSONS RD

A B C D s52E E F G K L M s54E N P Q R s55E

MAP 103
1 KILOMETRE EQUALS 4 GRID SQUARES

JOINS 93

JOINS 102

JOINS MAP AT D20 INSET

CUDGEN
2487

KINGSCLIFF
2487

CASUARINA
2487

KINGS
FOREST
2487

CASUARINA
2487

New Tweed Valley

Hospital Site
(due for
completion
early 2024)

TAFE NSW
Kingscliff

Kingscliff
High

Cudgen
Foreshore

Cudgen
Headland

Sutherland
Point
Kingscliff

Robert Dixon
Pk

Ed
Parker
Rotary

Kingscliff Lions
Pk

Faulks Park

The Jack Julius
Park

CORAL

SEA

Tweed

Old
Bogangar
Bridge

Casuarina
Village

Casuarina
South
Sportsfield

Casuarina
Central
Park

Beachcomber
Cov

Bogangar
Cabarita Beach
Hastings Point
Pottsville

Tweed

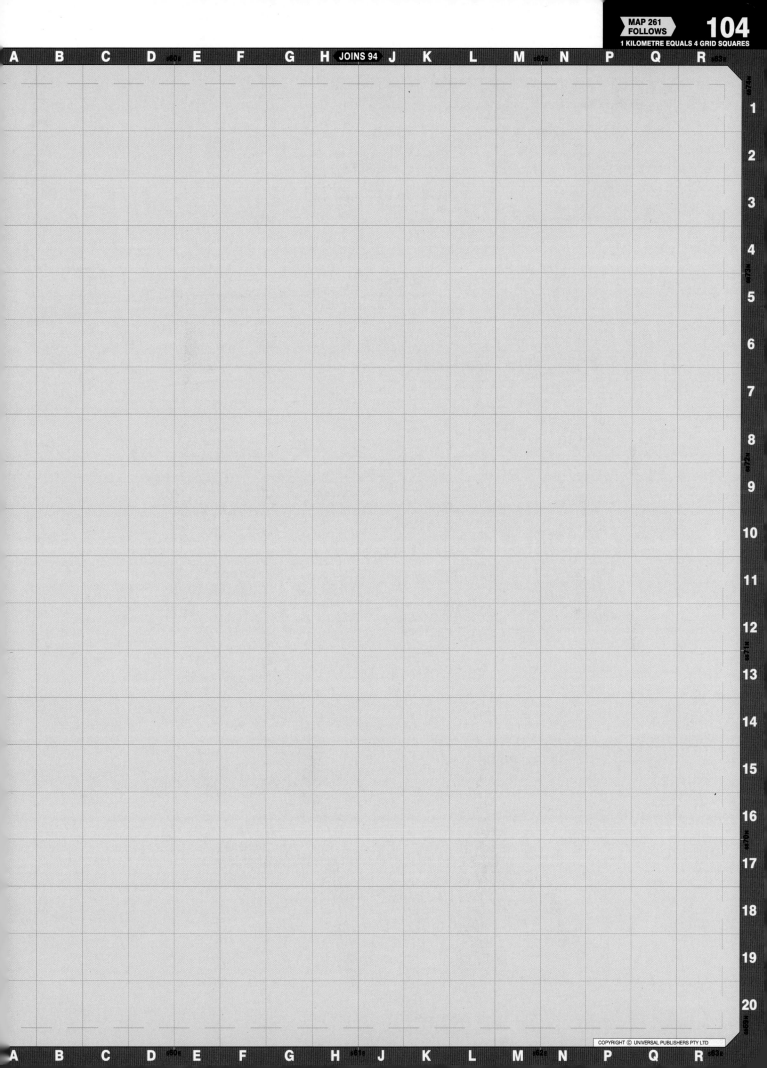

MAP 261
FOLLOWS
104
1 KILOMETRE EQUALS 4 GRID SQUARES

JOINS 94

LIMIT OF MAPS

BERRINBA
4117

MARSDEN
4132

Burrowes Primary

Marsden Gardens

Crestmead Industrial Estate

Crestmead Primary

Marsden Primary

Marsden High

CRESTMEAD
4132

Crestmead Park

Judith Park

St Francis College

Brabham Park

Pony Club

Cmnty Cntr

PCYC

Logan

Lake Cooroibah

PARK RIDGE
4125

Park Ridge District Park

Claremont Resort Over 50's Village

LOGAN RESERVE
4133

LIMIT OF MAPS

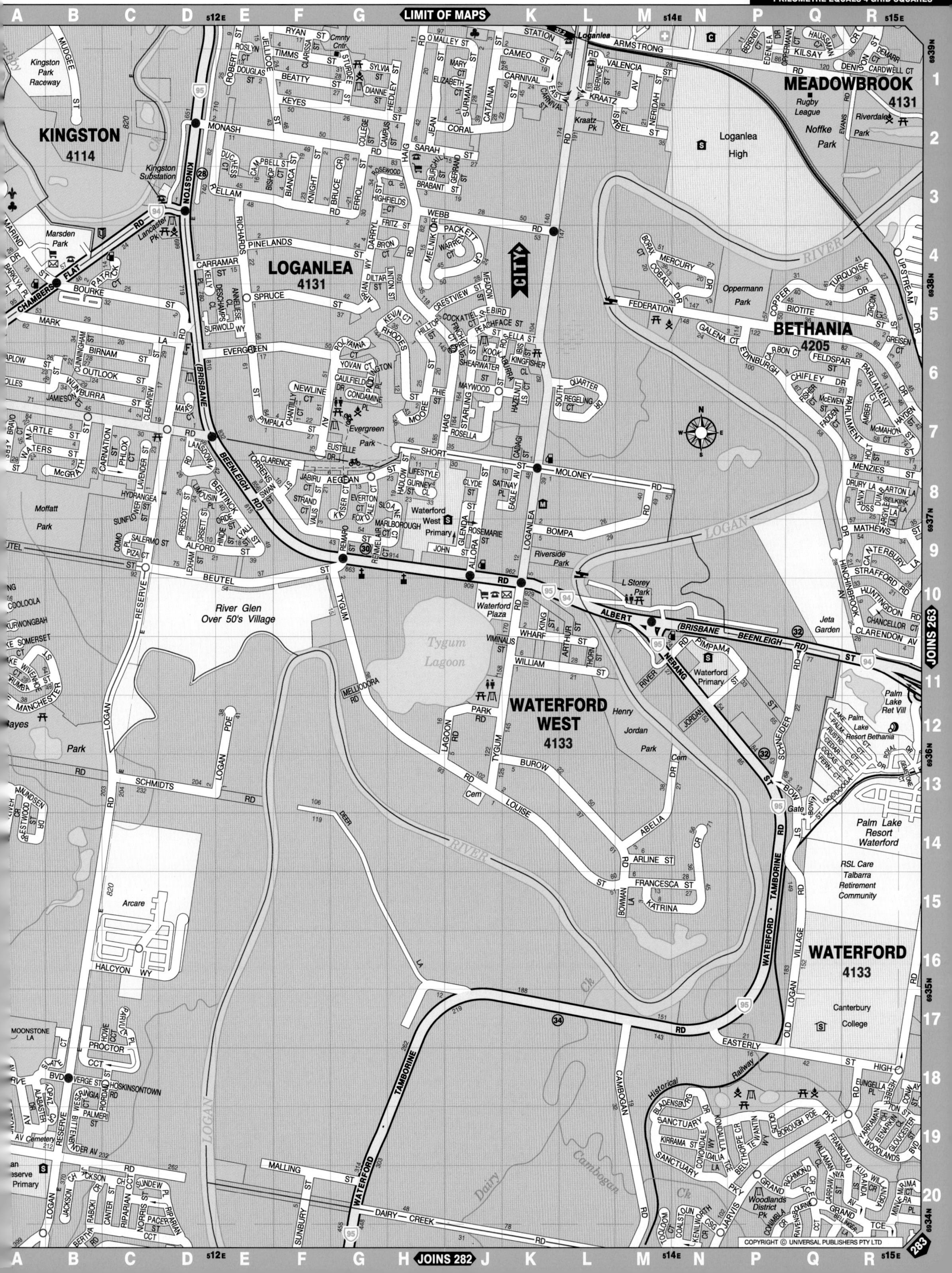

MAP 262
1 KILOMETRE EQUALS 4 GRID SQUARES

LIMIT OF MAPS

KINGSTON 4114

LOGANLEA 4131

MEADOWBROOK 4131

BETHANIA 4205

WATERFORD WEST 4133

WATERFORD 4133

Loganlea High

Oppermann Park

Palm Lake Resort Bethania

Palm Lake Resort Waterford

RSL Care Talbarra Retirement Community

Canterbury College

Tygum Lagoon

River Glen Over 50's Village

Waterford Plaza

Waterford West Primary

Waterford Primary

Marsden Park

Moffatt Park

Kingston Substation

Kingston Park Raceway

JOINS 263

JOINS 282

MAP 263
1 KILOMETRE EQUALS 4 GRID SQUARES

LIMIT OF MAPS

MEADOWBROOK
Riverdale 4131
Park

TANAH MERAH
4128

BETHANIA
4205

LOGANHOLME
4129

Logan River Parkland

EDENS LANDING
4207

Alexander Clark Park

Bill Norris Oval

HOLMVIEW
4207

WATERFORD
4133

MAP 264
1 KILOMETRE EQUALS 4 GRID SQUARES

LIMIT OF MAPS

CORNUBIA
4130

CARBROOK
4130

Carbrook Pmy

Kimberley College

Riverlakes
Country Club

LOGAN RIVER

Skinners Park

Water Pollution
Control
Works

EAGLEBY
4207

BORONIA DR	5
EUCALYPTUS PARK AV	6
KOOKABURRA AV	4
LORIKEET AV	2
MELALUECA PARK CR	1
PALMVIEW AV	3

Palm Lake Resort

Eagleby Primary

Eagleby Learning Centre

Herbst Memorial Pk

Olympic Park

Cec Clark Park

Booiurragum Park

Beenleigh Cemetery

Eagleby Shopping Plaza

Oxford Crest Eagleby

Eagleby South Primary

Jimbelunga Nursing Centre

Olivers

Eagleby Sports

BEENLEIGH
4207

BMX Track

Trinity College

Davy Gooding Bridge

St Josephs Pmy

PCYC

Dauth Park

Ruby Gardens

Sapphire Gardens

Sewage Treatment Plant

Wetlands

Beenleigh High

STAPYLTON
4207

Mt Stapylton

Gold Coast

ALBERT

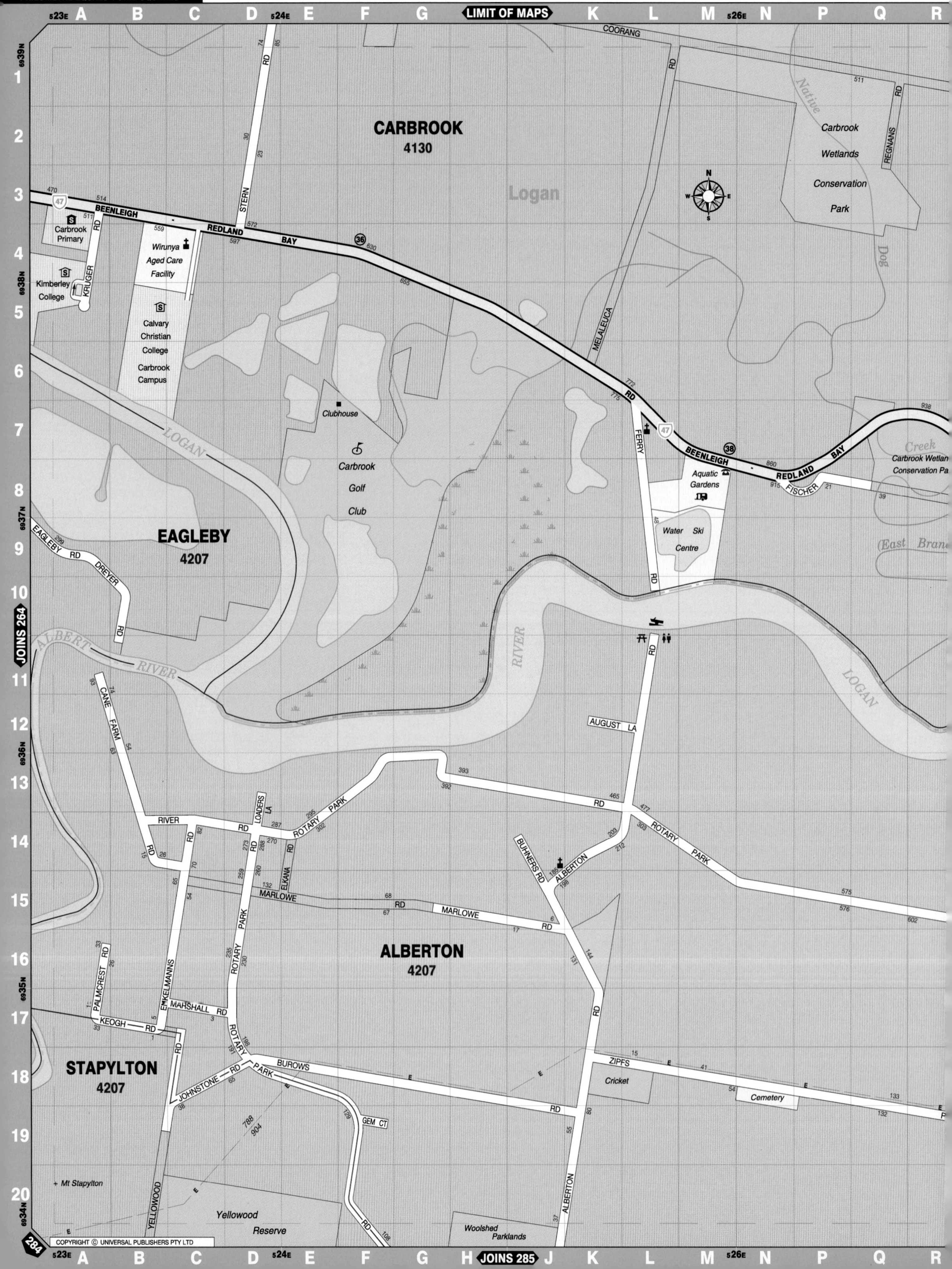

MAP 265
1 KILOMETRE EQUALS 4 GRID SQUARES

LIMIT OF MAPS

CARBROOK
4130

Logan

Carbrook
Wetlands

Conservation

Park

N
W E
S

BEENLEIGH
REDLAND
BAY

Carbrook
Primary

Wirunya
Aged Care
Facility

Kimberley
College

KRUGER

Calvary
Christian
College
Carbrook
Campus

Clubhouse

Carbrook
Golf
Club

EAGLEBY
4207

LOGAN

MELALEUCA

RD

FERRY

BEENLEIGH
REDLAND BAY

Carbrook Wetlan
Conservation Pa

FISCHER

Creek

Dog

Aquatic
Gardens

Water Ski
Centre

(East Branch)

RD

RIVER

RIVER

LOGAN

ALBERT
RIVER

CANE
FARM

AUGUST LA

RD

ROTARY PARK

River
RD

LOADERS LA

ROTARY PARK

ALBERTON
4207

ELKANA

BUHNERS RD

Alberton

ROTARY PARK

MARLOWE
RD

MARLOWE
RD

PALMCREST
RD

ROTARY
PARK

EMKELMANNS

MAHSHALL RD

ZIPFS

Cricket

Cemetery

STAPYLTON
4207

KEOGH
RD

JOHNSTONE
RD

ROTARY
PARK

BUROWS

GEM CT

Mt Stapylton

YELLOWOOD

Yellowood
Reserve

Woolshed
Parklands

RD

ALBERTON

MAP 266
1 KILOMETRE EQUALS 4 GRID SQUARES

LIMIT OF MAPS

Serpentine Creek
Conservation
Area

Carbrook Wetlands
Conservation Park

Carbrook   Wetlands

Conservation   Park

NATIVE   DOG

43

Serpentine

Creek

KUA
CT
38
27
2

JRRINGA
CT
30
23
2

39

HAVEN
RD
1
9

552

132
121

RD

SERPENTINE   CREEK

RD

47

42

LAGOON   VIEW
2
15

ROCKY
99
30
PASSAGE

47

LONGLAND   RD)

RD

40

1046

1010

1035

RD   RIEDEL   FISCHER

135

190
213

RD

RD   4

56

RD

65

ORCHARD
110
156

RD
134
145

MURIEL
ST
16

ST

REDLAND
BAY
4165

Redland

CITY

WALLABY
61
39
RD
120

ZIPFS
24
72
96
RD
132

124

211

ROAD
298
297

BEITZ
RD
3

FACILES
6
59
52
115
121

RD

RD
217

637

172

144

ZIPFS
788
904

E

E

E

RD
375
E

LOVES
RD 260

Stoney   Ck

RIVER

Gold Coast

WOONGOOLBA
4207

MUDLO
AILSA
ST
VINE
PEAR
ST
37

102

MAP 267
1 KILOMETRE EQUALS 4 GRID SQUARES

LIMIT OF MAPS

A B C D E F G K L M N P Q R

5 31E 5 32E 5 34E

◄CITY

Long

Moreton Bay

Marine Park

Redland

Bay

Lagoon

Channel

VINE ST
PEAR
MURIEL
ALBERT
ST
WALLABY RD

Island

JOINS 266

ZIPFS RD

RIVER

**REDLAND
BAY**
4165

ROCKY
PASSAGE
RD

LOGAN

RD

MARKS

Gold Coast

WOONGOOLBA

4207

Cecil Zipf
Park

MARKS
RD

ROCKY
POINT RD

285

A B C D E F G H **JOINS 287** J K L M N P Q R

5 31E 5 32E 5 34E

MAP 281 FOLLOWS

268

1 KILOMETRE EQUALS 4 GRID SQUARES

LIMIT OF MAPS

Browns

Bay

Turtle

Island

Rubbish Tip

Turtle Swamp Wetlands

Swamp

Passage

RUSSELL ISLAND 4184

Channel

Water Mouse Wetlands

Rocky Point

Rocky Point Park Res

Redland

LIMIT OF MAPS

Moreton Bay

Marine Park

Main

Little Rocky Point

Canaipa

SOUTHERN MORETON BAY ISLANDS

Cobby Cobby Island

Southern Moreton Bay Islands National Park

Mosquito Islands

JOINS 261

PARK RIDGE
4125

St Philomena School

Chambers Pines Lifestyle Resort

Ingenia Lifestyle Chambers Pines

LOGAN RESERVE
4133

LOGAN

Logan

Henders Street Park

Cemetery

Chambers

CHAMBERS FLAT
4133

Chambers

PLEASANT VIEW

RFB

Chambers Flat Logan Reserve Cmnty Cntr

LOGAN

WATERFORD

JOINS 303

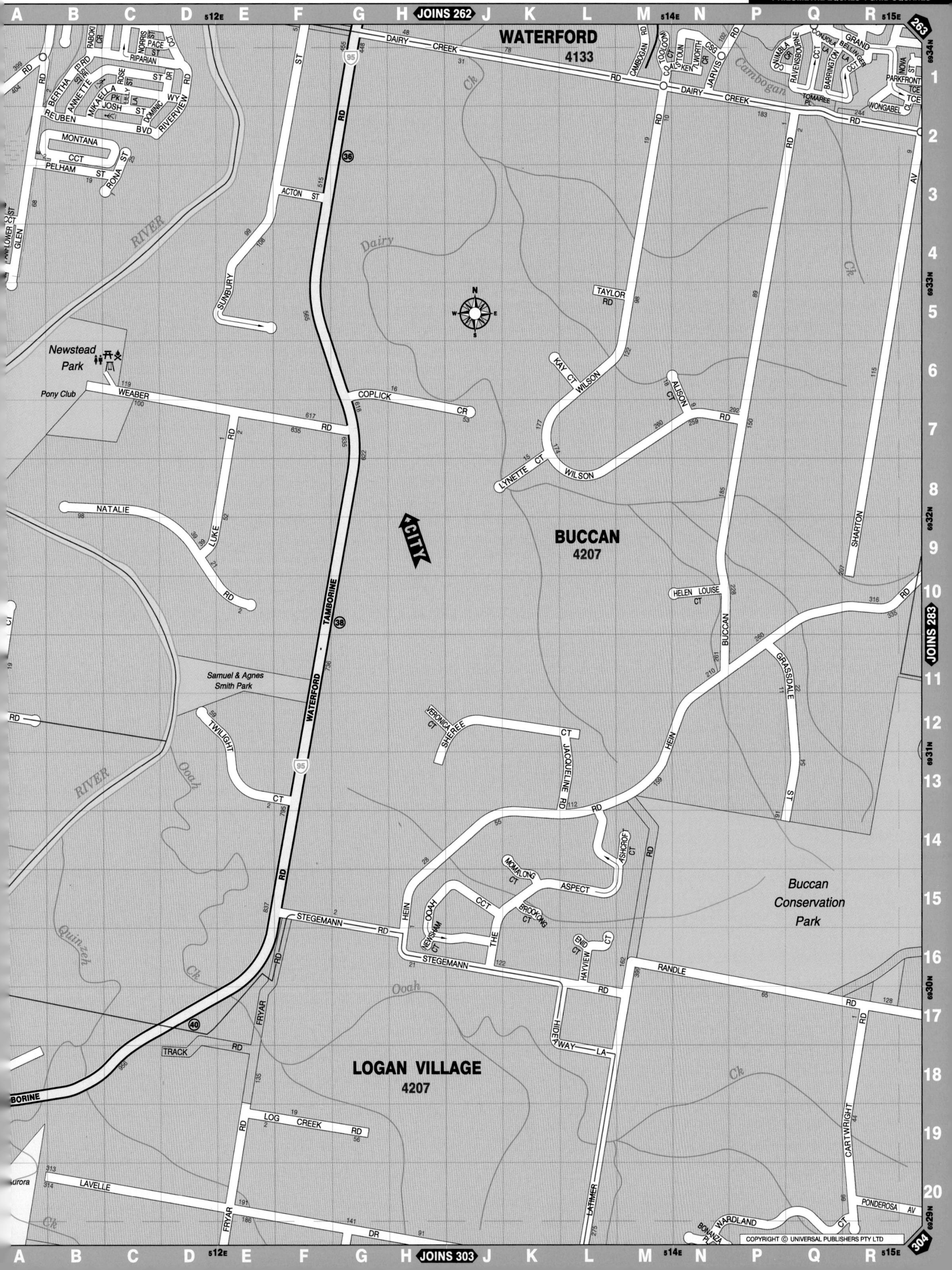

MAP 282
1 KILOMETRE EQUALS 4 GRID SQUARES

JOINS 262

WATERFORD
4133

263

BUCCAN
4207

LOGAN VILLAGE
4207

Buccan
Conservation
Park

Newstead
Park

Pony Club

Samuel & Agnes
Smith Park

JOINS 283

304

MAP 283
1 KILOMETRE EQUALS 4 GRID SQUARES

JOINS 263

HOLMVIEW
4207

Logan

BAHRS
SCRUB
4207

Buccan
Conservation
Park

Windaroo Valley
High

Windaroo

Transfer
Station

BUCCAN
4207

BELIVAH
4207

BANNOCKBURN
4207

MAP 284
1 KILOMETRE EQUALS 4 GRID SQUARES

JOINS 264

JOINS 304

BEENLEIGH 4207

MOUNT WARREN PARK 4207

WINDAROO 4207

EAGLEBY 4207

STAPYLTON 4207

YATALA 4207

Mt Warren Park

Golf Course

Windaroo Lakes Golf Course

Rivermount College

Gold Coast Motocross Club

Archery Club

Stanmore Park

Gold Coast

Noyea Riverside Retirement Village

Historical Village

Hugh Muntz Park

ALBERT RIVER

PACIFIC MWY

BIRCHWOOD CL 2
CYPRESS CR 7
FERN TREE CR 8
MAPLE CL 3
MOUNTAIN ASH CR 9
POPLAR CR 5
SILKY OAK CR 1
WARATAH CL 6
WILLOW TREE CL 4

JOINS 285

MAP 285
1 KILOMETRE EQUALS 4 GRID SQUARES

JOINS 265

JOINS 305

ALBERTON
4207

STAPYLTON
4207

GILBERTON
4208

ORMEAU
4208

YATALA
4207

Gold Coast

Yellowood
Reserve

Quarry

Woolshed

Visy

Parklands

Proposed

Quinns Hill

Wildflower
CT

Ironbark CT

Eco
Memorial
Park

Mitchell
Enviro
Industrial
Estate

Stonemaster DR

Rotary Park

Stapylton · Jacobs Well

Jacobs Well

Quarry

Angel RD

Penny LA

Beenleigh
Twin Drive-In

DJR
Team
Penske

Yellowood

De Burton ST

Emer ST

Eastridge

Homestead

Fairway DR

Hillside DR

Rossmanns

Stapylton
Landfill &
Recycling
Centre

Christensen

Majella ST

Christensen RD

Sandy

Proximity PL

Yatala

Industrial

Estate

Eastern

Elliot DR

Service

Pacific

Elderslie

Dixon ST

Darlington Dr

Cuthbert

Industrial
Area

Auction House

Burnside

Prairie

Christensen RD S

Greyhound RD

Transport

Sandy

Burnside

Creek

Reginal

Intra

Jacosa

Jacobs Well

RD

RD E

Carlton
Brewhouse

Yatala
Delivery
Centre

Binary

Progress ST

Rom ST

Progham RD

Computer

Octal

Mavis CT

Lahrs RD

Notar DR

MWY

Halfway

Bridge Ck

Halfway

Goldmine RD

Corridor

Ck

MAP 286
1 KILOMETRE EQUALS 4 GRID SQUARES

A B C D s28E E F G H **JOINS 266** J K L M s30E N P Q R s31E 267

JOINS 287

307

RD
LOVES
RD
RD
LOVES
RD
Creek

788
904

JACOBS WELL
(ST APYLTON - JACOBS WELL)
44

Sandy

N
W E
S

WOONGOOLBA
4207

WOHLSEN RD
RD
(ST APYLTON - JACOBS WELL)

GIBSONS
COOKS
RD
RD

48

Tennis
Pimpama Island
Sports Complex

SHORT CUT RD
RD

RD
Creek
RD)
46
JACOBS WELL
RD

Woongoolba
Conservation
Park
RD
RD

NORWELL
46

Norwell
Motorplex

SUGARCANE

FISCHERS

SUGARCANE

NORWELL
4208

CITY

RD

RD

NEW NORWELL

COPYRIGHT © UNIVERSAL PUBLISHERS PTY LTD

1
2
3
4
5
6
7
8 s32N
9
10
11
12 s31N
13
14
15
16 s30N
17
18
19
20 s29N

MAP 287
1 KILOMETRE EQUALS 4 GRID SQUARES

266

531E

JOINS 267

JOINS 286

WOONGOOLBA
4207

MARKS RD

SCHOOL RD

GIBSONS RD

MILL RD

SWAMP RD

HOLMSTEAD

Rocky Point
Sugar Mill

ROCKY POINT

HOLMSTEAD ROAD

BERNDT RD

SHORT CUT

SHORT CUT ROAD

MILL RD

SCHOOL RD

Woongoolba
Primary

JACOBS WELL RD

Cmnty
Cntr

STAPYLTON - JACOBS WELL RD

NEW NORWELL RD

FINGLAS RD

CITY

GROSS RD

JACOBS WELL RD

STAPYLTON - JACOBS WELL RD

CABBAGE TREE POINT ROAD

Private Road

Horizon Shores
Marina

Admin

STEIGLITZ
4207

Gold Coast

STEIGLITZ RD

KLEINSCHMIDT RD

FLOODGATE RD

FLOODGATE

ROAD CECIL ZIPF RD

Cecil Zipf
Park

Cabbage Tree
Point
Conservation
Park

**Cabbage Tree
Point**

POINT

CABBAGE TREE DR

MADAGASCAR PL

ROYAL PALM DR

PANDANUS PL

BANGALOW

CORAL DR

Lake

WALKERS JETTY

SHED

HIRSCH ST

SEABR

SEABIRD ST

RD

COPYRIGHT © UNIVERSAL PUBLISHERS PTY LTD

NORWELL
4208

**JACOBS
WELL**
4208

Behm Creek

MAP 293 FOLLOWS
288
1 KILOMETRE EQUALS 4 GRID SQUARES

JOINS 268

Moreton Bay

Marine Park

Channel

Mosquito   Islands

Southern Moreton
Bay Islands
National Park

Cobby   Cobby

Island

SOUTHERN
MORETON
BAY ISLANDS

Short

Island

Cabbage
Tree
Point

Charlie
Hammel Pk

Tabby   Tabby

Island

LIMIT OF MAPS

Eden

Island

Southern Moreton
Bay Islands
National Park

Moreton Bay

Marine Park

Kangaroo

(Boonnahbah)

Island

JOINS 281

CHAMBERS FLAT
4133

STOCKLEIGH
4280

JOINS 280

JOINS 302

LOGAN

RIVER

Creek

Creek

Logan

Allans

Kooruhman

Kings Christian College

Logan Village Campus

John Nevell Memorial Park

Geoff Philp Bridge

Logan Village Dog Park

Towns Avenue Park

Logan Village Primary

Logan Village Retirement Village

Community Centre

Skatepark

Mus

Cemetery

SES

Waste Disposal Facility

RFB

Daybreak Park

The Markets

Darlington Parklands

Yarrabilba Camp Cable Pk

Shaw St Oval

St Clares Pmy

Stockleigh Environmental Park

Yarrabilba to Logan Village Rail Trail

Logan Village Park

CITY

Street names (partial):
WENDT RD, KENNY RD, KIRK RD, KUMILE CT, ANZAC, MANUKA RD, STOREY ST, NORTH ST, WHARF ST, QUINZEH, CADMERE CT, CENTENARY, INDUSTRIAL, OPAL, WATERFORD-TAMBORINE RD, ALBERT ST, RIVER, FERRY, PAGET, PERSE, ENTRANCE AV, BURKE ST, WESTERN, ROBYN CT, LUCINDA RD, POTTS ST, ARDEE PL, LAUREMEG PL, LEONIE, TOWNS RD, VILLAGE CT, ARDEE, PIONEER, SARAH CT, JILLIAN CT, KATHERINE CT, BENJAMIN RD, WANDEARA, POSSUM CT, LAIDLAW CL, PIONEER, GAYLE CT, RAILWAY, GEORGINA, CULGOA, CULL, PEPPERINA DR, FIGWOOD CT, STOCKLEIGH RD, HASTINGS CT, MOLLENHAGEN CT, ALFRED RD, KOORUHMAN, ARDEE CCT, ROGIUS CT, BIGAL AV, LADY ARDEE, CARABEN RD, GEOFF PHILP DR, ARDARA CT, MYE PL, YORE RD, WARREN CT, KOORUHMAN CT, BOBERMIEN, FROG HOLLOW CT, FLORENCE CT, HOTZ, NOSF FARM, VIRGINIA WY, TRAVIS RD, CAMP CABLE RD, AMBER CR, DAYBREAK, SKYBLUE, LAMBENT, VERMILLION, MYERS ST, BLOSSOM ST, BRIGHT ST, SUMMERVIEW, SIENNA, VERO, DEW ST, EVERGLADE, HIGHLANDS, YARRABILBA, SHAW ST, WALDRON ST, DARLINGTON, TAPPEN, GARRAGILBA

COPYRIGHT © UNIVERSAL PUBLISHERS PTY LTD

MAP 299 FOLLOWS
294
1 KILOMETRE EQUALS 4 GRID SQUARES
283

JOINS 282

JOINS 304

LOGAN
VILLAGE
4207

ARRABILBA
4207

CEDAR
CREEK
4207

Merv & Ollie
Musch Park
RSL

Quinzeh Creek

Quinzeh Creek Park

Big River
Country
Park
Soccer

Former
Village Links
Golf Couse

Wickham
Timber
Reserve

Wickham Plunkett Horse Trail

Wickham Peak

Wickham Peak
Lookout

Buxton
Park

Yarrabilba
Secondary
College

Jinnung Jali
Park

Sandstone
Park

LAVELLE
MILLER
STEELE
QUINZEH CREEK
FRYAR
MINEHAN
HAMILTON
CHALLEN
HINCHCLIFFE
QUINZEH CREEK
FORBES CT
STANFORD CT
LATIMER
SWANBOROUGH
CAMEL CT
INSPIRATION
MURRAY
COOINGIE VIEW
DUKES CT
BUENA VISTA
WARDLAND
BONANZA PL
PONDEROSA AV
ANEMBO CT
LAWAH CT
ELLEN CT
KENNEDY CT
TYSON CT
DIAMENTINA
DAINTREE
DIAMENTINA DR
CANAIPA CT
CONDAMINE
BOOLONG CT
BURDEKIN CT
WEMLOCK CT
JARDINE CT
MARANOA
STEELE
PINEVIEW
LOUISE CT
CONIFER CT
QUINZEH CREEK
ROSEWOOD CCT
WILLOW CCT
WINDSOR AV
CAMBRIDGE CCT
HARMONY CCT
HIDDENVALE CCT
PARADISE
ARCADIA
GLENDOUR CCT
OLIVINE CT
BENGAL ST
STRATA
ARCHES
CHALK
GOSSAN
BRECCIA
MICA
MORION
SHILIN
BIRON
DARRAU
MASON
GREENSTONE
WOODWARD
BASALT
MANGANO
LOWTHERS
SCORIA ST
SLATE
MICA ST
GRANITE ST
MARL
SOAPSTONE
DUSTONE
Wickham Plunkett Horse Trail

COPYRIGHT © UNIVERSAL PUBLISHERS PTY LTD

JOINS 293

302

JOINS 302

JOINS Gold Coast 1

JOINS 293

330

A B C D E F G H J K L M N P Q R

CITY

Logan

Quinzeh

LOGAN VILLAGE
4207

JIMBOOMBA
4280

TAMBORINE
4270

Range

Binam

Clutha

Creek

AMBER CR

EUCALYPT

TITREE CT

TRAVIS

VIRGINIA

RD

WATERFORD - TAMBORINE

WATERFORD - TAMBORINE

DOLLARBIRD

TEAL CT

NAYLOR

DR

CURLEW CT

WEDGE - TAIL CT

NAYLOR

DR

MARKS

McDONALD

RD

DAVIDSON RD

KESTREL CT

CURRAWONG CT

WILLIAMSON AV

DELLCAL

PL

NOLAN CT

FAIRWEATHER CT

DRYSDALE CT

GREENSWARD

MONA DR

SAWREY

KILLIGREW

GREENSWARD

RD

FROND RD

RD

BAILEY ST

DARLINGTON

TULLIS CL

LELAND

KURGAN LA

MASSEY ST

GARRAGULLO

SOMMER GR

HESSEL ST

DR

95

40

WY

507E

508E

510E

6924N

6923N

6922N

6920N

6919N

CHAMBERS FLAT
4133

STOCKLEIGH
4280

LOGAN VILLAGE
4207

Stockleigh Environmental Park

Logan Village Park

Quinzeh Creek Park

Big River Country Park Soccer

Buxton Park

FOR MORE DETAIL SEE MAP 293

FOR MORE DETAIL SEE MAP 294

JIMBOOMBA
4280

FOR MORE DETAIL SEE MAP 299

FOR MORE DETAIL SEE MAP 300

KAIRABAH
4207

TAMBORINE
4270

Logan

LIMIT OF MAPS

CITY

ARCHES LA 55	HANTLEMANN LA 17	RIDGEVIEW LA 8
AUTUMNFIELD AV 1	HERSHEY CL 38	SANDELL ST 22
BAILEY ST 26	HILLARD ST 41	SCHROEDER ST 18
BENGAL ST 54	HUGGINS AV 19	SHILIN ST 57
BERNARD CCT 27	JENSEN LA 50	SIGWELL ST 46
BLOSSOM ST 36	JUBERA CL 47	SPRINGRISE PL 11
BOICE ST 21	KURGAN LA 37	TALLWOODS CCT 13
CAREW ST 15	LATHAM ST 43	TAPPEN ST 51
CARPENTER ST 16	LOWTHERS ST 44	TASKER ST 40
CERULEAN PL 35	MACNAB ST 20	TERRACE LA 33
CHERNEY LA 31	MANGANO CT 59	TREELINE CCT 32
COOLRIDGE CCT 29	MASSEY ST 42	TREETOPS ST 3
DOMES LA 53	MILBY ST 30	TULLIS CL 28
ELMER LA 12	MYERS ST 34	VANTAGE LA 5
EVERGLADE ST 4	PEABODY LA 24	VERMILLION LA 14
FOLLIT ST 49	PEAK LA 9	WILDFLOWER ST 7
FULMER ST 23	PERSELLS LA 45	WINKLER CT 58
GRASSLANDS ST 6	PUMICE LA 56	WINTERPEAK CL 10
GRAYSON ST 39	REESE LA 48	

BUCCAN 4207

BELIVAH 4207

WOLFFDENE 4207

Corbould Land Trust (Wolffdene) Nature Refuge

Gold Coast

LUSCOMBE 4207

YATALA 4207

Empire Industrial Estate

Darlington Park Industrial Estate

Private Rd
Gate

Quarry

Quarry

Quarry

ORMEAU 4208

ORMEAU HILLS 4208

THE PLATEAU

LUSCOMBE BRIDGE

Ecopark Fishing World

CEDAR CREEK 4207

KINGSHOLME 4208

Darlington Range

Parkhouse Cem

Plunkett Conservation Park

Plunkett Tamborine Village Cem

Scenic Rim

Cedar Creek Primary

(Low level narrow bridge)

Cedar Creek Pk

Tamborine National Park

ALAN WILKE BR STANMORE (Causeway)

RIVER

Rocky Ck

Cedar Ck

ALBERT

MAP 305

1 KILOMETRE EQUALS 4 GRID SQUARES

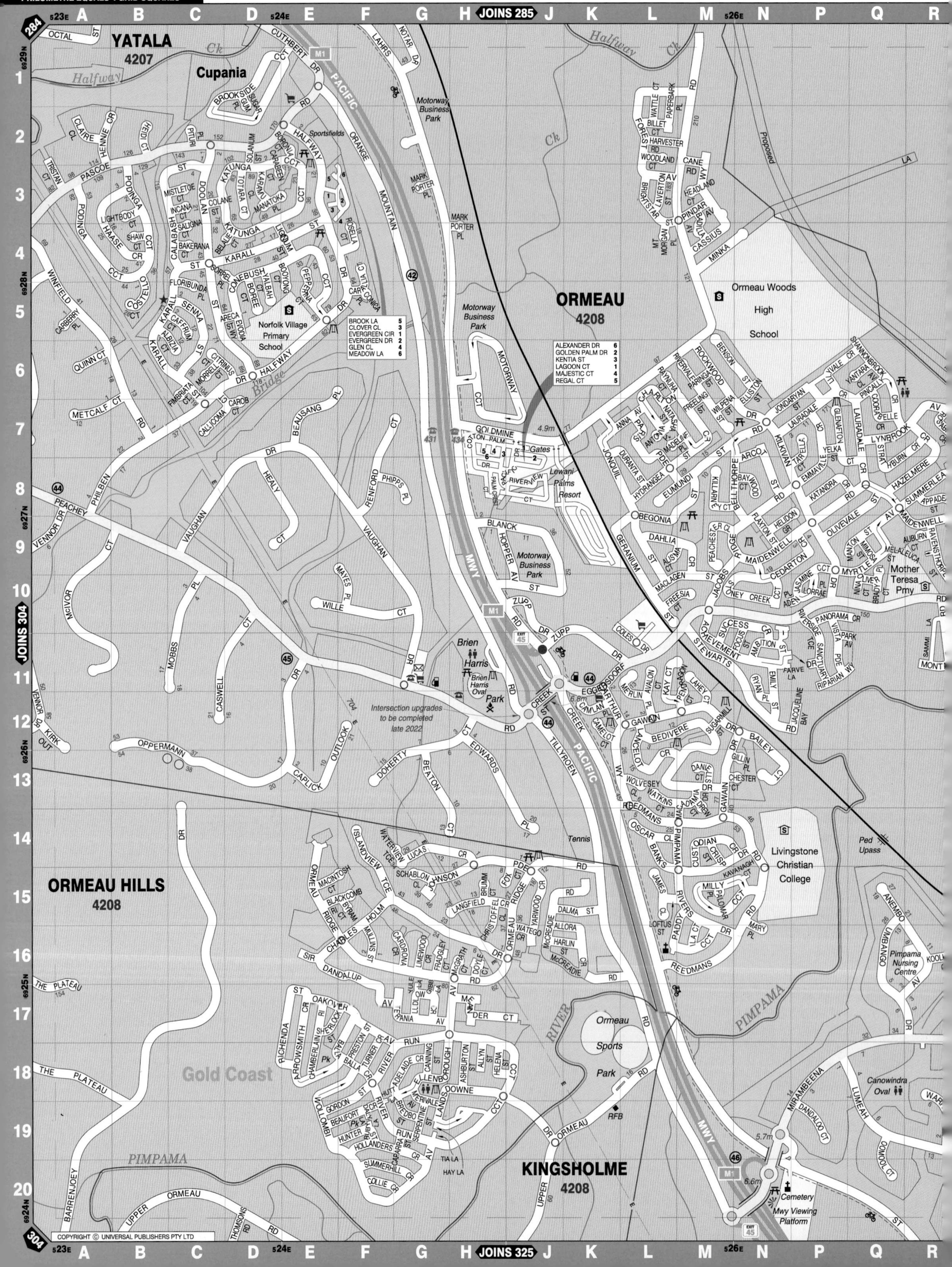

MAP 306
1 KILOMETRE EQUALS 4 GRID SQUARES

A B C D E F G H JOINS 286 J K L M N P Q R

287

WOONGOOLBA
4207

NORWELL
4208

NEW NORWELL RD

COWLEY RD

NORWELL RD

PIMPAMA

RIVER

JOINS 307

Transport

RIVER

Xtreme Karting

JACOBS WELL

PIMPAMA
4209

Ck

PIMPAMA

CITY

BINNOWEE WY

Ormeau

Lutheran
Ormeau Rivers
District School

Ormeau Pmy

GUARA GR E

OLD WHARF RD

WHARF RD

JACOBS WELL RD

PIMPAMA RD

Corridor

Hotham

KYEWONG CT

COBRADAH CT

NYRANG DR

GUARA GR

A B C D E F G H JOINS 326 J K L M N P Q R

327

MAP 307
1 KILOMETRE EQUALS 4 GRID SQUARES

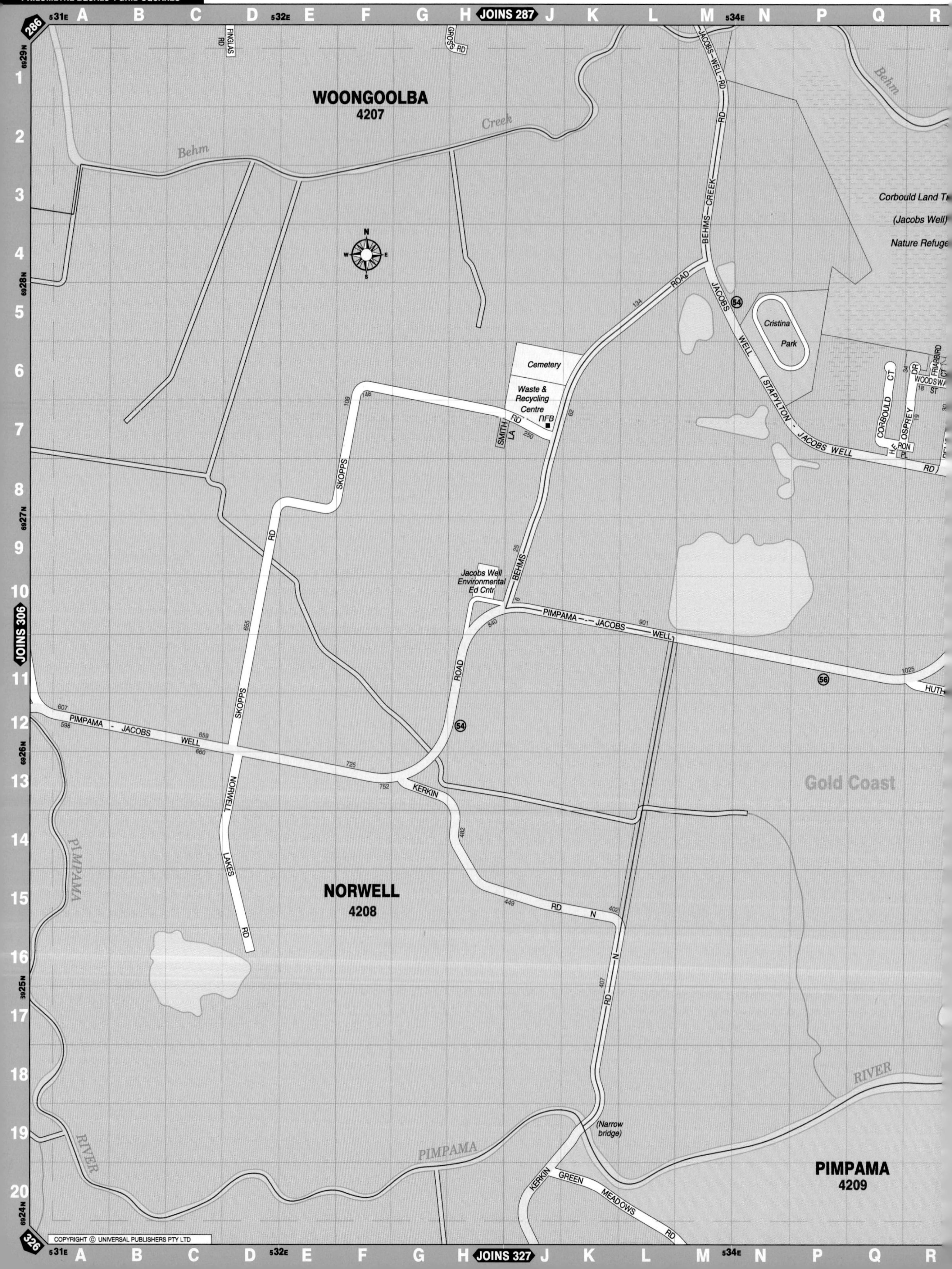

JOINS 287

286

531E S32E JOINS 287 534E

FINGLAS RD

GROSS RD

WOONGOOLBA
4207

Behm Creek

Behm

N
W E
S

Corbould Land T

(Jacobs Well)

Nature Refuge

134

BEHMS CREEK RD

JACOBS WELL ROAD

54

Cristina Park

Cemetery

Waste & Recycling Centre

RFB

250

62

SMITH LA

SKOPPS RD

146

109

STAPYLTON - JACOBS WELL

CORBOULD CT

OSPREY DR

FRIARBIRD ST

WOODSWA

RON PL

HE

18

19

34

RD

BEHMS

25

Jacobs Well Environmental Ed Cntr

6

840

PIMPAMA -- JACOBS WELL

901

1025

56

HUTH

ROAD

54

RD

655

SKOPPS RD

JOINS 306

PIMPAMA - JACOBS WELL

607

598

659

660

725

752

KERKIN

482

Gold Coast

NORWELL LAKES RD

NORWELL
4208

449

RD N

400

N

RD

407

PIMPAMA RIVER

RIVER

RIVER

PIMPAMA

(Narrow bridge)

KERKIN

GREEN MEADOWS RD

PIMPAMA
4209

JOINS 327

Grid references: 6929N, 6928N, 6927N, 6926N, 6925N, 6924N

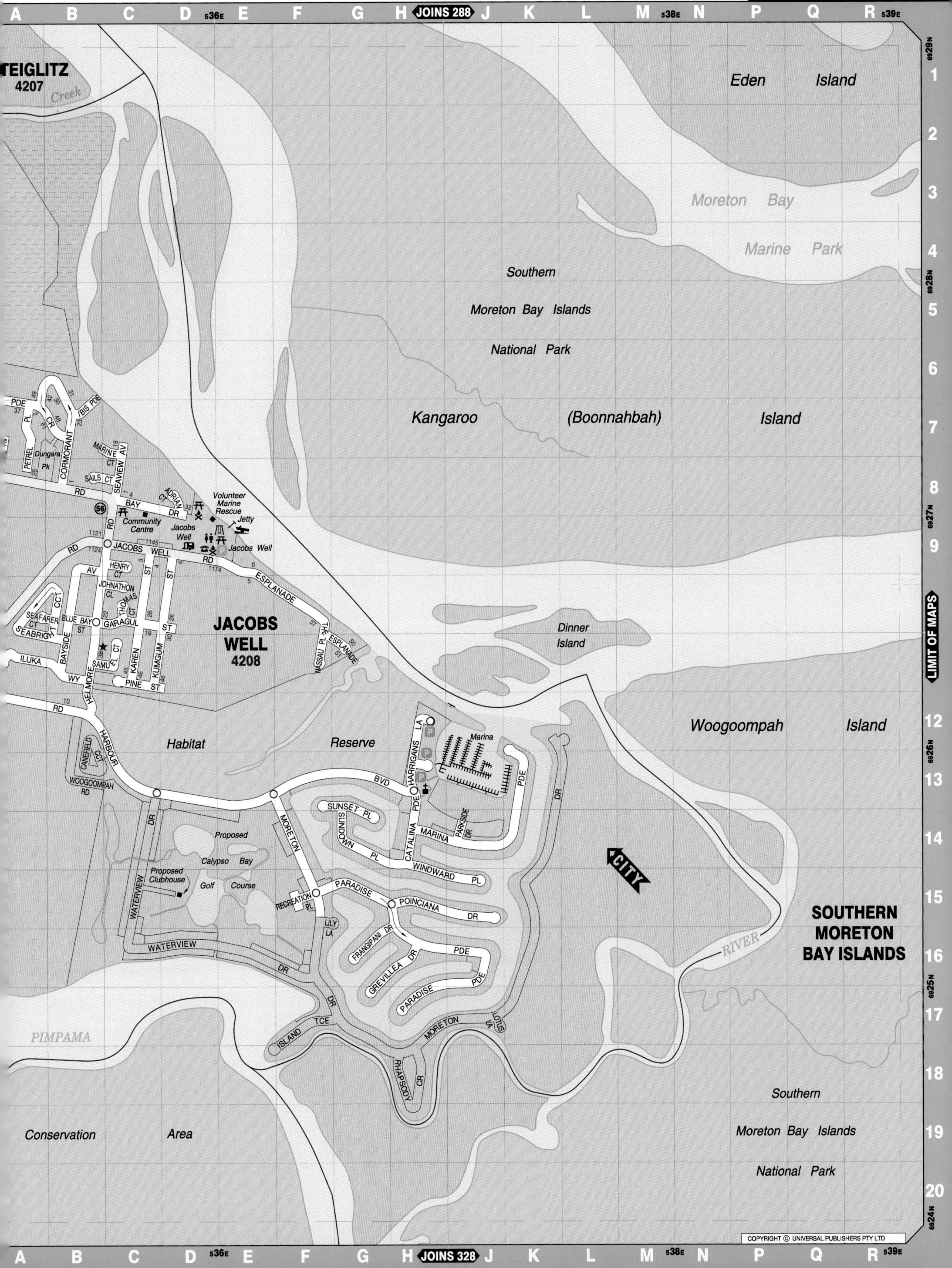

MAP 325 FOLLOWS

308

1 KILOMETRE EQUALS 4 GRID SQUARES

A B C D 536E E F G H JOINS 288 J K L M 538E N P Q R 539E

1
TEIGLITZ
4207
Creek

Eden Island

2

3
Moreton Bay

4
Marine Park

5
Southern

Moreton Bay Islands

6
National Park

7
Kangaroo (Boonnahbah) Island

8

PDE
PL 37
CR 48
CORMORANT
BIS PDE
MARINE CT
SEAVIEW AV
Dungara Pk
SAILS CT
RD
BAY
ADRIAN CT
Volunteer Marine Rescue
Jetty

9
56
Community Centre
Jacobs Well
Jacobs Well
JACOBS WELL RD
ESPLANADE
THE ESPLANADE
NASSAU ST

HENRY CT
JOHNATHON CL
THOMAS CT
JACOBS WELL ST
GARAGUL
KAREN ST
KUMGUM ST

SEAFARER CT
BLUE BAY ST
BAYSIDE
SAMU CL CT
PINE ST

ILUKA WY
HELMORE
RD

10
JACOBS WELL 4208

Dinner Island

12
HARBOUR CCT
CANEFIELD CCT
WOOGOOMPAH RD
Habitat
Reserve
HARRIGANS LA
Marina
PDE
Woogoompah Island

13
BVD
CATALINA PDE
MARINA
PARKSIDE DR
DR

14
MORETON
SUNSET PL
SUNDOWN PL
WINDWARD PL
CITY

15
WATERVIEW
Proposed Calypso Bay
Proposed Clubhouse
Golf Course
RECREATION PL
PARADISE
POINCIANA DR
SOUTHERN MORETON BAY ISLANDS

16
WATERVIEW DR
LILY LA
FRANGIPANI DR
GREVILLEA DR
PDE
PARADISE PDE
RIVER

17
PIMPAMA
ISLAND TCE
DR
MORETON VA
LOTUS VA

18
RHAPSODY CR

19
Conservation Area
Southern Moreton Bay Islands

20
National Park

JOINS 305

JOINS 304

KINGSHOLME
4208

WILLOW VALE
4209

Gold Coast

PIMPAMA RIVER

Mwy Viewing Platform
Cemetery

PACIFIC

M1

EXIT 45

BARRENJOEY DR
UPPER ORMEAU RD
COUNTRYVIEW
HEREFORD CL
BRIDLE CL
HOLSTEIN CL
MONTEGO HILLS
RED CEDAR
WOODLAND CL
CCT
DRIFTWOOD CCT
HILLS ST
MONTEGO DR
ELM CL
HOMESTEAD
SAWMILL CR
STOCKMAN
FERN HILL
STUCKEY
LILLY MUNTZ DR
THOMAS DOHERTY PL
HOTHAM RD
COACH
STAGE
THOMSONS RD
HIDDEN CT DR
GERRALE DR
FAIRVIEW
FAIRVIEW DR
NIJINSKY
HYPERION PL
HOTHAM CREEK DR
PROUDLOCK DR
HOTHAM CREEK WY
Richardson Family Park
SUNNYSIDE (Private) Rd
LA
RUFFLES
COULTER
ELLEN GRANT
WILLOWVALE DR
BLACKS
WHITES RD
PITTAS PL
RUFFLES RD
CRYSTAL CREEK
FERN TREE GULLY DR
MAIDEN HAIR PL
PEA RD

HIDEAWAY RD

JOINS 5

COPYRIGHT © UNIVERSAL PUBLISHERS PTY LTD

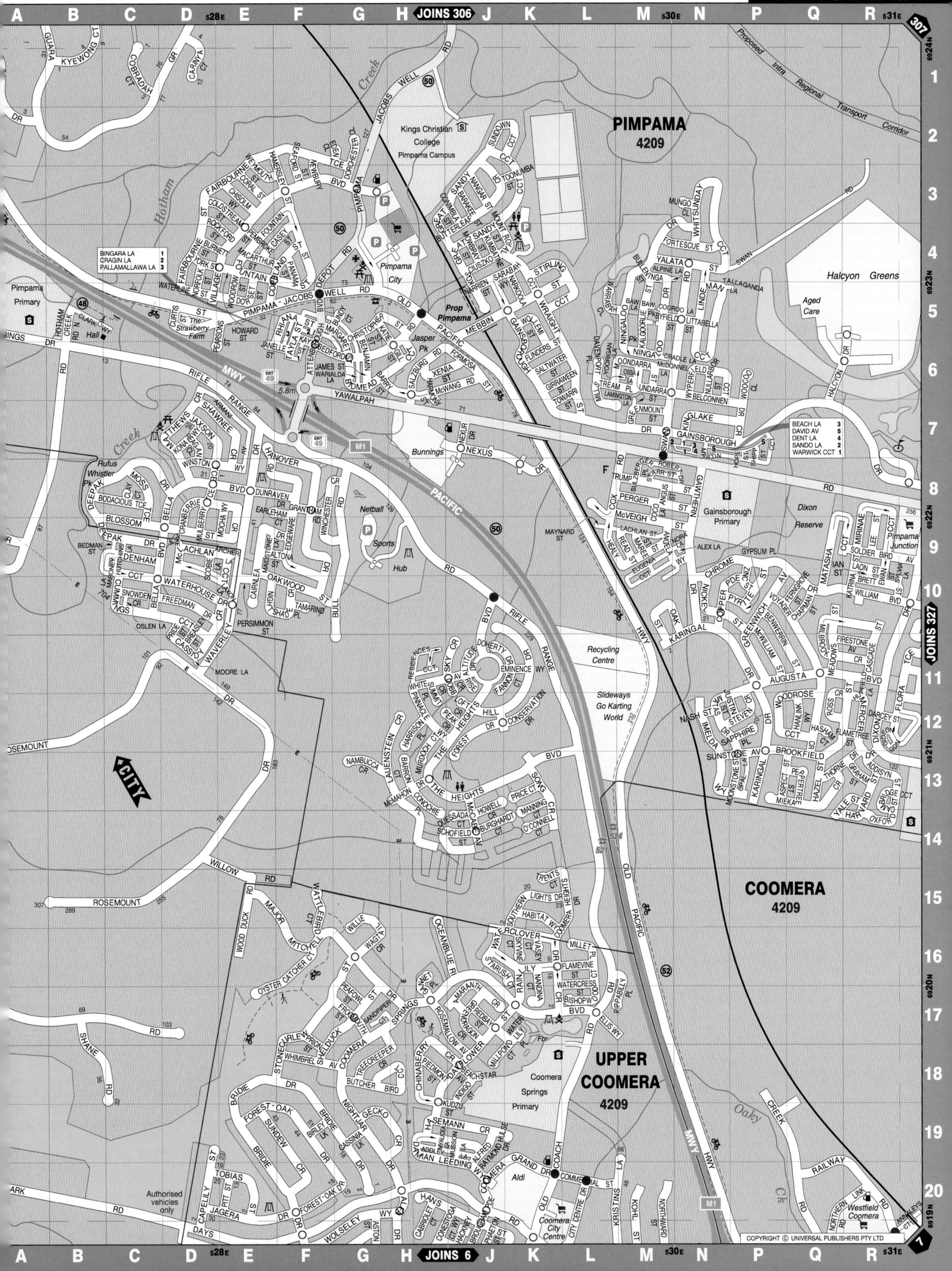

MAP 326
1 KILOMETRE EQUALS 4 GRID SQUARES

JOINS 306

307

PIMPAMA
4209

Kings Christian College
Pimpama Campus

Pimpama City

Prop Pimpama

Pimpama Primary

Halcyon Greens

Aged Care

Pimpama Junction

Gainsborough Primary

Dixon Reserve

BINGARA LA	1
CRAGIN LA	2
PALLAMALLAWA LA	3

BEACH LA	3
DAVID AV	5
DENT LA	4
SANDO LA	2
WARWICK CCT	1

Bunnings

Netball Sports Hub

Recycling Centre

Slideways Go Karting World

COOMERA
4209

UPPER COOMERA
4209

Coomera Springs Primary

Coomera City Centre

Aldi

Westfield Coomera

CITY

Authorised vehicles only

JOINS 327

JOINS 6

MAP 327
1 KILOMETRE EQUALS 4 GRID SQUARES

PIMPAMA 4209

JOINS 307

JOINS 326

Conservation

Halcyon Greens

Gainsborough Greens Golf Course

Bim Binga Park

Pimpama State Primary College

Pimpama State Secondary College

St Josephs College

Cassab St

Parkside Community Park

Picnic Creek Primary

Coomera Rivers State School

Coomera State Sp Sch

Billabong Fields

Billabong Ponds

Foxwell Road Reserve

Sanctua Cove

Coomera East Shop Cntr

McCoys

Picnic Creek

JOINS 7

MAP 328
1 KILOMETRE EQUALS 4 GRID SQUARES

A B C D 536E E F G H **JOINS 308** J K L M 538E N P Q R 539E

6924N
1
2
3
4

Southern Moreton Bay Islands

National Park

Woogoompah Island
6923N
5
6

Area

7

Moreton Bay Marine Park

Creek

8
6922N

**SOUTHERN
MORETON BAY
ISLANDS**

9

Gold Coast

LIMIT OF MAPS

ENDEAVOUR CT

ENDEAVOUR

12
6921N

KATINKA CCT

COLMAN

COOMERA
4209

Spoonbill
Lagoons

IMPECCABLE

SEABIRD LA
SEABERRIMA LA

CCT

SALTASH

SERENADE DR

RAGAMUFFIN CT

LINTAIL LA

JASNAR LA

BENECIA

SKANDIA

TCE

QUEST

DR

13

PACHA
CCT

RAINBOW

IMPECCABLE

BRILLIANT LA

FLAMINGO
LA

Natures

Escape

EOLO LA

TIERCEL

PENDRAGON

AMBERMERLE
WY

LA

14

SOLOS

CRUSADE CT

FIRST
LIGHT CT

CONDOR

RFB

ELUSIVE

ICEBERG LA

RD

BOBSLED

JOSEPHINE RD

ELLIDA

15

COLMAN

RAGAMUFFIN

KIRREEL

VENINDE LA

RIVAL LA

AINSMAID

TRADITION

Wasp

Creek

Broadwater

16

FOXWELL

Isle of
Wings

KINGSTIDE LA

BALMARA

Middle
Cove

17

Serenity Bay

Melaleuca
Lagoons

BUCCANEER

Sandy
Bay

VILLAGE
DR

Rec
Cntr

Butterfly
Pk

Environmental

18

TOORANEEDIN

Dragonfly
Ponds

Reserve

Southern Moreton Bay Islands

National Park

19

Jetty

Marina

6920N

4212
HOPE
ISLAND

InterContinental
Sanctuary Cove
Resort

RIVER

Coomera Island

The

20
6919N

A B C D 536E E F G H **JOINS 8** J K L M 538E N P Q R 539E

9